THE BEST AMERICAN MOVIE WRITING 2001

THE BEST AMERICAN MOVIE WRITING 2001

EDITED BY

JOHN LANDIS

SERIES EDITOR, JASON SHINDER

THUNDER'S MOUTH PRESS ■ NEW YORK

The Best American Movie Writing 2001

Published by
Thunder's Mouth Press
An Impring of Avalon Publishing Group Incorporated
161 William St., 16th Floor
New York, NY 10038

Library of Congress Cataloging-in-Publication Data is available from Avalon Publishing Group
ISBN 1-56025-344-4

9 8 7 6 5 4 3 2 1

Printed in the United States of America
Distributed by Publishers Group West

GUEST EDITOR'S DEDICATION

for Deborah, Rachel, and Max (the real writer in the family)

ACKNOWLEDGMENTS

Best American Movie Writing features only a selection, of course, of the previous year's outstanding writing about films, writings that show an awareness of style, craft, and thoughtfulness as determined by the guest editor. To better reveal the changing conditions and directions of writing about film each year, the guest editor is given some flexibility in the scope of his research and decision-making. This year, the guest editor is given some flexibility in the scope of his research and decision-making. This year, the guest editor John Landis, for example, selected some pieces published in books as well as magazines, and included, for the first time in the series, book reviews.

In addition to Mr. Landis, I want to thank his assistant Sharon Dolin for her invaluable support and assistance, especially as regards communication and follow-through as the book was being edited. Thanks to the writer Sarah Ann Johnson, senior researcher and permissions editor, and to Katie Adams, Angelo Verga, Nina Kudler, and Edith Grundfust for their help with research and permissions as well. This edition would not be possible without the editorial direction and support of Neil Ortenberg and Dan O'Connor at Thunder's Mouth Press. Thanks also to Ken Brecher, Executive Director of Sundance Institute, who first suggested I consider John Landis as a guest editor. Finally, and most importantly, thanks to the writers for their work and to those who granted permission to reprint pieces in this collection.

CONTENTS

Preface Jason Shinder xiii

Introduction John Landis xix

Some Thoughts on Critics compiled by John Landis xxiii

1: ACTORS

Molly Haskell **HIGH WIRE ARTIST (Burt Lancaster)** 3

Robert Polito **BARBARA PAYTON: A MEMOIR** 8

Jack Kerouac **CODY AND THE THREE STOOGES** 16

Tom Weaver **HATS OFF TO CHARLES GEMORA, HOLLYWOOD'S GREATEST APE** 20

2: CENSORSHIP

Sam Staggs **excerpt from ALL ABOUT ALL ABOUT EVE, THE COMPLETE BEHIND THE SCENES STORY OF THE BITCHIEST FILM EVER MADE** 37

Mary Harron **THE RISKY TERRITORY OF AMERICAN PSYCHO** 53

Doug Atchison **HOW THE MPAA RATES INDEPENDENT FILMS** 59

Leonard J. Leff **GONE WITH THE WIND AND HOLLYWOOD RACIAL POLITICS** 70

3: WRITERS

Russell Banks — NO, BUT I SAW THE MOVIE 89
John Irving — THE TWELVE-YEAR-OLD GIRL 105
David Leavitt — LOST AMONG THE PINAFORES 112
Daryl G. Nickens — THE GREAT ESCAPE—OR THE FIRST TIME I DIDN'T PAY FOR IT 120
Walter Bernstein — New Introduction & Last Chapter INSIDE OUT: A MEMOIR OF THE BLACKLIST 123

4: DIRECTORS

Lawrence Kasdan — POV 151
Michael Herr — KUBRICK 171
Stanley Kubrick — 2001: A FILM 179
Rick Lyman — WHOA, TRIGGER! AUTEUR ALERT! 184
Rebecca Mead — CHEESE WHIZ: SAM RAIMI, THE AUTEUR OF THE EVIL DEAD 193
Natalie Zemon Davis — CEREMONY AND REVOLT: BURN! 203
David Geffner — PEOPLE WHO NEED PEOPLE 213

5: NAZIS

Stuart Klawans — AN INTERLUDE 228
J. Hoberman — WHEN THE NAZIS BECAME NUDNIKS 238

6: TECHNOLOGY

John Bailey — FILM OR DIGITAL? DON'T FIGHT, COEXIST 246
Michael Atkinson — STOP-MOTION JIMJAMS: RAY HARRYHAUSEN 254

7: GENRE

David Remnick **IS THIS THE END OF RICO?** 262
Maria DiBattista **FEMALE RAMPANT** 278

8: SHANGRI-LA

Ian Buruma **FOUND HORIZON** 310

Afterword by John Landis 319
Contributor's Notes 321
About the Series Editor 327
About the Guest Editor 329
Permissions 330
Index 334

PREFACE

The next best thing to watching movies is perhaps to read about them. And when you read and reread hundreds of pieces, especially over a short span of time, as John Landis and I did, you should be able to draw a few conclusions.

Perhaps the most obvious is that there are clearly a growing number of good pieces these days about the movies by a growing number of writers dedicated almost entirely to the art, as well as by some of our most distinguished writers of other genres. (There are plenty of pieces, of course, that aren't so good or realized for reasons, I suspect, to do with limits of space in magazines, and a prevailing misunderstanding that the audience is only interested in whether a film is violent or not, and/or sexually explicit or not.)

As writing about film, good and not-so-good, flourishes, it continues to be characterized by a greater and greater sense of variety. In fact, like cinema itself, its diversity may be one of its most noticeable characteristics. In light of the form's transformations and forms (essays, reviews, memoirs, historical studies, profiles, interviews, etc.), other literary arts can, for a moment, appear stagnant. Perhaps it is this variety that James Agee was referring to when in the 1940s he called writing about film one of the "greatest dramatic literary forms."

Taken together, the essays in this year's collection rest the growing contrasting and often contradictory, but clearly rewarding, varieties of form and content characteristic of cinema. More than any other guest editor of the series, the award-winning director and writer, John Landis, has chosen pieces without any predetermined theme. Last year's guest editor, for example, director and writer Peter Bogdanovich, was interested in "retrospectively-minded pieces," and another previous guest editor, writer and editor George Plimpton, was looking for "a sympathetic and passionate quality, especially regarding the changes occurring in cinema." As Mr. Landis notes in his introduction, he was looking only for those pieces that inspired and engaged him—as director, as writer, as moviegoer, nothing more, nothing less. As one of the cinema's most thoughtful, learned, skilled, and passionate practitioners, Landis's interest in cinema (and life) are so extensive (and generous) as to resist categories or definitions. As a result, this year's collection reinforces a major strain of contemporary writing about the movies: variousness of subject and form.

As Landis's interests and passions, especially about the movies (he seems not to have missed anything about the history of cinema and its masters, many of whom he had the good fortune to work with) are hard to nail down, so is this collection. With selections ranging from those about movie gorillas to Nazi films to movie ratings to Mafia films to video filmmaking to racial politics to the Three Stooges to Burt Lancaster, his collection reflects several literary forms, including book reviews, memoirs, and interviews, profiles, as well as the more traditional essay-form of movie writing.

Despite the diversity of his selections, Landis was able to organize them into organic, if imperfect, sections. With each section, he then brought a keen appetite and eye to observing further the reasons for his selections and/or their shared characteristics. The result is a collection that, once assembled, provides an opportunity for the reader to move through the pieces as if with a personal guide—the voice and presence of its editor, John Landis. Along the way, Landis suggested that the reader would enjoy photographs of many of the films and personalities written about and so, for the first time, this annual series offers a generous selection of photos chosen, from a limited pool of artwork, by Landis himself. As in his movies, Landis is always looking for new and innovative ways to approach people and places—and I'm pleased he brought this gift to this collection.

Given the depth and reach of films, it's no wonder that many writers are no longer producing film writing on their way to their novels, but as a form in itself. J. Hoberman, Molly Haskell, and Natalie Zemon Davis are just a few of such dedicated film writers appearing in this collection. And for the same reason, it is no wonder that some of our most distinguished writers of fiction, screenplays, and nonfiction are turning more and more toward writing about film, including Russell Banks, John Irving, David Leavitt, Lawrence Kasdan, and Walter Bernstein, all of whom have work in this collection.

What makes writing about film such a distinct and exciting literary form? It may be at first that writing about film is more an inclusive rather than limited art, offering authors the ability to shift from episodic retelling to compressive illustration to anecdotal analysis. It may also be that the common language and life of film creates a shared background, a unique, unparalleled canvas, upon which one can cover and uncover experience and themes in a way not possible in other literary forms—and, at the same time, reaching audiences not necessarily interested in other mediums beside cinema. Apart from all that, writing about film may also be, what Flannery O'Connor calls "an intense awareness of human possibilities."

James Agee, who brought the modern form of writing about film to a level of great intensity and power, showed us that its point of entry for the public may be close, or not close, to the film itself—but act as a springboard for everything else in life. Of the many pieces in this collection which demonstrate this point, one need look no further than Robert Polito's *Barbara Payton* or Mary Harron's *The Risky Business of American Psy-*

cho. Perhaps the only news regarding writing about film in the future that this collection suggests—is that it may drift more and more away from the classic model of writing about film where the film is the central component of the piece.

One of the benefits of serving as series editor of this annual collection is that I get to talk with, and occasionally meet, several of the writers and directors I admire. Many of John Landis's movies have had an unparalleled way of giving critical stories of several generations their due, especially perhaps the stories of those outside traditional communities and environments. Movies such as *Animal House, Trading Places, Blues Brothers, Coming to America, An American Werewolf in London*, and *Michael Jackson's Thriller*, among others, provide a temporary, if sometimes bizarre and humorous, haven for those who may feel temporarily exiled from everyday life. Such insight and dedication were evident as he read each piece with utmost care, appreciating every author's efforts and intentions, even as he made the sometimes very difficult decision not to include in the collection.

Except for a few selections, the pieces Landis finally chose for this anthology were originally published in magazines and books (published and distributed in the United States) from December 1999 to January 2000. Yet the pieces, of course, are, I hope, timeless in their qualities of craft and in their ability to illuminate, surprise, entertain, and move the reader toward new levels of engagement with the power and beauty of an art in crisis and celebration.

Jason Shinder

You could fit all the sincerity of Hollywood into a flea's navel and still have room left over for two caraway seeds and an agent's heart.

—Fred Allen

INTRODUCTION

John Landis

When I was approached by Jason Shinder to edit this edition of *Best American Movie Writing*, I hesitated at first. I've always disliked the word "best," as in *Best Picture* or the *Ten Best Films of the Year*. So I've decided that the title of this particular edition in this series really means that the "Guest Editor" will do the "best" he can.

I have chosen an eclectic and diverse selection of pieces for this volume from traditional and nontraditional sources. Included are magazine articles, book chapters, book reviews, newspaper articles, and even two interviews (one of those from the Internet).

Perhaps a better title for this collection would be *Stuff Written About Many Different Aspects of Film That Interest John Landis*. I've broken down the contents in eight chapters: Actors, Censorship, Writers, Directors, Nazis, Technology, Genre, and Shangri-La.

Many of these pieces overlap chapters; others pertain to specific pictures or personalities. They all share only one thing in common: they are about films and filmmakers.

I have written an introduction to each chapter to explain each choice. So much ink is devoted to the movies that there is almost too much information, much of it is gossip or just wrong. With the Internet there is unprecedented opportunity to get both information and misinformation. Since I believe that it is impossible to be objective when reporting or even discussing a subject, I tend to be drawn to those writers who wear their agenda loud and clear.

A movie tells a story by the juxtaposition of images. The camera in individual "set-ups" captures each image. Each set-up requires the skills of many craftspeople: actors, technicians, carpenters, physical and optical effects people, electricians, grips, makeup, hair, wardrobe, sound recorders, etc. In fact, the narrative motion picture is the last handcrafted product available at low cost to the consumer. The movie patron pays whatever the going ticket price is (in Manhattan it's now ten dollars) regardless of the cost of the movie. If you see a film that cost one hundred and eighty million dollars to make in a movie theater in New York City, it's ten dollars. If you see a movie that cost one hundred thousand dollars to make, it's ten dollars. If you see a great work of film history, a true work of art, it's ten dollars. And, as you're well aware, a piece of dreck . . . ten dollars.

This is a holdover from the glory days of Hollywood, when each major studio in Los Angeles produced over 45 feature films and countless shorts, travel logs, newsreels, and cartoons a year. And equally important, a steady and appreciative audience would show up every week.

The history of film reflects the history of the Motion Picture Industry. From the earliest days it has been called the Movie Business, never even The Craft. This is the key thing to understand about those who struggle to make movies. The crazy-making paradox of the nature of what we do. There are directors who differentiate between their own pictures as "movies" (a commercial effort), and "films" (a picture with more artistic ambitions).

What is a "good" movie? The very real yardstick used by most is Box Office. Of course, bad movies often make a fortune, and good movies consistently fail. Should we go by the prevailing Movie Critic's response? Or, should we "trust the public"?

Two widely accepted American films now firmly established

as classics (and rightly so) are *It's A Wonderful Life* and *The Wizard of Oz*. Neither was particularly well received, and both had to wait many years to find their audiences through television. Liberty Films, the company that made the Frank Capra masterpiece, actually had to shut down because of the financial failure of Jimmy Stewart's greatest performance.

I will never forget reading Pauline Kael's negative review of *2001, A Space Odyssey* in the *New Yorker*. She called it "a monumentally unimaginative movie"! I always enjoyed her writing skill; in much the same way I enjoyed the bitchiness of John Simon. But, as a filmmaker I've learned the truth about reviews. The great danger, to paraphrase Lawrence Olivier, is that if you believe the good notices, then you must believe the bad ones too.

The real quality of a movie is down to the knowledge and life experience of the viewer.

The impact of the motion picture on world culture has been, and continues to be, gigantic. As technology advances daily, the tools the filmmaker uses changes, but the craft itself does not. As the invention of the computer has changed the way books are composed, and printed, the actual creation of text, the human part, has remained constant. So it is with the movies.

New delivery systems (television, the home computer, etc.), will never replace the shared experience of sitting in a large theater and watching a movie with an audience. We have been sitting around campfires telling stories for thousands of years, and I'm confident we shall continue to huddle around whatever new means of projection comes our way.

To judge a film is easy. It was wonderful. It was terrible. I loved it. I hated it. The important thing is not only whether or not one enjoys a movie; it is also why.

I trust that if you are reading this book, it's because you are interested in the movies. I hope the following essays illuminate and entertain you.

SOME THOUGHTS ON CRITICS

compiled by John Landis

"Critics are like horseflies which prevent the horse from ploughing."

ANTON CHEKHOV

"Listening to critics is like letting Mohammed Ali decide which astronaut goes to the moon."

ROBERT DUVALL

"Listen carefully to first criticisms of your work. Note just what it is about your work that critics don't like, and then cultivate it. That's the part of your work that's individual and worth keeping."

JEAN COCTEAU

"Critics are like eunuchs in a harem: they know how it's done, they've seen it done every day, but they're unable to do it themselves."

BRENDAN BEHAN

"Taking to pieces is the trade of those who cannot construct."

RALPH WALDO EMERSON

"A gong at a railway crossing clanging loudly and vainly as the train goes by."

CHRISTOPHER MORLEY

"The critic's symbol should be the tumble-bug: he deposits his egg in somebody else's dung, otherwise he could not hatch it."

MARK TWAIN

"In the arts, the critic is the only independent source of information. The rest is advertising."

PAULINE KAEL

"Oh, fuck Pauline Kael, fuck her! And I don't use that language all the time. I don't care what she has to say. She's a bitch. She's spiteful, and she's wrong."

GEORGE CUKOR

"Time is the only critic without ambition."

JOHN STEINBECK

"The best thing you can do about critics is never say a word. In the end you have the last say, and they know it."

TENNESSEE WILLIAMS

"The criterion for judging whether a picture is successful or not is time."

PETER BOGDANOVICH

"A critic is a man who knows the way but can't drive the car."

KENNETH TYNAN

"Criticism is the art wherewith a critic tries to guess himself into a share of the artist fame."

GEORGE JEAN NATHAN

"It is the will of God that we must have critics, and missionaries, and Congressmen, and humorists, and we must bear the burden. Meanwhile, I seem to be drifting into criticism myself. But that is nothing. At the worst, criticism is nothing more than a crime, and I am not unused to that."

MARK TWAIN

1

"Memorize your lines and

don't bump into the furniture."

—Spencer Tracy

ACTORS

WE BEGIN WITH a book review by Molly Haskell of *Burt Lancaster, An American Life* written by Kate Buford. Why a review and not an excerpt from the book itself? Because of the nature of many book reviewers, their reviews will contain their own viewpoints on the subject of the book as well as an assessment of the author's. Burt Lancaster is a movie star of icon status, and represents the power shift from the studios to the star that began in the fifties. In Lancaster's case, he was directly responsible for some truly great films (*Marty, The Sweet Smell of Success*) and many great and indelible performances. Read this review, and then read the book.

"Barbara Dayton: A Memoir" by Robert Polito reads like an Edgar Ulmer movie, tough and sad. It is almost the perfect antidote to dreams of Hollywood stardom.

The Three Stooges are probably the most popular and successful film comics of all time. There is never an instant when one of their Columbia shorts is not shown somewhere in the world on television. Like all comics with long careers, their huge body of work collapses under its own volume. Laurel and Hardy, Abbot and Costello, The Marx Brothers, Martin and Lewis, and others found it impossible to sustain a standard of excellence in part because they were so prolific. Stand-up comedian Jay Leno had an early routine on how what really differentiated the sexes was an appreciation of the Three Stooges. Men loved them, women hated them. They have always amused me, not only for their straightforward stage-bound routines, but also sometimes for their sheer artlessness. A total lack of pretension goes a long way in my book.

I found the Jack Kerouac story "Cody and the Three Stooges" printed as an appendix to *Larry, the Stooge in the Middle*, a biography of Larry Fine by his brother Morris "Moe" Feinberg with G.P. Skratz. Kerouac's style wonderfully captures the lunacy of the Stooges' best work.

Since the studios evolved into a factory system of production, film companies tended to regard their sets, props, and costumes, etc., as industrial by-products. The physical ephemera of production was recycled or more usually, trashed. Over the years, much of what remains of film history has been the work of private individual collectors. Eccentrics like Henri Langlois, Forrest J Ackerman and Bob Burns saved priceless material that otherwise would be lost forever.

There is a new book, *It Came From Bob's Basement* by Bob Burns with John Michlig, which is lavishly illustrated with photographs of Bob's collection. On the flyleaf Bob's bio reads, "After a long and varied career spent in the company of monsters, space aliens, and gorillas, Bob has accumulated what may be the world's largest private collection of props and artwork from our favorite creature features and sci-fi pics." Bob actually has the genuine King Kong!

I have always had a love of and fascination with apes, especially gorillas. I have only met three others in my lifetime with my own passion for the great apes, Rick Baker, Ray Harryhausen and Bob Burns. All of us agree that the original *King Kong* is a perfect film. All of us collect gorilla figures (Rick Baker gave my wife Deborah and I as a wedding present a life-size fiberglass sculpture of a male Mountain Gorilla which still stands proudly in our living room, and a Ray Harryhausen sculpture in bronze of Kong battling the Tyrannosaurus with Fay Wray cowering nearby is in the hall), and three of us have actually portrayed apes in the movies.

We four are most likely the only ones who can hold forth on the different gorilla suits, masks, and performances of Emil van Horne, Crash Corrigan, George Barrows, Janos Prohaska, Bob Burns, Rick Baker, and the greatest "gorilla man" of them all, Charlie Gemora. These were the men inside all those Hollywood gorilla and monster costumes in all those movies.

The Monster and the Girl, a Paramount picture released in 1941, is a delirious mixture of film noir/white slavery/mad scientist-transplants-human-brain-into-gorilla/revenge picture, with an outstanding performance by Charlie Gemora. Check it out to understand why I've included him.

John Landis

HIGH-WIRE ARTIST

by Molly Haskell

To fly through the air with the greatest of ease is what we expect of the young man on the flying trapeze; to enthrall women sexually in the name of the Lord is the dubious gift of the religious revivalist. Yet Burt Lancaster, onetime circus performer (see him swing through *The Crimson Pirate* in 1952 and *Trapeze* in 1956) and Oscar winner for his Bible-thumping evangelist in *Elmer Gantry* (1960), was neither a natural athlete nor a natural seducer. He had a great many qualities—leonine beauty, acrobatic dexterity, physical strength, street smarts, serious ambition, a political conscience, and, by the end of his career, a number of good and a few great performances under his belt. But ease, natural ease, eluded him; too often he had a deliberate, overheated quality on the screen, mirrored, it seems, in the way he played golf: he never managed the relaxed swing essential to the game that attracted and frustrated him.

He had charisma—in many scenes, as Kate Buford points out in this splendid biography, he is the only person you watch on the screen. But not being able to blend in with one's fellow actors is hardly an unqualified asset. That sort of megawattage defines star cinema, and Lancaster, who had it in spades, almost could not not be a star. But charisma, with its overtones of divinity, is one thing; charm on the human scale is something else. A few stars have both, the blast of star power and the quieter lure of intimacy, but Lancaster was like those Olympians who bestrode the earth and laughed at puny mortals, whose gestures were larger, whose words were weightier and whose diction was more precise than anybody else's.

Indeed, and not just incidentally, in the many interesting descriptions quoted by Buford from friends, directors, and journalists, phrases like "golem," "Adam," "young Sun god," "sculptural," "Greek hero," "hyper-man," and "wounded colossus" are used, and the people most often doing the describing in this biography are men. Lancaster's was a male ideal of power and grace, classical in form: the sculptured physique, the exultation in the body, the sense of being complete without a woman.

At least that was how he appeared to us in the 1950's—strenuously physical, preeningly patriarchal, decidedly uncool, almost an embarrassment, or, as Buford says in the prologue to her first book, "too earnest to be chic." But as time went on, that earnestness paid off. In the retrospective view that *Burt Lancaster: An American Life* invites, his career now looks infinitely more interesting—richer and more ambitious on the whole than Brando's, the more gifted contemporary who beat him out for coveted roles like Stanley Kowalski and the Godfather but languished in middle and old age. Lancaster used his autumn years not just to make a few bucks or stay in the game but to explore new facets of his character and come to terms with age itself, to risk losing his fans in wildly unconventional roles. Not only did he allow himself to be Luchino Visconti's alter ego as the Sicilian aristocrat of *The Leopard* (1963) and the fussy professor of *Conversation Piece* (1975) and, no less perversely, Bernardo Bertolucci's randy landowner in *1900* (1976), but he wanted desperately to make a film of *Kiss of the Spider Woman* and play the gay hairdresser!

Descended from Protestant Irish immigrants, Lancaster (1913–94) grew up in a raffish East Harlem neighborhood like that of another pugnacious Irishman, James Cagney. Along with other kids in the area, he was a lucky protege of the Union Settlement House, that extraordinary church-run institution that got young people off the streets with a range of activities, from sports to theatricals, and helped the immigrant poor organize within their communities. Encouraged by an artistic, opera-loving mother and two inspirational pastors, he discovered a talent for acting—balanced always by the more "masculine" love of sports.

Preferring to express himself physically rather than emotionally (he would later block love scenes carefully, according to one co-star, in order to "hide his feelings from the camera"), he was disdainful of Stanislavsky's Method, which was overtaking the New York theater and its settlement offshoots, and felt that acting the same role night after night was "sissy." He had "no intention," Buford adds, "of playing dour Russian peasants when he could dream of emulating Douglas Fairbanks in *The*

Mark of Zorro." But from the settlement-house ethic he also developed the progressive and reformist impulses that would characterize his leftist politics, from his mostly staunch solidarity with the Hollywood targets of the witch hunt in the 50's to the underdog sympathies of his films to major personal and financial contributions to the American Civil Liberties Union and other organizations in his later life.

Lancaster figured out what was needed in postwar Hollywood and was way ahead of the game as an independent, forming his own production company in 1945 with the agent and onetime actor Harold Hecht as his partner. Called Norma Productions after his wife, it was one of the first and most successful of its kind, boosting the fortunes of all concerned. With different studios (they eventually put United Artists back on the map), Lancaster and Hecht made offbeat movies like *Marty* (1955) and serious adaptations like *Come Back, Little Sheba* (1952) and *The Rose Tattoo* (1955), as well as more profitable adventure pictures. Lancaster always insisted he was making movies, not films, and if a picture didn't score with an audience it was by definition a failure. Yet best regarded today are not the ambitious ego trips, one-man shows *Elmer Gantry* and *Birdman of Alcatraz* (1962), but the less pretentious movies that did not become box-office hits. The cult classics and acknowledged masterpieces are the noirish pictures in which the smiles are few, Lancaster's "Chiclet" teeth are least visible and the endings bleaker than a cold moonless night.

In *The Killers* (1946), he makes one of the most dazzling debuts on film, lying in the shadow, awaiting death, his bare arms by his side, the muscularity in repose implying both strength and sensitivity. In *Criss Cross* (1949), also directed by Robert Siodmak, his bank guard gone bad greets death almost passively, the noir antihero as fallen idol. As J. J. Hunsecker, the malicious gossip columnist in *Sweet Smell of Success* (1957), he scored a critical triumph and gave Tony Curtis the role of his life. As the hawkish and half-mad General Scott in *Seven Days in May* (1964), he played his own philosophical opposite. Closer to his real-life character was the shrewdly tolerant American Indian scout in Robert Aldrich's brilliant *Ulzana*'s *Raid* (1972), who dies in the end, victim of a massacre, while lighting a cigarette.

There was gossip about his unorthodox sex life (on which the omnipresent Federal Bureau of Investigation kept a running file), and Buford reports the rumors as such. Through many affairs—he was a compulsive womanizer but not a ladies' man—he nevertheless remained dutifully with his alcoholic wife and their five children until circumstances finally drove them apart. However, by all accounts, he nevertheless lived on the wild side, took advantage of the multiplicity of offerings—orgies, sharing women with his associate James Hill, forays into homosexuality. He was a man of broad appetites and black rages, difficult and sometimes impossibly rude. Siodmak was so disgusted with his behavior on location for *The Crimson Pirate* that he left Lancaster and Hollywood for good. Yet he could be kind and generous, loyal to friends and indifferent to the Hollywood power game, rarely cultivating the socially important and unconcerned with what people thought.

He could make fun of his own virility and though *Mad* magazine might parody him and Gary Cooper in *Vera Cruz* (1954) as "Lambaster" (who takes forever to die) and "Chickencooper," the two stars were already halfway there in this entertaining buddy tale of two laconic he-men cowboys outhustling each other. It was his coming to terms with growing old and the loss of masculine power that makes his later films so engaging, even moving. In *Atlantic City* (1981), coming full circle back to his runaway felon in *The Killers,* he plays a has-been mobster who voyeuristically ogles, then befriends, Susan Sarandon's croupier-in-training. Sarandon describes how difficult it was for Lancaster, whose instinct was to take a woman by force, to accept the idea that the woman "gave herself to him." The man who had shocked audiences of *From Here to Eternity* (1953) by making graphic love to Deborah Kerr on the sand had never really exposed his emotional vulnerability. Now that the famous torso was past displaying, and the emperor had to wear clothes, there was, after all, as Kate Buford's biography makes clear, more to him than met the eye.

BARBARA PAYTON: A MEMOIR

by Robert Polito

For a few years during the early 1960s my father tended bar at The Coach and Horses on Sunset, in Hollywood. Weekdays he inventoried the sale of stamps, money orders, and Pitney Bowes machines as supervisor of a Santa Ana Post Office, close to where he lived in a tidy dingbat studio. But I was about to turn thirteen, and he hoped to send me to a "real college." The Post Office discouraged second jobs for Government employees of his rank, so my father moonlighted only at bars, all transactions cash.

The Coach and Horses lured patrons with the natty coat of arms of a British pub, but inside the landscape registered saloon. This was residential Hollywood. Cocktail lounges unattached to hotels or eateries still tended to be rare in Los Angeles, and survived on local drunks who could swing the tab—wall drinks sixty-five cents. Fourteen stools along a runty bar, half as many booths strung in a miniature railroad, the vibes at The Coach and Horses read dark: dusky paneling, blackout drapes, shaded lamps. Haul in a couple of slot machines and you might feel transported to Vegas, even Barstow.

* * *

The summer of 1962 my father let me join him for his Saturday stints. My parents already were separated, and he took custody of me weekends. In the beginning I was too shy to connect with anyone but him, but I loved the overheard chatter, wisecracks, complaints, the provocative fragments of confessions. The silent drinkers, draining the day over the *Citizen-News*, I also admired, because they were harder to figure out. I read novels and music magazines sitting at a desk in the ruins of an office that the staff tagged the "Black Hole of Calcutta," up a shaky flight of stairs at the back; or sometimes I moved to the last booth, where we covertly replaced the mood lighting with a forty-watt bulb—still too dim to menace the perpetual twilight. We made a day of it, before heading off to supper and a movie. The whole experience was a lot like going to a loud library.

We were about three or four weeks into our routine when a day-manager, probably Rodney, an occasional DJ at Hollywood High dances, started to lecture my father. He felt sorry for me, he said, rotting away doing nothing on another beautiful LA afternoon. His concern could also have betrayed the sodden departure the previous night of his latest barback—a fiftyish ex-race car driver fleeing overdue alimony. (The Coach and Horses rotated help nearly every payday.)

Rodney suggested I could better occupy myself. For exactly a dollar less than minimum wage, he put me to work retrieving bottles and splits, sweeping cigarettes off the black-and-red carpeting, soaking glasses. My father and I opened the bar Saturdays at noon. Quickly I graduated also to Friday evenings.

I was too thrilled to tell my mother about my secret employment, but lied cautiously.

Ralph and Leo from Holloway House stopped at The Coach and Horses evenings after work, and Leo usually returned Saturday. Back then, Holloway House—situated up on Holloway Drive—published bottom-feeder Hollywood autobiographies along the lines of *Jayne Mansfield's Wild, Wild World*. Earnestly sensational scientific exposes, such as *Psychodynamics of Unconventional Sex Behavior* by Paul J. Gillette, Ph.D., and unexpurgated classics, *Satyricon: Memoirs of a Lusty Roman*, rounded off the list.

Leo was an old columnist for the *Hollywood Reporter*, a squat mischievous man. He would discover me with a book at the bar during the ordinarily vacant afternoons, and he started to joke with me about school. Leo could talk to anyone.

One day he arrived lugging a fat brick of loose pages—"What's your spelling like?," he quizzed me. His company needed a person to fix galleys. Leo said he was sick of doing everything himself. For exactly a dollar more than minimum wage I signed on as the exclusive proofreader at Holloway House.

This was perfect, since I would now be paid double for reading at The Coach and Horses. The first titles I remember were *Hollywood Screwballs* and *The Many Loves of Casanova.*

The Coach and Horses swirled with legends of famous lushes who boozed there—Hitchcock, Jason Robards, Richard Harris, William Holden. But the only star—if star's the right name for her—we ever saw was Barbara Payton.

Someone, no doubt Leo, told me about "the scandal." Back in the early 1950s Payton was coming off a leading role in *Kiss Tomorrow Goodbye,* when she met B-movie actor Tom Neal at a party. Within days she ended a relationship with Franchot Tone, proclaiming her engagement to Neal. But believing marriage to the more prominent and accomplished Tone might advance her Hollywood stature, Payton ditched Neal—only to return again. "He had a chemical buzz for me that sent red peppers down my thighs," she subsequently explained to *Confidential.* But the night before Payton was to marry Neal, she contrived a date with Tone. Neal waited up for them. The former boxer smashed Tone's nose, and sent him to the hospital with a concussion and fractured cheekbones. Tone secretly underwent plastic surgery.

Payton wed Tone upon his recovery. She divorced him fifty-three days later. Neal and Payton toured in a backwater road production of *The Postman Always Rings Twice,* but both careers derailed.

Connecting *that* Barbara Payton to the woman in The Coach and Horses demanded impossible time-travel. Our Barbara Payton oozed alcohol even before she ordered a drink. Her eyebrows didn't match her brassy hair, her face displayed a perpetual sunburn, a map of veins by her nose. Her feet swelled, and she carried an old man's pot belly that sloshed faintly when she moved. Her gowns and dresses looked more like antique costumes than clothes, creased and spotted. She must have weighed two hundred pounds.

She didn't resemble anyone two actors would fight over.

Barbara Payton was then thirty-four years old—younger than my father. She didn't come across as bitter, or angry, or crazy. She clearly wasn't rich, but she always carried ten or twenty dollars for her drinks.

Beyond the Rose, Barbara emanated a chronic self-abdication that outmaneuvered most humiliations. If a new customer of The Coach and Horses wondered whether there might be any regrets, she'd pause, taste her wine, and answer as though she had never considered the question. "You know if I had to do it all over again, I'd do the same. It's all in heaven in a little black book with neat lines. You are what you are and there's no out. You do what you have to do."

She was the first person I met who spoke like she lived in a movie. She conversed through hard-boiled maxims.

"I got news for you baby—nobody's civilized. You peel off a little skin and you got raw flesh."

"But forever is just a weekend—more or less."

She had a theory different sleeping pills will give you different sorts of dreams. She couldn't recall any brandnames—only colors, red for passionate dreams; white for horror dreams. Barbara maintained she told this to Gregory Peck while they were filming *Only the Valiant*. He jotted it down.

She enjoyed washing men's dirty shirts—said she liked it the way someone liked playing golf.

Barbara entered The Coach and Horses every Saturday afternoon at five o'clock, and she left at seven, as methodical as a stopwatch conductor. Fridays she would land around eleven and remain on her stool until we closed at one. Leo sometimes would escort Barbara home—Friday, anyway, but never Saturday, when she always insisted on leaving alone. Her apartment, it turned out, was right on Holloway Drive.

Ralph once joked that Leo could smell a book in a Hollywood toilet. Soon after my proofreading chores started for Holloway House, Leo advanced Barbara Payton $250 for her life story.

He loaned her a tape recorder to reconstruct her memories. A young woman Leo knew named Nancy—I heard later she dated, maybe even married one of the Wilsons, of the Beach Boys—would actually write the text. My job was to transcribe the tapes.

Leo titled Barbara's story after a line she regularly used around the bar: *I Am Not Ashamed*.

I typed on a sleek Remington Portable (courtesy of Holloway House) up in the "Black Hole of Calcutta." Barbara's tapes came as a revelation—to me, though hardly, I suspect, to Leo and Ralph. If her Hollywood past loomed a distant mystery, her present amounted to an "other life." Five minutes into the first reel Barbara was describing her practices as a hooker along the Sunset Strip.

On the tapes she compared her book to "a kind of detective story. I—or we—want to find out what happened that started me on the skids, down, down, down, down." Yet Barbara was short on motive or responsibility. Even "the scandal" seemed less a life-transforming watershed than another spongy anecdote.

Barbara herself charted her fall as an inverse pyramid of declining cash. There was stardom, and $10,000 a week. Then, all but inexplicably, no roles—instead $300 "gifts" tactfully deposited inside her purse by producers. Then, $100 gifts, left less discreetly on her dresser. She bounced a check at a Hollywood grocery store to purchase liquor. She slept with her landlady's husband for the rent, and on Christmas Eve with an actor friend for $50, then $20 johns, then $10.

Now—her voice oozed from the speaker—"The little money I accumulate comes from old residuals, poetry and favors to men. . . . I love the Negro race and I will accept money only from Negroes. . . . White men don't seem to go for me anymore. . . . Wine and bare bodies and nightmare sleep and money that was never enough to pay the bills. . . . One night I realized I was in bed with a Negro. He was gentle and kind to me. . . . He gave me five dollars. . . . Five dollars!"

The hooking explained Barbara's meticulous timetable in The Coach and Horses. Friday she drank after she roused a few bucks. Saturday she braced herself against the evening ahead.

The poems, though, appeared to scratch a revenant of pride amid the drift. "I decided it was alright to be a hustler as long as I wrote poetry," Barbara declared on the tapes. "Even in bed with a trick I could think of lines." Her poems zigzagged like her stories—the few poems she showed us. Fragments, essentially: some phrases about Tom Neal, followed by an image from her Texas childhood, ending on a hymn to Rose wine. A writer friend, she mentioned, sold them to a "way-out Beatnik journal" for her.

I asked my father if he knew about Barbara's secret. He laughed. Anything she did was OK, he said, assuming she didn't do it in The Coach and Horses—and provided she stayed away from me.

* * *

He did allow Barbara to take me to the movies, twice, each occasion one of her old films. While we were working on the book, *Kiss Tomorrow Goodbye* played at the Oriental, a few doors down Sunset. Another afternoon we rode the bus over to the Encore at Melrose and Van Ness for *Trapped.*

Watching seated alongside Barbara, I was startled by her glamour—slim, blonde, beautiful—and the strangeness of actually knowing someone who made movies.

Seeing those films again, and some others for this history, I'm struck more by her obvious disquiet as an actress. Barbara Payton starred in roughly eleven features between 1949 and 1955, but she flashes anxiously from the margins of her movies. Her presence is fleeting—even when she attained top billing for *Only the Valiant* or *Bride of the Gorilla* her on-screen time amounted to staggered cameos; her command of role is hesitant, uneasy. As Holiday Carleton in *Kiss Tomorrow Goodbye* Payton wobbles from ingenue to she-devil. When facing into the camera she scarcely moves, except her mouth, to deliver her lines. Her transitions roll as a succession of production stills, a flip-book of faltering moods.

She does not so much inhabit a character as impersonate a starlet—an act, I suppose, she merely extended to The Coach and Horses, or the Sunset Strip. In her movies Payton is a doll dropped into a scene to insinuate sex. Directors took to filming her from the side, her breasts vaulted in silhouette.

Only Edgar Ulmer understood how to spin her anxiety into an advantage. For *Murder Is My Beat*—Payton's last film—he cast her as Eden Lane, a nightclub singer convicted of murder. On the way to prison Lane is convinced she sees the supposed victim from her train, and escapes. For much of the action the viewer is uncertain whether Lane committed a crime. Payton's tension plays as suspense, her hesitations as possible instability, the intimation that she might indeed be a murderess.

On the tapes Barbara asserted she bankrolled the completion of *Murder Is My Beat* by sleeping with a prosperous stockbroker. "Mr. Shellout" she christened him.

She even put me—or someone like me—into the book. "One night when a friend brought over another friend," she suggested, "and the first one left leaving me with this kid. . . . He was so awed by me I went to bed with him and then wouldn't take his money. That's how lousy a hooker I was."

This never happened. But many of Barbara's implausible stories weren't so readily dispelled. She also clutched secrets—her first husband, their son in Texas.

Nancy and I probed, and verified what we could; then we camouflaged the rest against lawsuits. The whole process took us about a month.

I Am Not Ashamed finally appeared in 1963. When Barbara Stanwyck read Payton's autobiography, she apparently quipped, "Well, she damn well should have been!"

Tom Neal married, and his wife died of cancer. He remarried, and opened a landscape business in Palm Springs. During a domestic dispute his new wife was shot to death. Like his character Al Roberts at the conclusion of Edgar Ulmer's film *Detour*, Neal maintained the killing was an accident. Barbara attended the trial wearing dark glasses. Neal served six years in the California Institute for Men at Chino before being paroled.

On her way back from Mexico in 1967, Barbara Payton died of complications from alcoholism in the bathroom of her parents' San Diego home. "A blonde movie actress in Mexico," she once said, "is always cause for celebration."

My parents divorced, and my mother never discovered The Coach and Horses. But my father sent me as far East from the bar as possible—to Catholic Boston College. By then he had moved on to the more upscale Firefly Lounge.

Holloway House discovered Iceberg Slim, and everything changed.

CODY & THE THREE STOOGES

by Jack Kerouac

BUT THE LATEST AND PERHAPS REALLY . . . best vision, also on high, but under entirely different circumstances, was the vision I had of Cody as he showed me one drowsy afternoon in January, on the sidewalks of workaday San Francisco, just like workaday afternoon on Moody Street in Lowell when boyhood buddy funnyguy G.J. and I played zombie piggy-backs in mill employment offices and workmen's saloons (the Silver Star it was), what and how the Three Stooges are like when they go staggering and knocking each other down the street, Moe Curly (who's actually the bald domed one, big husky) and meaningless goof (though somewhat mysterious as though he was a saint in disguise, a masquerading superduper witch doctor with good intentions actually)—can't think of his name; Cody knows his name, the bushy feathery haired one. Cody was supposed to be looking after his work at the railroad, we had just blasted in the car as we drove down the hill into wild mid-Market traffic and out Third past the Little Harlem where two and a half years ago we jumped with the wild tenor cats and Freddy and the rest . . . we passed Third Street and all its *that*, and came, driving slowly, noticing everything, talking everything, to the railyards where we worked and got out of the car to cross the warm airy plazas of the day . . . began somehow talking about the Three Stooges—were headed to see Mrs. So-and-So in the office and on business and around us conductors, executives, commuters, consumers rushed or sometimes just maybe ambling Russian spies carrying bombs in briefcases and sometimes ragbags I bet—just for foolishness—and the station there, the creamy stucco suggestive of palms, like the Union Station in L.A. with its palms and mission arches and marbles, is so unlike a railroad station to an Easterner like myself used to old redbrick and sootirons and exciting gloom fit for snows and voyages across pine forests to the sea, or like that great NYCEP whatever station . . . that I couldn't imagine anything good and adventurous coming from it . . . when it came into Cody's head to imitate the stagger of the Stooges, and he did the luck bone, luck bone's connected to the, foul bone, foul bone's connected to the, high bone, high bone's connected to the, air bone, air bone's connected to the, sky bone, sky bone's connected to the, angel bone, angel bone's connected to the, God bone, *God bone's connected to the bone bone;* Moe yanks it out of his eye, impales him with an eight-foot steel rod; it gets worse and worse, it started on an innocent thumbing, which led to backhand, then the pastries, then the nose yanks, blap, bloop, going, going, gong; and now as in a sticky dream set in syrup universe they do muckle and moan and pull and mop about like I told you in an underground hell of their own invention, they are involved and alive, they go haggling down the street at each other's hair, socking, remonstrating, falling, getting up, flailing, as the red sun sails—So supposing the Three Stooges were real and like Cody and me were going to work, only they forget about that, and tragically mistaken and interallied, begin pasting and cuffing each other at the employment office desk as clerks stare; supposing in real gray day and not the gray day of movies and all those afternoons we spent looking at them, in hooky or officially on Sundays among the thousand crackling children of peanuts and candy in the dark show when the Three Stooges (as in that golden dream B-movie of mine round the corner from the Strand) are providing scenes for wild vibrating hysterias as great as the hysterias of hipsters at Jazz at the Philharmonics, supposing in real gray day you saw them coming down Seventh Street looking for jobs—as ushers, insurance salesmen—that way. Then I saw the Three Stooges materialize on the sidewalk, their hair blowing in the wind of things, and Cody was with them, laughing and staggering in savage mimicry of them and himself staggering and gooped but they didn't notice . . . followed in back. . . . There was an afternoon when I had found myself hungup in a strange city, maybe after hitch-hiking and escaping something, half tears in my eyes, nineteen or twenty, worrying about my folks and killing time with B-movie or any movie and suddenly the Three Stooges appeared (just the name) goofing on the screen and in the streets that are the same streets as outside the theater only they are photographed in Hollywood by serious crews like Joan Rawshanks in the fog, and the Three Stooges were it wild, crazy, yelling in the sidewalk right there by the arches and by hurrying executives, I had a vision of him which at first (manifold it is!) was swamped by the idea that this was one hell of a wild unexpected twist in my suppositions about how he might now in his later years feel, twenty-five, about his employers and their temple and conventions, I saw his (again) rosy flushing face exuding heat and joy, his eyes popping in the hard exercise of staggering, his whole frame of clothes capped by those terrible pants with six, seven holes in them and streaked with baby food, come, ice cream, gasoline, ashes—I saw his whole life, I saw all the movies we'd ever been in, I saw for some reason he and his father on Larimer Street not caring in May—their Sunday afternoon walks hand in hand in back of great baking soda factories and along deadhead tracks and ramps, at the foot of that mighty red brick chimney a la Chirico or Chico Velasquez throwing a huge long shadow across their path in the gravel and the flat—

Supposing the Three Stooges were real? (and so I saw them spring into being at the side of Cody in the street right there in front of the Station, Curly, Moe and Larry, that's his bloody name, *Larry;* Moe the leader, mopish, mowbry, mope-mouthed, mealy, mad, hanking, making the others quake; whacking Curly on the iron pate, backhanding Larry (who wonders); picking up a sledgehammer, honk, and ramming it down nozzle first on the flatpan of Curly's skull, boing, and all big dumb convict Curly does is muckle and yukkle and squeal, pressing his lips, shaking his old butt like jelly, knotting his Jell-O fists, eyeing Moe, who looks back and at him with that lowered and surly "Well what are you gonna do about it?" under thunderstorm eyebrows like the eyebrows of Beethoven, completely ironbound in his surls, Larry in his angelic or rather he really looks like he conned the other two to let him join the group, so they had to pay him all these years a regular share of the salary to them who work so hard with the props—Larry, goofhaired, mopple-lipped, lisped, muxed and completely flunk—trips over a pail of whitewash and falls face first on a seven-inch nail that remains imbedded in his eyebone; the eyebone's connected to the shadowbone, shadowbone's connected to bopping one another . . . until, as Cody says, they've been at it for so many years in a thousand climactic efforts superclimbing and worked out every refinement of bopping one another so much that now, if it isn't already over, in the baroque period of the Three Stooges they are finally bopping mechanically and sometimes so hard it's impossible to bear (wince), but by now they've learned not only how to master the style of the blows but the symbol and acceptance of them also, as though inured in their souls and of course long ago in their bodies, to buffetings and crashings in the rixy gloom of Thirties movies and B short subjects (the kind made me yawn at 10 A.M. in my hooky movie of high school days, intent I was on saving my energy for serious-jawed features which in my time was the cleft jaw of Cary Grant), the Stooges don't feel the blows any more, Moe is iron, Curly's dead, Larry's gone, off the rocker, beyond the hell and gone, (so ably hidden by his uncombable mop, in which, as G.J. used to say, he hid a Derringer pistol), so there they are, bonk, boing, and there's Cody following after them stumbling and saying "Hey, lookout, houk" on Larimer or Main Street or Times Square in the mist as they parade erratically like crazy kids past the shoeboxes of simpletons and candy corn arcades—and seriously Cody talking about them, telling me, at the creamy Station, under palms or suggestions thereof, his huge rosy face bent over the time and the thing like a sun, in the great day—So then I knew that long ago when the mist was raw Cody saw the Three Stooges, maybe he just stood outside a pawnshop, or hardware store, or in that perennial poolhall door but maybe more likely on the pavings of the city under tragic rainy telephone poles, and thought of the Three Stooges, suddenly realizing—that life is strange and the Three Stooges exist that in 10,000 years—that . . . all the goofs he felt in him were justified in the outside world and he had nothing to reproach himself for, bonk, boing, crash, skittely boom, pow, slam, bang, boom, wham, blam, crack, frap, kerplunk, clatter, clap, blap, fap, slapmap, splat, crunch, crowsh, bong, splat, *BONG!*

HATS OFF TO CHARLES GEMORA, HOLLYWOOD'S GREATEST APE

Bob Burns on Charles Gemora
As Told to Tom Weaver

As a kid growing up in Oklahoma and California, I always loved jungle movies because I always loved the gorillas. And, little by little, once I began meeting actors and makeup artists and other people who worked in the movie industry, I made it my business to find out who Hollywood's "gorilla men" were. I knew from Glenn Strange that "Crash" Corrigan played gorillas in a lot of pictures, and I knew about Emil Van Horn (*Perils of Nyoka, The Ape Man*, etc.) from Roy Barcroft. I found out all the names through perseverance, mostly by asking the makeup guys. And whenever I would ask about one of my *favorite* gorillas—"Who played the gorilla in *Murders in the Rue Morgue*?", "Who played the gorilla in *The Monster and the Girl*?", "Who played the gorilla in *Phantom of the Rue Morgue*?—the answer would always come back the same: Charlie Gemora.

I started getting friendly with the various makeup men in the early 1950s, when I was about 18. One of them was a fellow named Emile LaVigne, who had worked on some of the Universal Frankenstein films and later made-up the mutants for *World Without End* [1956]. He'd been around a long time and I'd known him since I was a kid. One day he told me, "If you want to *really* learn about this stuff, they always need people to sit in for makeup tests. They don't care how old you are, they just need a *face*." He made a call for me, and soon I was sitting in for tests at the makeup union. Makeup "interns"—young guys who were trying to get into the makeup union—would take a makeup test consisting of an oral test, a written test, and then, of course, the makeup itself. They would do hair work on me, the bald caps, the beards, the cuts, the bruises, *all* that kind of stuff. A lot of people didn't like to do it—it's pretty uncomfortable—but I didn't care. I loved it. In fact, the more junk they put on me, the *more* I loved it! After they finished up on me, the old makeup guys would come in and see how the hair looked and examine the bald cap looking for "ends" and so on, then grade them. This was before there were makeup "classes" at places like the Joe Blasco Schools, this was at a time when the only way you could pick makeup tips was by sitting in for these guys. It only paid ten bucks a day, but I knew I'd "pick up" some information on how to do this stuff, and that was the idea.

The way I was introduced to Charlie Gemora was, again, through an old makeup guy I knew, Abe Haberman. In talking to him one day, I mentioned Charlie Gemora doing apes, and Abe said, "He's over at Paramount now." I'd had no idea. I knew Gemora did the Martian for *The War of the Worlds* [1953] at Paramount, but I thought Paramount just called him in for that—I didn't know he *worked* there. But he did: At that time, 1957, Wally Westmore was head of makeup at Paramount, and Charlie Gemora was head of the lab.

Once Abe realized how interested I was, he said he'd make a call for me—and he did. And Charlie Gemora said, "Sure, come on over!", and we arranged to meet at Paramount a couple of days later. I had a pass that got me through the famous Paramount gate and I proceeded to the makeup lab. I knew him as soon as I saw him, mainly from his size—he was only about five-five, a very short man. He was Filipino, and at that time he was probably 54 or 55 years old. It was really exciting for me; and, funnily enough, *he* was really excited that *I* was excited, because he probably didn't have a whole lot of fans asking him about his work. He said a few people had talked to him about making the *War of the Worlds* Martian suit and playing the Martian in the movie, but nobody had ever talked to him about doing the gorillas—nobody had ever even *mentioned* that. I was probably the first "fan" to ever mention the gorilla side of his career. So we got along famously.

We talked right there in the lab: He had a little desk in a corner of the lab and that's where we sat down, across the desk from each other. I pulled up a chair and we sat and talked for hours. Man, sitting across from Charlie Gemora—how cool is that? He asked, "Well . . . what do you want to know?", and I told him I thought he made the greatest gorillas in the world. And once I told him that someday I was hoping to build a gorilla suit, it opened up that whole avenue. He began telling me *every*thing he knew about gorilla suits, what to do and what *not* to do and so on and so forth.

Charlie got started building gorilla suits back in the 1920s, when he realized that there was a need for them. On some picture that he was working on as a makeup man, somebody said, "We need a gorilla suit"—and so Charlie built one! I've seen photographs from silent films with gorillas that aren't Charlie, so obviously costumers built gorillas from the '20s on, and probably put extras in them most of the time. But Charlie was the first to actually build his own gorilla suit and then portray the gorilla as well. He was a makeup artist who simply thought to himself, "Well, there's a need for a gorilla suit, so I'm gonna build one." It was a great idea, one that gave him a whole second career.

My main questions were about building gorilla suits, and Charlie was very open about it. He had no secrets at all, he told me *every*thing. Anything I wanted to know, he would tell me. He said, "You're going to need a cast of your face if you want it to fit well. That's one of the main things you gotta worry about: If you have daylight through those eyeholes, you're in trouble." That *was* one thing that put Charlie's suits above *all* the other gorilla suits: He put black makeup around his eyes to make it blend, and then his eyes fit right up against the eyeholes. You could shoot an extreme closeup on his face and the eyes blended right in with the gorilla face, and it didn't look like a mask. All the other gorilla guys, if the camera got too close, it didn't quite work right, you could tell there were eyeholes. But even in the early days, you could get real close on Charlie's face and it would look great. (The only guy that came close to that was George Barrows [*Gorilla at Large, Black Zoo,* many more], because he also did a casting of his face and it worked pretty good.) So when I did my first gorilla head, one that Don Post Sr. made for me, we took it off my head cast and it was perfect. The inside of my gorilla face was a total "negative" of my face, so it fit *very* close around my eyes. You could get closeups, everything, without a problem. That was because I listened to Charlie.

Charlie's gorilla suits were padded with kapok, the silky stuffing they used to use in mattresses and sleeping bags. It's fine, it's good padding, but you *sweat* to death because *insulation* is what it is! He told me, "If you ever build a gorilla suit, *don't use kapok,* what*ever* you do. It'll kill you!" That was a very good suggestion, and I certainly *didn't* use it. Unfortunately for Charlie, kapok was probably just about all he knew in those days, and he just didn't think about changing. Something else he advised me against doing was wearing the sort of iron mask that he and Emil Van Horn and "Crash" Corrigan wore, with the rubber gorilla face would be glued to that. What I did instead was make a gorilla face that was strictly all rubber—to make a dense foam rubber, a thicker type of foam. Instead of having the metal armature, the armature that the gorilla face fit on, around my face, my gorilla face fit right to my face.

Charlie was also the first guy to ever come up with what he called "a water bag." He put it in the stomach of his later gorillas so there would be totally realistic movement—it moved the way a chubby person's stomach would movie if he was bouncing around. It was incredible, the extra realism he got by having the belly move. He also did extension arms, because gorillas' arms are a lot longer than human arms. You don't need them on a gorilla suit unless you have to walk on all fours, but *then* you really do, because the human body doesn't bend the way a gorilla's does. Emil Van Horn used arm extensions, and George Barrows later on, but (again) Charlie was probably the first because, here again, he wanted it as realistic as he could get it. The gorilla actor's hands reach down the gorilla sleeve to about the elbow, and there would be a grip that he would hold onto. The arm extensions would go on down the rest of the way from there. Usually the gorilla hands were in a clenched position, because gorillas clench their fists when they're walking. Charlie only used them when he was walking or moving around; otherwise he didn't have to use them at all. Believe it or not, he could go back and forth between regular arms and extension arms in the same movie, all depending on the scene. For some reason, you can get away with that, audiences just don't notice it. For example, in *Phantom of the Rue Morgue*, he isn't wearing the arm extensions for the scene where he's in his cage, reaching through the bars and touching Karl Malden and Patricia Medina. But in later scenes where you see him walking on all fours, he *is* wearing them.

Charlie made all of his own suits from scratch, every one of them. Heads, hands, feet *and* the suit, he built; the only thing he didn't build was that "iron mask" armature. In addition to telling me everything I wanted to know about building a gorilla suit, he gave me lots of advice on how to move. For gorilla guys, the right "body English" is essential, and Charlie had it down pat because he'd done his homework: He used to go to the San Diego Zoo (the only place in California that *had* gorillas in those days) to observe them, he studied up on gorillas as much as he could and even got some scientific pictures. That was back in the '20s and '30s, when gorillas were still very "mysterious." (Back then, people used to think they were monsters and hunt them just because of their size and the fact that they were pretty ugly, grisly-looking things. You can tell that by the early movies, where the gorilla was always the monster—always.) The fact that Charlie had done his homework showed in his suits and also in his performances.

According to Charlie, what "makes" the performance is 90 percent body English and eye movement. He told me to do a lot of head movements and things like that; open and close your eyes; and, if you want to make the gorilla look *really* mean, when you open the mouth, throw your head back so that people are now looking up *inside* the mouth. It gives the illusion that the mouth is open a lot wider than it actually is. Just tilt your head back, open your mouth as wide as you can get it, and it looks like you're really growling. I had seen him do these things 100 times in his movies, and yet these were things that I'd never thought about. Ever. And it was all true. People think that the gorilla brow moves up and down and everything. But it doesn't move at *all*, it's strictly an illusion. When I played gorillas, I've heard people say about me, "Man, that gorilla really looks mean. Look at that brow!"—when the brow wasn't doing *any*thing. It's strictly the eyes and your body English. My gorilla faces were exactly like Charlie's as far as movement went: The mouths of my gorilla suits opened and closed, and that's *all* they did.

Charlie got up out of his chair and moved around and did all his gorilla stuff. He showed me how he walked and how he beat his chest and how he threw his head back—he demonstrated all of that for me. I think he was having a lot of fun. The other guys in the makeup lab, I don't remember if they watched—I was so engrossed, I don't even know if they were even still *there*. I was flabbergasted. Here's the God of Gorillas, showing me how he did his gorillas. To me, it was like the biggest thing in the world. I think he had a lot of fun . . . I know *I* sure did!

I know for sure that Charlie built at least six gorilla suits; he could have made *more* than that, but no less. He did three in the silent days, including one that he wore in a Tarzan picture. Then there was the gorilla suit that he wore in both versions of Lon Chaney's *The Unholy Three* [1925 and 1930], which was a slight variation, and one that was in the short *The Chimp* [1932] with Laurel and Hardy. So there were those three suits in the early days, and then he did one for *The Monster and the Girl* (1941), which was the best gorilla suit he ever made; one that ended up in *Africa Screams* [1949] and some other films; and then the *Phantom of the Rue Morgue* suit, which was the last one he ever built. He might have built more suits in between that I'm not familiar with, but I know he did at least those six.

Of course, he also talked about some of the experiences he'd had making those movies, and some of the stars he'd worked with. He did both versions, silent and sound, of *The Unholy Three*—I'll bet that was on account of Lon Chaney telling someone, "I want the same gorilla guy." He said Chaney was a very generous, kind man, but that was about it. But Laurel and Hardy he loved to death, he absolutely adored those guys and told me that they were two of the nicest, most friendly guys he'd ever met. I knew Stan Laurel real well, and that was exactly the same thing Stan used to tell me about Charlie Gemora, that *he* was the sweetest, greatest guy that he ever worked with. Charlie worked with them twice, in *The Chimp* and then in *Swiss Miss* [1938], where he played the gorilla on the suspension bridge. He loved working with Laurel and

Hardy and he talked about those guys more than he did anybody else.

I don't know how physically strong Charlie was back when he was in his prime. When you're playing gorillas, it helps a lot if you *are*, but you don't *have* to be. You have to be in pretty good health, though, and obviously Charlie was because he did it a number of times in the '20s, '30s and '40s. It's hard work, I can certainly vouch for that. He didn't mention any injuries, even though I don't believe he was stunt-doubled very often in his gorilla roles. In *Murders in the Rue Morgue*, Charlie did tell me that strongman Joe Bonomo doubled him in the scenes where he's climbing up to the Paris rooftops. But the thing about *Murders in the Rue Morgue* that stuck in Charlie's craw a little was the fact that closeups of an actual chimp were inserted into the film.

One of Charlie's more unusual credits was *Magic Island*, which was shot in color around 1935. It was a short in which puppets of various movie stars (like the Marx Brothers and Mae West) are menaced by a giant gorilla (Charlie) and a dragon (played by Wah Chang, who built the puppets as well as his own dragon suit). It was directed by LeRoy Prinz, a choreographer who had to shoot *Magic Island* at night because he was shooting dance sequences for other movies during the day. I never talked to Charlie about it, I didn't even know that it ever existed when Wah Chang told me about it. Wah told me that in one scene he and Charlie had a fight, and that at one point Charlie fell on top of him. Poor ol' Wah was a very thin little guy, and he said the weight of Charlie *and* his gorilla suit almost squished him! Wah said he believed that *Magic Island* was never completed, and I can believe that; I've never seen it, and never talked to anyone who has.

Phantom of the Rue Morgue was the last gorilla portrayal Charlie did. He had suffered a major heart attack some time before he began work on that movie, so Nick Cravat, the actor-acrobat who worked with Burt Lancaster in swashbucklers like

The Flame and the Arrow (1950) and *The Crimson Pirate* (1952), doubled him in the more strenuous scenes. (Lancaster and Cravat were friends from childhood who worked as an acrobatic circus act throughout the 1930s.) Charlie did all the closeup work, like (as I mentioned earlier) the scene where he and Patricia Medina are touching each other through the bars of his cage. At that point in his life, Charlie's gorillas could do minimal movement—he could do *some* stuff, but he couldn't do any of the stuntwork, like climbing up the side of Karl Malden's home or climbing the tree or tearing up the mannequin in the dressmaker's shop window. Nick Cravat doubled him in all those physical scenes. (Cravat was uncredited, of course—as was Charlie. I believe the only time Charlie got screen credit for playing a gorilla was *Swiss Miss*—and there they misspelled his name!) Charlie did a very minimal of work in *Phantom of the Rue Morgue*, but all the closeups were him because nobody could do the body English the way he did.

The only monster Charlie ever played was the Martian in *The War of the Worlds*, and of course I was real interested in that too. And, again, he filled me in on the whole story, including how he made the suit. (There was no secrecy about this man—none at all.) Building a Martian suit for *War of the Worlds* was a last-minute decision. Since George Pal had done the Puppetoons, the original idea for the Martian was to stop-motion-animate it the way the Puppetoons characters were animated. But then they decided that animation would be too costly—Paramount already had a lot of money in the film anyway—and that they would go ahead and make a Martian suit instead. Art director Al Nozaki quickly designed the Martian guy—this was a *very* last-minute thing—and Charlie built it just as fast. He made a chicken wire framework and laid what he called rubber sheeting over it. The Martian's three-color eye was made out of plastic and glass. (I'm sure somebody in the Paramount prop shop, not Charlie, made *that*.) For the Martian's pulsating veins, he used very, very thin rubber tubing. A guy off-screen could work the tubes, sucking the air out to make them collapse and then letting air back in again. That's what made them fluctuate and look like pulsating veins.

Charlie built the suit from Al's design and also wore it in the film (again uncredited, of course). He played the Martian, I believe, just because of the time constraints. He was used to wearing gorilla suits, so he knew it wouldn't bother him, and it was easier to build it for himself than to build it for somebody else. He didn't *say* that to me, but that's *my* speculation: The time was short, so he just figured, "I'll build it for myself, that'll be a lot easier." Also, Charlie would know how to manipulate everything. If Paramount had put an extra in that suit, it would have probably taken him hours or days to figure out how to work it. So it was just easier for Charlie to do it.

People have sometimes wondered what the bottom of the Martian looked like—you only see the top half of it in the movie. Well, a bottom half was never designed, there *was* no bottom to the Martian. The suit went down below Charlie's waist to probably just a little bit above his knees. Here again, as with his gorilla arm extensions, his arms went into the sleeves of the Martian suit but his hands went only to the elbows. At the elbows, there were three little rings that he put on three fingers. By pulling on those rings, which were attached to cables, he could make the Martian's fingers move. If he moved *his* fingers inside, opened and closed them, the Martian hands would open and close. When they were ready to shoot the scene, Charlie kneeled down on a small dolly and a grip just wheeled him around on it. At the end of the scene, when you see him streaking out of the room, they literally just *yanked* him across the room on that dolly! Balancing himself on his knees the way he was, he almost fell off and busted his head. He said that was perhaps the only time in his gorilla-monster career that he almost *did* get hurt! But Charlie thought playing the

Martian was real fun. He said it was a quick and easy scene, that there wasn't really all that much to it, and that they got it done in just one day.

I sat with Charlie in the Paramount makeup lab that day for at least four or five hours. We even went to lunch at the studio commissary—his treat. Like Stan Laurel said, he was absolutely the sweetest guy on Earth. He was a humble man—extremely humble—and very, very nice. In fact, I think he was maybe even a little bit embarrassed, because I don't think he was used to having fans wanting to talk to him. That was the feeling I got. It's so neat, when you finally meet someone whose work you admire so much, and they turn out to BE that kind of person. Often you meet people you think are going to be great, and they turn out to be so full of themselves. But he was just the opposite. In our meeting, he even promised to send me some photos of himself in his various movies, and sure enough he mailed them to me about a week later. I still have them today. I saw Charlie just that one time, but I talked to him at Paramount on maybe five or six occasions over a period of the next few months. I would think of another question about gorilla suits—what about the padding?, what about the size of the hands?, that kind of thing, and he was always *extremely* nice. If somebody else would answer, no matter what he was doing, he'd come right to the phone.

Charlie worked as a makeup man and mask maker on other science-fiction and fantasy films after I met him (*The Colossus of New York, I Married a Monster from Outer Space, Curse of the Faceless Man, Jack the Giant Killer,* more), but his days of working in front of the camera were over. He was the makeup man on a movie called *Flight of the Lost Balloon* (1961) with Marshall Thompson and Mala Powers, and one of Charlie's old gorilla suits was also used in the movie. But I doubt very much if it was Charlie wearing it; they weren't his mannerisms at all. He never did another gorilla after *Phantom of the Rue Morgue* that I know of. He'd had his heart attack in the '50s and *Flight of the Lost Balloon,* shot in May-June 1961, was one of his last films. I don't think health-wise he *could* have done it.

Charlie passed away in August of 1961. When I heard that he had died, I was devastated. Even though I couldn't say he was a close friend, I *felt* like I had lost a close friend because I had followed his career for so many years, and then he'd been so kind to me. It was like, "The king of gorillas is dead. The King is dead. There'll never be another one like him." And that's true—I don't think there ever *will* be another quite like Charlie Gemora.

In his obits, it was reported that his last work was as a makeup man on Paramount's *One-Eyed Jacks (1961)* with Marlon Brando—and that he had "achieved his first measure of fame as the oversize gorilla of the film, *King Kong*." Charlie never in his life said he played King Kong—never—but for some reason, people believed that he *had* played Kong in some scenes. According to the rumor, it was Charlie climbing up the side of the Empire State Building. Well, I've got a picture of Buzz Gibson animating the Kong puppet for that scene! There was *never* a guy used in a suit in that film, ever. Charlie was never even sure how the rumor got started, but it had gone around for a long time. At some point, somebody who knew that Charlie played gorillas must have been talking about *King Kong* and said, "it must have been Charlie Gemora . . . ", and the story spread from there. Charlie never claimed that he did, and when people would mention to him that he did, he would tell them [*emphatically*], "No, I did *not* play King Kong. I never played King Kong." That was a sore point with him. He would always say, "*No*, I had *nothing* to do with that film."

What Charlie did with his gorilla suits, I don't know. I think most of them rotted away. The last one, the *Phantom of the Rue Morgue* suit, ended up years ago with some makeup artist at NBC. I don't know how or where he got it, but he brought it over to Don Post Studios one day. It was just *totally* rotting away—the face was about gone. It was in real bad shape, and it's completely gone by now, I'm sure. What ever happened to the rest of his suits, I never even thought to ask him, and he didn't say.

Strangely enough, about a year ago I talked to *Mrs*. Gemora, who was still alive and in her late 80s. It was funny, *she* found *me*: I appeared in a TV special about guys who played gorillas in movies, *Hollywood Goes Ape*, and there was a good piece about Charlie in there and we dedicated the whole show to him. Well, somebody sent her a tape of *Hollywood Goes Ape* and she somehow tracked me down and called to thank me for saying all those nice things about Charlie. I told her the whole story of meeting Charlie, and she said, "Yes, I think Charlie mentioned you a couple of times. He'd talk about this young fellow who wanted to be a gorilla man. . . . " Unfortunately, she didn't remember a whole lot about Charlie's career—she was a housewife. At one point I brought up the fact that Charlie had given me some stills, and she said, "Oh, my gosh, speaking of stills . . . " and she told me that a very sad thing had recently happened: A few years earlier, she had gone on a vacation and the lady who was taking care of her house decided to clean up. She went up into the attic and found this big suitcase *full* of Charlie's pictures and everything . . . and *threw it away*. She thought it was junk, and that she was helping clean the place up. Once I heard that, I took all the stills of Charlie that I had and I made up copies and sent them to her so that she could have *some*thing again.

Charlie Gemora was *the* gorilla guy, the most realistic of any of 'em—Emil Van Horn, "Crash" Corrigan, whoever. Probably the one who came closest to acting like him was George Barrows. George did a pretty darn good gorilla; he was probably the only one of the latter-day guys that *tried* to do a real gorilla. (*I* never really got to try to do a *real* gorilla, most of *my* stuff was comedy. But that was okay with me.)

Unfortunately, I didn't make my first gorilla suit within

Charlie's lifetime. We didn't build my first suit until 1962, when Charlie had been dead for several months or a year. Don Post Sr. sculpted my original head, hands, and feet, and my wife, Kathy, built the costume. (It was kind of weird, the way she built the suit. There were no such thing as "gorilla patterns," not in *those* days, so she based it on a clown suit, because clown suits are kind of "full.") I remember we were over at Post Studios when we first got the suit all together, because they wanted to take pictures. Once I got the suit on, I looked in one of those big, full-length mirrors. I looked at myself the first time and, I wanna tell you, I got a thrill that I've never gotten over. I had chill bumps on top of chill bumps. Here was a lifelong dream fulfilled: I'm looking in the mirror, and looking back at me is this incredible gorilla. And as I tried that suit on for the first time, who was in my mind but Charlie Gemora. He was forefront. I was thinking, "Now, what would Charlie do? How would *he* move? How would he tilt his head?" And I did every move he did—or *tried* to, anyway. I wasn't thinking about real gorillas and how real gorillas moved, I was thinking about Charlie Gemora. I emulated him the whole way.

2

"I believe in censorship. After all, I made a fortune out of it."

—Mae West

CENSORSHIP

CENSORSHIP IS ALWAYS arbitrary. Standards change constantly and what is permissible one moment is forbidden the next. To avoid government censorship (which is alive and well all over the world), the American motion picture industry has over the years used its own ratings system. These ratings are meant as a guideline for the public on what the individual movie may or may not contain in the way of sex or violence. The sheer hypocrisy of our media and politicians in dealing with these ratings would be laughable if it wasn't often so scary.

Whenever a senator or congressman or even president wants to deflect the people's attention from the real problems in our society, Hollywood has always been a reliable target.

"Suppose you were an idiot, and suppose you were a member of Congress, but I repeat myself." Mark Twain said that even before the Congressional impeachment proceedings against President Clinton.

While it may be true, in the words of Henny Youngman, that "Motion pictures have ruined a lot more evenings than morals," the Republican release of the prurient Kenneth Starr report to the press has done more to lower the level of discourse in television, newspapers, magazines, and radio than any other event this century.

While the Starr report itself is funny and sad, the prosecutor's insistence on impeachment for lying about sex is stooping to a new low in American politics. Presidents Reagan and Bush lying about Iran/Contra apparently did not warrant impeachment I guess because no oral sex was involved, or at least none that we're aware of.

Censorship comes in all shapes and sizes. While technically the movies in America are not censored, in reality this is not the case. The economic restraints put on mainstream films are immense. Filmmakers are obligated by contract to deliver G, PG, PG13 or R rated films. Since the ratings are supposed to reflect contemporary standards, the process is never rational.

I've made films in the past which would definitely receive different rating classifications if rated now. Every director I know has tales of their struggles with the MPAA.

The X rating was meant to indicate adult themed subjects. *Midnight Cowboy* was an X rated film that won an Academy Award for Best Picture in 1969. However, the Porno Industry started using the expression "Triple X" (XXX) and hence the association with pornography was born. To get away from the porno taint that came with an X rating, the MPAA changed the rating for an adult themed picture to NC17. The television networks and major publications like *The New York Times* refuse to print ads for NC17 films. They will print ads for unrated films, usually foreign or independent pictures that aren't submitted to the MPAA for fear of an NC17 rating. This is blatantly dishonest.

This chapter has discussions of movie censorship of different kinds now and in the past.

The excerpt from *All About All About Eve* by Sam Staggs offers a fascinating look at the "routine but surreal correspondence" between Joe Mankiewicz and the Breen Office concerning his screenplay for *All About Eve.*

Mary Harron is the director of the film *American Psycho*. She writes clearly about the hysteria surrounding her production.

I have made feature films for Universal, Paramount, Warner Brothers, Disney, and independently. All of them have been submitted to the MPAA for ratings. My own experience has been the usual silliness but I have never felt unfairly treated. Doug Atchison has a different perspective.

I believe *Gone With the Wind* is a remarkable film. Although there is much to admire in it, I am uncomfortable with the inherent racism that comes directly from Margaret Mitchell's novel. The movie stands as a monument to Hollywood craftsmanship and to producer David O. Selznick's talent and energy. Leonard J. Leff's in-depth examination of *Gone With the Wind and Hollywood's Racial Politics* demonstrates the process by which the filmmakers dealt with the built-in pitfalls of the book.

John Landis

ALL ABOUT "ALL ABOUT EVE"

by Sam Staggs

In the spring of 1950 Joe Mankiewicz received his first two Oscars—Best Director and Best Screenplay—for *A Letter to Three Wives*. By that time 20th Century-Fox, where Mankiewicz was under contract as a writer-director, had optioned Mary Orr's story. A year earlier this story had been given to Mankiewicz, who read it an apparently knew from the start that here, in a few pages, was the embryo of the picture he wanted to make about the theatre.

On April 29, 1949, Mankiewicz had written a memo to Darryl F. Zanuck, production chief of the studio. The memo recommended that Fox exercise its option on "The Wisdom of Eve." Mankiewicz also noted in his memo to Zanuck that the story "fits in with an original idea [of mine] and can be combined. Superb starring role for [Fox star] Susan Hayward."

The deal with Mary Orr and her agent was soon made, but Mankiewicz had little time to think about how he world treat the material, for he had just finished directing *House of Strangers* with Edward G. Robinson and Susan Hayward. With an opening date of July 1, Mankiewicz still had to supervise post-production work on the film.

Much more demanding was his next assignment, *No Way Out,* a tense racial drama staring Richard Widmark, Linda Darnell, and Sidney Poitier. During the early summer he and Lesser Samuels collaborated on the screenplay for this movie, which was shot from October 28 through December 20. (The picture was not released, however, until August 1950.)

Between completing the screenplay of *No Way Out* and the start of production, Mankiewicz in the summer and early fall of 1949 also wrote the treatment of the movie that would become *All About Eve*. To do so, he left home and sought the relative isolation of the San Ysidro Guest Ranch near Santa Barbara. There he followed his habit of writing at night: "I was alone and I would write from about eight P.M. until two or three in the morning, while listening to the radio. Next day I would play tennis and go for long walks, then start back to work after dark."

Like many writers of the time, especially male writers, Mankiewicz never learned to type. As the *Hollywood Reporter* once phrased it, he "penned his scripts in longhand." From these manuscripts his secretary, Adelaide Wallace, would make typescripts with impeccable margins and faultless spelling.

Mankiewicz said later that he worked on the treatment for three months, and the rough draft of the screenplay for six weeks. The treatment—which is a synopsis or detailed plot outline—was called *Best Performance*, Mankiewicz's original title for *All About Eve.* It ran to eighty-two pages, double-spaced.

It is impossible to reconstruct a complete and precise chronology of *Eve*'s evolution from story, to treatment, to script, and finally to completed film. But the copy of Mankiewicz's treatment that Zanuck used to write his suggested revisions is dated September 26, 1949. This indicated that Mankiewicz worked on this treatment during the summer and early fall of 1949, spending as he recalled later, three months on it.

He would not, of course, have worked on treatment and script simultaneously. It seems likely, therefore, that with so many projects underway, Mankiewicz waited until he had finished shooting *No Way Out* in late December of 1949 before he began transforming his *Best Performance* treatment into the actual script that would later be renamed *All About Eve.* Zanuck was eager to see it.

Darryl Zanuck's biographer, Mel Gussow, describes the producer's collaboration with Mankiewicz as one of "mutual trust with a healthy degree of mutual suspicion . . . they worked superbly together. Each one honestly admired the other. Zanuck knew that there was no one better with dialogue on the lot and Mankiewicz knew that his outspoken comedies could not be made except in such an atmosphere of freedom as provided by Zanuck."

Zanuck produced three of the films Mankiewicz directed at Fox: *No Way Out, All About Eve,* and *People Will Talk.* Their actual collaboration, however, was more intricate than the above statistic indicates, for Zanuck, as studio production chief, was to some extent de facto producer of every film done on the lot. He and Mankiewicz retained their wary cordiality until 1963, when Zanuck fired Mankiewicz as director of *Cleopatra* and recut that ill-fated epic. ("He *rechopped* the picture," said Mankiewicz.)

Zanuck ran the show at Fox. He was responsible for all A products (as opposed to cut-rate B pictures), in addition to which he personally produced one or two films a year. Naturally, he reported to the president of the company and the board of directors, most of whom were in New York, but generally they left the day-by-day business of *making* the movies up to him.

Reading Mankiewicz's treatment of *Best Performance*, Zanuck followed his custom of making notes in pencil throughout the text and inside the back cover. At one point he underlined a phrase in Addison DeWitt's voice-over narration: "Eve . . . but more of Eve, later. All about Eve, in fact." The phrase Zanuck underlined was "all about Eve," which may have been the first dawning of the new title. At any rate, sometime during January 1950 the project acquired its new name.

Elsewhere in the pages of Mankiewicz's initial treatment, Zanuck expressed his concern about premature revelation of Eve's villainy to the audience. "Beware of Birdie's jealousy as it will tip off that Eve is a heel," he wrote. Where Eve makes a sexual overture to Bill Sampson in her dressing room and kisses him, Zanuck's reaction was: "This is all wrong. She is too clever to jump in so quickly." The kiss was eliminated, but the overture stayed. Several long speeches were reduced to a few lines, with Zanuck's marginal note, "This should cover it all." There were professorial admonitions to "Make clear. This can be confusing." Perhaps anticipating audience incredulity and wondering if viewers would suspend disbelief, Zanuck reacted to Karen's draining the gas tank of Richards' car to make Margo miss her performance with: "This is difficult to swallow." It stayed in, and it's still a bit difficult to swallow.

A major concern to the producer was a series of scenes, in the treatment, that depicted Eve's calculated designs on Lloyd Richards. Zanuck wanted to cut the entire four pages that showed Eve and Lloyd spending time together in little cafés on side streets, in Lloyd's apartment with Karen present and later without Karen, in Eve's furnished room, and Lloyd going to see Eve late at night after a phone call from a friend of Eve's. Zanuck noted: "Dull, obvious, dirty. . . . This is wrong. . . . All relationships with Eve and Lloyd [should be] played offstage by suggestion. . . . We get it by one brief scene at rehearsal." Most of the superfluous material was deleted.

Like most treatments, Mankiewicz's is a typical writer's "workshop" where he lays out all his materials, from which he will soon extract and polish the actual script. What sets this treatment apart, however, is the degree to which Mankiewicz has already nailed down the structure of his screenplay. Even at this stage, the material is unmistakably Mankiewicz's own; it bears his fluency, his wit, and also his excesses. It's an excellent example of how to transform a well-tailored treatment into an even better script.

Perhaps most surprising is the discovery that many of the film's best lines—"Fasten your seat belts, it's going to be a bumpy night," and "You can always put that award where your heart ought to be," to cite two of the most famous—were already there at this early stage of *All About Eve.*

Instructive, too, are the changes and omissions made either by Mankiewicz or Zanuck. For example, in the treatment Karen and Lloyd "wish Bill all sorts of bad luck" as he leaves to go to Hollywood. In the film Karen says, "Good luck, genius," and Lloyd merely shakes Bill's hand. Someone realized that most moviegoers would be confused by the theatre shibboleth "break a leg."

There's even a whiff of deference to McCarthyism. In the treatment, Mankiewicz has Eve tell Margo, in a cab from LaGuardia after they've put Bill on the plane, that she—Margo—needs galoshes. Eve knows this because she has watched Margo's comings and goings so closely. Referring to Eve's surveillance, Margo quips, "You're not on one of those congressional committees, are you?" This sly political reference must have given Zanuck the willies, for he slashed through it with a heavy pencil—markedly heavier than elsewhere—as though the House Committee on Un-American Activities were reading over his shoulder.

At the end of the treatment, the young girl, Phoebe, doesn't slip into Eve Harrington's apartment as she was to do later, in both script and film. Rather, she calls out from the shadows near the entrance to Eve's Park Avenue building. Eve invites her in for a drink. And the girl is not a high school student but a young working woman who "worships Eve from afar." Nor does Phoebe hold Eve's award to her breast while bowing into an infinity of mirrors; that cinematic finale came later. The treatment ends as Addison DeWitt's taxi "drives off and is lost in the lights of the city."

After incorporating various changes suggested by his producer, Mankiewicz delivered his first draft of the screenplay—dubbed the "temporary script"—to Darryl Zanuck on March 1, 1950. According to 20th Century-Fox's records, Mankiewicz's services as writer (for accounting purposes) terminated on March 24, 1950. Adhering to studio bookkeeping policy, Fox subsequently started Mankiewicz's assignment as director" at the beginning of April.

Mankiewicz was luckier than most screenwriters: His scripts were lightly edited, if at all. (Unlike the writer who once told a companion at the premiere of a film he had written, "Shh! I thought I just heard one of my lines.") In the case of *All About Eve,*, the trajectory from treatment, through various drafts of the shooting script, to the actual film was uncluttered by compromise. In this sense, *Eve* "belongs" to Mankiewicz as a novel belongs to its author. He owns it as few studio directors ever owned their films.

Zanuck, of course, served as "editor" to the Mankiewicz screenplay, as he had done on the treatment. After reading Mankiewicz's lengthy first-draft "temporary script" in March 1950, he praised it highly but suggested some changes and cuts. Zanuck wrote in a memo, "I have tried to sincerely point out the spots that appeared dull or overdrawn. I have not let the length of the script influence me. I have tried to cut it as I am sure I would cut it if I were in the projection room."

The "temporary script" of March 1 ran to 223 pages. After Zanuck's cuts and Mankiewicz's own, the next—and final—version had slimmed to 180 pages. Most of the changes involve shortening or condensing.

Overall, the "temporary script" is not radically different from the final version. But there are some intriguing changes. For example, the "temporary" has a five-page scene in Max Fabian's limousine after Margo's cocktail party. Karen and Lloyd ride with Max and they all talk about Margo's outrageous behavior at the party. They also discuss Eve as a possible understudy for Margo. Karen and Lloyd urge Max to give Eve the job. Max demurs. It's a long, chatty scene that stops the story dead.

Deleted, also, was a four-page scene in the Richards' country house. Dialogue from this scene was saved, however, and added to the lines spoken in the car by Margo, Karen, and Lloyd.

Elsewhere in the "temporary script" are such unpolished, rather pedestrian speeches as this, spoken by Addison to Eve: "What do you take me for? A talented newsboy like Bill Sampson? Or Margo—a gifted neurosis? Or Lloyd Richards—a poetic bank clerk? A refined Girl Scout—like Karen? Look closely, Eve, it's time you did. I am Addison DeWitt. I am nobody's fool. Least of all yours."

In the revision Mankiewicz turned it into this trenchant exchange:

ADDISON

What do you take me for?

EVE

I don't know that I take you for anything. . . .

ADDISON

Is it possible—even conceivable—that you've confused me with that gang of backward children you play tricks on? That you have the same contempt for me as you have for them?

EVE

I'm sure you mean something by that, Addison—but I don't know what.

ADDISON

Look closely, Eve, it's time you did. I am Addison DeWitt. I'm nobody's fool. Least of all yours.

Anyone comparing these two versions of the *All About Eve* screenplay would likely agree that the deleted passages were love handles on an otherwise shapely script. Since Mankiewicz, as screenwriter, was inclined to overindulge, we can assume that it was Zanuck who reduced *Eve* from 223 pages to a svelte 180 by toning the muscle and losing the flab.

Zanuck, unlike the semi-literate moguls of Hollywood legend, was considered an astute judge of scripts, and his editorial suggestions were usually followed—even by Mankiewicz, who had enough power and prestige to buck the front office when necessary. While many of Zanuck's suggestions at the time of the first draft of *Eve* were reflected in the revised shooting script, Mankiewicz disregarded one change that Zanuck recommended. "On page 32," Zanuck wrote, "I think the use of my name in a picture I am associated with will be considered self-aggrandizement. I believe you can cut it with no loss." The producer's name occurs four times just after Bill Sampson, making his first appearance, flings open the door of Margo's dressing room.

BILL

The airlines have clocks, even if you haven't! I start shooting a week from Monday—Zanuck is impatient, he wants me, he needs me!

MARGO

Zanuck, Zanuck, Zanuck! What are you two—lovers?

The in-joke stayed in the script. Gary Merrill and Bette Davis read their lines as written, their exchange was filmed, and the scene remained in the picture. To this day it gets a laugh, one reason being that it's an early tip-off—although a red herring—to the movie's gay subtext.

Across town at Paramount, Billy Wilder, Charles Brackett, and D. M. Marshman, Jr., were also dropping names in their *Sunset Boulevard* screenplay. "Seems like Zanuck's got himself a baseball picture," sneers producer Fred Clark when he rejects one of William Holden's Casey-at-the-bat story ideas. "I think Zanuck's all wet," says Holden, the failed screenwriter.

By early April, Mankiewicz had finished revising the draft of his screenplay. The version that now emerged was the shooting script, identified on the title page as "Revised Final—April 5, 1950." (This designation appears on Bette Davis's copy of the script, which I consulted at Boston University, where her papers are deposited. Other members of the cast and crew would have used copies of the same version.)

Much had happened to the material between Mary Orr's "The Wisdom of Eve" and this completed version of the screenplay. Most obviously, it had grown from a prose work of fewer than a dozen pages into 180 pages of narrative and dialogue. Included in this metamorphosis was Mankiewicz's recharacterization and expansion of Mary Orr's characters—Margola Cranston, now rechristened Margo Channing; Karen Richards, Lloyd Richards, Eve Harrington, Miss Caswell—and his invention of half a dozen new ones: Addison DeWitt, Bill Sampson, the Old Actor at the Sarah Siddons Awards, Birdie Conan, Max Fabian, and Phoebe. (Mankiewicz had also dropped a character from the story: producer-director Clement Howell, Margola's English husband.)

In Mary Orr's story Karen Richards is the narrator. There she, too, is an actress, but Mankiewicz, in his script, has made her just a "happy little housewife." Margola's maid, who bears no resemblance to Birdie, is named Alice; she neither speaks nor is she described. Margola lives in Great Neck, Long Island, in a forty-room house called Capulet's Cottage. In the story, Margola is not forty but somewhat older. Karen Richards says, "If she ever sees forty-five again, I'll have my eyes lifted."

Mankiewicz kept not a line of dialogue from Mary Orr's story, but he did retain what served him far better: the breezy, brittle tone. The story's high-gloss opening sentences match Addison DeWitt's lacquered narration at the start of the movie. We don't know to what extent Mankiewicz consciously mimicked Mary Orr's tone, but he must have recognised the story's hard-edged irony as the right key in which to play his own composition.

Mankiewicz and Zanuck, while in basic agreement on the *All About Eve* screenplay, were not the final arbiters on all points, however. The imprimatur of Joseph Ignatius Breen, chief administrator of the Production Code, was necessary for this picture as for virtually every other one. Breen was, in effect, the head censor of Hollywood at the time, an ardent Catholic who had been director of Code Administration since 1933, first under Will Hays and, since 1945, under Eric Johnston.

References to "the Hays office" and later to "the Johnston office" actually meant the Motion Picture Producers and Distributors of America (MPPDA), which was created by the film industry in 1922 and whose grip tightened in 1934 after Catholic bishops formed the Legion of Decency and threatened to bar American Catholics from seeing all movies. (Some attributed this more rigid enforcement of the Code to Mae West's racy on-screen dialogue and suggestive wiggles. Pauline Kael, for example, says that if West's on-screen bosom-heaving and dirty songs "led to the industry's self-policing Production Code, they were worth it. We enjoyed the crime so much that we could endure the punishment of family entertainment.")

Breen and his minions were empowered to review scripts as well as films, suggesting changes at all stages and granting a seal of approval to films that met the standards of the Code. Only rarely would a producer buck the power of the Production Code by releasing a film without the requisite seal. Two famous instances of Code nonapproval are Howard Hughes's *The Outlaw* in 1943 and Otto Preminger's *The Moon Is Blue* ten years later.

Familiar Code regulations included these: "Scenes of passion should not be introduced when not essential to the plot"; "Sex perversion or any reference to it is forbidden"; "The sanctity of the institution of marriage and the home shall be upheld"; and "Pointed profanity . . . or other profane or vulgar expressions . . . is forbidden."

Although the Code was not only fussy but also obsessive, its guardians often missed subtle suggestiveness, both verbal and visual. Screenwriters and directors knew this, and so a script usually included bargaining material—that is, scenes or bits of business and lines of dialogue that moviemakers didn't expect to get Production Code approval for, but that they included for trading purposes.

Today *All About Eve* strikes viewers as "adult" in the sense that it is sophisticated, but in 1950 much of its dialogue stopped just short of raciness and some of its situations didn't conform to Code standards of "good taste" (e.g., Bill, explaining to Margo why he didn't immediately come up to her room: "I ran into Eve on my way upstairs and she told me you were dressing." Margo: "That's *never* stopped you before.")

Like the other studios, 20th Century-Fox employed experts

to forewarn of anticipated problems when the script was submitted for Production Code approval. Colonel Jason S. Joy, Fox's director of public relations, acted as ex officio liaison to Joseph Breen and the formidable script-vetters of the Johnston office.

Colonel Joy was ideal for the job, since he himself had formerly worked in the Hays office. A native of Montana, he came to Hollywood in 1926 from the American Red Cross. He left the Hays office in 1932 to join the Fox Film Corporation—three years before it merged with 20th Century to become 20th Century-Fox.

By the time of *All About Eve*, Colonel Joy was a gray-haired man in his sixties. With his conservative eyeglasses and loose-fitting business suits, he might have belonged to that multitude of character actors who played uncles and businessmen and politicians in movies and television shows. Even his voice, which was pleasantly staid, added to the typecasting.

During Colonel Joy's time at the Hays office, the Production Code lacked real teeth. Tolerant and enlightened, Joy did not have a large appetite for censorship, and his admonitions were frequently ignored. According to film historian Kenneth Macgowan, "Some producers played ball, some did not. Others sent in only parts of their scripts, and paid little or no attention to Joy's criticism."

But the Code, and its enforcers, grew increasingly rigid under Breen, who blamed the Jews in Hollywood for just about everything. Writing to Father Wilfrid Parsons, editor of the Catholic publication *America*, in 1932, he characterized the Jews as "a rotten bunch of vile people with no respect for anything beyond the making of money. Here [in Hollywood] we have Paganism rampant and its most virulent form. Drunkenness and debauchery are commonplace. Sexual perversion is rampant . . . any number of our directors and stars are perverts. Ninety-five percent of these folks are Jews of an Eastern European lineage. They are, probably, the scum of the earth."

Despite Breen's anti-Semitism, he seems not to have singled out Jewish writers, directors, and producers for increased scrutiny. To Breen, perhaps, after years of stanching the corrupt ooze of Hollywood, there was neither Jew nor gentile but only a vast freemasonry of debauched pagans. Mankiewicz was Jewish; Zanuck was not. Breen's fiery righteousness engulfed them both.

Beginning in March 1950, a routine but surreal correspondence started up, first among those at 20th Century-Fox who were concerned with making *All About Eve*, and later between them and the resident censors at the Johnston office. Surviving letters and memoranda from these exchanges convey some of the difficulties that moviemakers faced. No one escaped the pinch of the Code straitjacket.

On March 15, 1950, Colonel Joy delivered the Mankiewicz script to Joseph Breen. Two weeks later, in a letter dated March 30, Breen wrote: "We have read the final script for your proposed production titled *All About Eve*, and wish to report that this basic story seems acceptable under the provisions of the Production Code.

"However, we direct your attention to the following details: At the outset, we direct your particular attention to the need of the greatest possible care in the selection and photographing of the dresses and costumes of your women. The Production Code makes it mandatory that the intimate parts of the body—specifically the breasts of the women—be fully covered at all times. Any compromise with this regulation will compel us to withhold approval of your picture."

This curious opening of Breen's letter wouldn't surprise us if it were addressed to Howard Hughes. After all, *The Outlaw* had made Jane Russell's breasts notorious and wags were still joking that the title should have been "The Sale of Two Titties." But Joseph Mankiewicz? Nowhere in the script was there a hint that decolletage might upstage drama. Nor was any female star in the cast known for cheesecake. It's possible, of course, that Marilyn's starlet reputation had preceded her. More likely, however, this mammary caveat was—to mix an anatomical metaphor—a knee-jerk reaction from Breen. It seems no one read the paragraph carefully, for in the party scene Marilyn ended up just about as strapless as possible.

Next, Breen asked that on page 15 "the use of the word 'sex' be changed to something less blunt in the circumstances." The offending line, spoken by Margo in the dressing room when she quotes the lady reporter from the South, was: "Ah don' understand about all these plays about sex-stahved Suth'n women—sex is one thing we were nevah stahved for in the South!"

Colonel Joy asked Mankiewicz for the change, and got it. "Sex" turned into "love."

On the next page of the script Margo said, "Honey chile had a point. You know, I can remember plays about women—even from the South—where it never even occurred to them whether they wanted to marry their fathers more than their brothers. Breen found this dialogue unacceptable. Later, when Colonel Joy suggested that the line be changed to the more Freudian "whether they had a fixation for their fathers or their brothers," Mankiewicz snapped in a memo to Zanuck, with a copy to Colonel Joy: "I do not like Jason's substitution of 'fixation' for 'marry' in Margo's teasing line about Lloyd's plays. I cannot imagine even censors objecting to the line as it is now written—delivered in a light, ribbing tone. The proper word, in any case, would be 'screw.' "

Mankiewicz sounds disingenuous. The censors *did* object, and eventually a compromise was made. Jack Vizzard, one of Breen's underlings, noted in a "memo for the files" on May 4 that "a protection shot will be developed at this point, since it sounds as though the dialogue is talking about incest." Mankiewicz kept the line in his script, but the protection shot was eventually used in the film.

In the script, Mankiewicz describes Margo's dressing room

and then adds, "A door leads to an old-fashioned bathroom." Birdie, of course, makes several trips into and out of this bathroom. But it made Breen nervous. His letter states, "We presume that there will be no notice of a toilet in the bathroom in these scenes."

When Colonel Joy, in a subsequent memo, conveyed Breen's apprehension to Mankiewicz, the retort was: "By my Oscars, I promise to show no indication of a toilet. Has it ever occurred to Joe Breen that the rest of the world must be convinced that Americans never relieve themselves?"

Next was a line that, if retained, would have made Thelma Ritter as notorious as Jane Russell, though for a different reason. Mankiewicz has Birdie say, in the dressing-room scene, "I'll never forget that blizzard the night we played Cheyenne. A cold night. First time I ever saw a brassiere break like a piece of matzo." Breen, not tickled, noted dryly that "the reference to the brassiere should be changed or eliminated."

And so it was, as Mankiewicz surely expected. It's likely he conceded that Borscht Circuit line as a gambit for retaining Birdie's crack. "Everything but the bloodhounds snappin' at her rear end." Breen also found this one "vulgar" and recommended that it be changed or eliminated, presumably because verbal references to the posterior were off limits although visual ones were not.

Colonel Joy, as go-between, reported Breen's request to Mankiewicz, adding helpfully, "Insomuch as Birdie's line is at the end of the shot, perhaps you can let it go the way it is and clip off 'rear end' if we have to, although I don't think we will." Mankiewicz replied impatiently, "The word *should* be 'arse.' What do you suggest we substitute for 'rear end'? 'Backside'? 'Butt'? What would you think of 'snappin' at her transmission'?"

In the pantry scene where Margo supplies Max Fabian with bicarbonate of soda for heartburn, the script reads simply, "Max burps." This troubled Breen, who wrote worriedly, "We presume there will be nothing coarse about the burp." But the

Production Code, to his chagrin, lacked a subsection on prohibited human rumbles, and so Gregory Ratoff, as Max Fabian, produced one of the great screen belches, perhaps surpassed only by Elizabeth Taylor's in *Secret Ceremony*—although hers seems unscripted, a comic fringe benefit of the fried chicken she devours in a scene with Mia Farrow.

Curiously, Breen had missed an earlier Max Fabian burp. On page four of the script, at the Sarah Siddons Awards, Mankiewicz had indicated that Max "drops the powder into some water, stirs it, drinks, burps delicately, and closes his eyes." Perhaps it was the word "delicately" that made this foreshadowing burp acceptable.

On page 119, the word "tart" was unacceptable to Breen and so it disappeared.

A few pages on, Breen and his fellow readers discerned a nuance that any literary critic might envy. Karen and Lloyd are arguing over Eve. Lloyd says, "That bitter cynicism of yours is something you've acquired since you left Radcliffe," and Karen snaps back, "That cynicism you refer to, I acquired the day I discovered I was different from little boys!" Her line always gets a laugh, one reason being that its meaning sounds submerged and elliptical. It could mean all sorts of things, or merely the obvious.

But Breen had little doubt. When told of it, Mankiewicz snorted. Zanuck swore. Colonel Joy pointed out diplomatically to Mr. Breen that perhaps someone had misconstrued the comic intent of that exchange between husband and wife. Breen wrote back: "The dialogue is still considered highly questionable. The lines seem open to an interpretation that the reference is to menstruation."

Joseph Breen yielded on the line, but the matter of bathrooms would not go away. We can imagine the grimace on Breen's face as he finished dictating a long memo: "We suggest that you soften the reference to the 'Ladies' Room' by possibly referring to it as the 'Lounge Room' or the 'Powder Room' or something similar. The line, 'I understand she is now the understudy in there' seems somewhat vulgar, and we ask that it be changed."

Now it was Mankiewicz's turn to grimace. Of all the idiotic, half-baked—He sighed and puffed harder on his pipe. "Changing 'Ladies' Room' to 'Powder Room,' " he wrote in an exasperated memo, "is not only childish but will most certainly hurt Bill's comment" (referring to Eve Harrington, Bill says, "I understand she's now the understudy in there."). Exhausted by such extreme literal-mindedness, Mankiewicz concluded rather pedantically, " 'Understudy' refers to *ladies* and not to *powder*."

On this point Mankiewicz prevailed, and on Breen's final point he also refused to budge. Referring to the hotel-room scene where Addison slaps Eve, Joseph Breen wrote demurely: "We ask that the slap across the face be eliminated."

It wasn't, and when Breen saw this slap on screen in its context of implied sado-masochism, he may well have bemoaned his leniency in letting the pagans retain such perversion.

THE RISKY TERRITORY OF *AMERICAN PSYCHO*

by Mary Harron

My first encounter with *American Psycho* should have prepared me for the trouble to come. This was in London, in 1991, shortly after the novel by Bret Easton Ellis was published. I was working for a BBC arts program, which was doing a segment on the controversy surrounding the novel, and heard the producer in charge exclaiming that the book was vile and should not have been published. I found out later she had not read it. Curious, I bought a copy and began reading it on the subway, braving the horrified glances of other passengers.

Nothing I had read about the controversy prepared me for what kind of book it was. The story of Patrick Bateman, a status-obsessed Wall Street executive who commits frenzied murders in his spare time, was not a slasher novel. It was a surreal satire, and although many scenes were excruciatingly violent, it was clearly intended as a critique of male misogyny, not an endorsement of it.

At the time, I had no thought of making a movie of *American Psycho*. When eight years later I was asked to do just that, it seemed to me that enough time had passed for the story to be seen as a commentary on the late 80's, and I hoped that by excising those graphic torture scenes, I would allow the novel's true meaning to appear. Of course that was naive, for if the forces of outrage had not bothered to read the book, why would they wait to see it on screen?

Before the film was even edited, the British tabloid *The News of the World* got hold of some innocuous photos of the actors standing around the set and published them with the headline, "The most disgusting film of the year!" Recently Eleanor Smeal, the president of the Feminist Majority Foundation announced "There are no redeeming qualities to a misogynist product like this"—without having seen it. And a lawyer in Florida threatened a lawsuit against *American Psycho* while admitting he had not read the book or the script, or seen the film.

Recently some critics have attacked the film for not being violent enough, but that hasn't slowed the controversy. I had not anticipated how panicky and confused the atmosphere around American movies has become since the rumblings from Washington about voluntary codes and the threatened lawsuits over *Natural Born Killers* and *The Basketball Diaries*. After *American Psycho* was shown at Sundance this year, I was asked over and over: "Aren't you concerned about violence in entertainment?" and "How can you release this film after Columbine?"—although even the novel's harshest critics have never accused it of causing violence in high schools.

This attempt to blame Columbine on entertainment seems to ignore the fact that America's culture is now the world's culture. Teenagers all over the globe now play exactly the same video games and watch exactly the same movies, and yet students in Belgium don't shoot up their high schools.

Perhaps other social factors—such as the Belgian teenager's lack of access to automatic weapons—might explain why.

At Sundance, the question I found most disturbing was this: "How would you feel if someone saw your movie and went out and killed someone?" I dislike the question because there is no way to answer it without sounding pathetic—"I would feel terrible"—and because I think it is unfair. When did a book or a film alone turn someone into a murderer? And what about all the other movies, books, and television dramas about serial killers? Would they be to blame too? But unfair or not, the question is still haunting. Because someone could commit a crime after seeing *American Psycho,* and blame it on the movie. Rightly or wrongly, I would have to live with that.

This issue came to the fore when we were in preproduction in Toronto. Before we started shooting, a group called C-CAVE—Canadians Concerned About Violence in Entertainment—sent a fax to local newspapers calling on concerned citizens to oppose the shooting of this "hideous and disgusting movie" in Toronto. Needless to say, they had neither read the script nor talked to me about what kind of film I intended to make.

The fax was headlined "Movie Version of Bernardo 'Bible' to Be Filmed in Toronto." This was a reference to Paul Bernardo, Canada's most notorious rapist and serial killer. Although C-CAVE sent its fax to all the Toronto newspapers, at first only one, the tabloid *Toronto Sun*, picked up on it. The *Sun*'s article reported that the book had been found by Bernardo's bedside and that it had inspired and acted as a "blueprint" for his crimes.

These initial press reports did not mention—although it was on the public record—that Bernardo's crimes had begun in 1987 with a string of particularly violent rapes, and his first killing took place in 1990, while the book was not published until 1991. Whatever effect *American Psycho* may have had on Paul Bernardo, it did not turn him into a monster: he was one already. It didn't matter. The mere name *American Psycho* set off a conflagration.

On the morning the *Sun* article appeared we were on our way to do a technical survey of our main location, which was to represent the office where Patrick Bateman works. Ten minutes after 9 the producer's cell phone rang with this message: "Don't bother showing up." The *Sun* article had reported that street protests against the film were being threatened, and the bank that owned the office building was scared of the potential bad publicity. It refused permission, as did all the rest of Toronto's financial institutions.

We were never able to find another office, and ended up shooting the scenes on a sound stage. Over the next two weeks, we fought to preserve the rest of our locations as restaurant and nightclubs began having second thoughts at the prospect of screaming demonstrators. We were nervous enough to take the film's title off the call sheet and parking permits.

We hired extra security and braced ourselves for the first day of filming. No protestors turned up. Not that day, or the next, or the next. During the whole of our seven-week shoot, not one person turned up to protest the filming of *American Psycho*. But it doesn't matter. Everyone I know in Canada, and every journalist I talk to, is convinced that the filming of *American Psycho* in Toronto took place surrounded by enraged crowds. When I got back to New York, I was met with concerned phone calls asking how I had coped with all the protests on the set. As so often happens, a tabloid frenzy had been mistaken for real life.

This being Canada, most of the press coverage of the controversy was eminently reasonable, with critics rushing to defend our right to film and even the *Sun* printing articles in favor of freedom of speech. The media frenzy subsided, but in Canada the name Paul Bernardo became permanently attached to *American Psycho.* One day in the ladies room I heard two extras discussing the film and realized they thought they were appearing in "the Paul Bernardo movie."

In fact, Stephen Williams, the author of *Invisible Darkness,* the most detailed book about that case, says that the copy of *American Psycho* belonged not to Mr. Bernardo (who was barely literate and is unlikely to have read a word of it) but to his wife and accomplice, Karla Homolka. In their police interviews neither she nor Mr. Bernardo ever described the book as their "bible" or as the "blueprint" for their crimes, or attached any special significance to it. Ms. Homolka was a voracious reader of all kinds of true crime books and crime fiction, and the prosecution tried to have two books from her collection introduced into evidence: *American Psycho* and Dostoyevsky's *Crime and Punishment.* The judge rejected both submissions as irrelevant to the case.

As absurd as it sounds, including *Crime and Punishment* in the prosecution's evidence is logically consistent with the current arguments for censorship, which revolve around the question of representation, and claim that portraying violence on the page or on the screen is enough to corrupt the audience, regardless of intention or message.

It is a sign of how unfocused the debate over violence in entertainment has become that this violence is never defined. *Crime and Punishment* can be described as a violent work. So can movies as various as *The Godfather, The Wild Bunch, Scream 2* and *Saving Private Ryan*; in fact, before it took on *American Psycho,* C-CAVE campaigned against *Saving Private Ryan.*

Once you accept the idea that the representation of violence is in itself harmful to society, much of the finest world cinema could be banned, from Eisenstein to Kurosawa to Kubrick and Polanski to Coppola and Scorsese. Most genre films would have to go too: film noir, horror, gangster films, westerns. This form of censorship, taken to its logical conclusion, clearly means the end of art. However, it does have a point, because no matter how moral or ironic or satirical a filmmaker might think a work is, he or she can have no control over how a member of the audience will receive it. No sane person could watch *Taxi Driver* and decide it was a good idea to shoot the president—but an insane person did. And who is to say that your audience will always consist of the sane? On the other hand, should you censor your own work because a fool or a madman somewhere might get it wrong?

In the end, as uncomfortable and disturbing as the process of making this film has been, I do not regret it. Although when I set out I thought I was making a social satire, it was only during filming that I realized how much I was drawing on my own deepest fears. I began to see *American Psycho* as a scenario of female terror, with Patrick Bateman as, quite literally, the date from hell. It is the fear of motiveless evil that lies at the heart of all horror movies—and in fairy tales and legends from time immemorial. There is something to be said for bringing those fears to light. Movies, after all, express not just our communal dreams but also our communal nightmares, and the director has responsibility for both.

If entering this territory is too risky, then what is the solution? Don't show violence, don't show evil, don't show any of the aspects of human nature that most frighten and distress us. In which case cinema and literature and drama will have to give up on providing a true reflection of society in favor of endless variations on life-affirming Robin Williams movies. And does anyone really believe that serial killers and violence against women and teenage shootings would then disappear?

SEPARATE AND UNEQUAL? HOW THE MPAA RATES INDEPENDENT FILMS

by Doug Atchison

Does the MPAA Rating Board treat independent movies more harshly than the motion pictures produced by the major studios which comprise its board of directors? It depends who you ask.

I'll start by saying that I cannot be a fully unbiased examiner of this issue. In the last edition of *MovieMaker*, I detailed my experiences with the MPAA when they bestowed an NC-17 rating upon my self-produced, low-budget feature, *The Pornographer*. After recutting the film twice, I was able to secure an R rating, thus meeting the requirements of Hollywood Video, which is exclusively carrying the film and forbids NC-17-rated fare in its stores. At the time, I firmly believed that if I had had the clout of a major distributor, I would have been able to appeal the Rating Board decision and secure a less restrictive rating without having to edit my movie.

MovieMaker asked me to follow up that article with an investigation into other indie moviemakers' experiences with the MPAA to see if a pattern of bias in favor of studio pictures exists. One of the first things I discovered is that many distributors and moviemakers are hesitant about going on the record with their true feelings about the MPAA for fear of possible reprisals when they need to have their future films rated.

Requiem for a Dream is the latest independent movie at the center of a rating controversy, and its producer, Eric Watson, is one moviemaker who isn't timid about speaking his mind. An intense and haunting portrait of four characters battling drug addiction in New York, *Requiem* was slapped with an NC-17—not for its shocking vision of drug use—but for several fleeting glimpses of sexual activity in the latter chapters of the movie. After receiving the rating, director Darren Aronofsky wrote a letter to the MPAA describing his intentions in making his "anti-addiction" film, but they were unmoved. When the film went before the Ratings Appeal Board, the NC-17 was upheld.

When I specifically asked producer Watson if he felt the MPAA discriminated against independent films like *Requiem*, his answer was unequivocal: "If you're a major studio film, you're in a position of having leverage over the MPAA because you're paying their budget. So, essentially, we're dealing with a paid jury. To me it's an unconstitutional concept. It's a jury that must answer to the people who are paying their paychecks. I think that's why films like *Scary Movie* and *8mm* get R ratings, even though the content is extremely shocking and the moral content of the film is suspect."

Watson applauds Artisan, *Requiem*'s distributor, "for not making us stick to the contract" in which they agreed to deliver an R-rated film—and allowing the movie to be released unrated. But he also agreed that the entire rating debacle could have been avoided had the movie been released by one of the seven studios who comprise the MPAA's board of directors. Those studios are Disney, Sony Pictures, MGM, Paramount, 20th Century-Fox, Universal, and Warner Brothers.

These echo the sentiments expressed by Matt Stone and Trey Parker, who have gone through similar battles with the MPAA over the ratings of their pictures *South Park* and *Orgazmo*. After multiple resubmissions, *South Park*, released by Paramount, was ultimately given an R rating, but *Orgazmo*, their first independent film, wasn't downgraded from its NC-17.

"The reason we got the NC-17 on *Orgazmo* was that it was released by October Films, which had no clout, and we didn't have the money to re-edit the film and continue to resubmit it," Parker told the *Los Angeles Times*. However, the Rating Board gave *South Park*, one of the most obscenity-laced pictures in recent memory, an R. "We got an R because Paramount was behind it," said Parker, simply. "But the independent filmmaker gets screwed."

The case of *Orgazmo* is a peculiar one, because of the lengths to which the movie goes to obfuscate its sexual content. A comedy about a Mormon missionary's stint as an actor in porno films, *Orgazmo* never seems interested in a realistic documentation of the world of adult moviemaking—but merely uses porno clichés to create laughs by juxtaposing them against its protagonist's prudishness. There isn't a single instance of full frontal nudity in the picture—in fact, whenever the actors are prepared to doff their clothing, a nude, male extra steps into frame so his bare backside covers the image. In the film's few scenes of bump-and-grind, the players even keep their clothes on!

So, in light of *South Park*'s acquisition of an R (with all its references to "rim jobs," "German scheise movies", and ping-pong ball-shooting vaginas) how did *Orgazmo* warrant an NC-17? If one were to momentarily put aside the notion that a flat-out conspiracy against non-studio fare exists, one can only surmise that the very notion of a Mormon boy in pornoland was too much for the Rating Board to stomach, and *Orgazmo*'s NC-17 was a fait accompli.

The same might be said for my film, *The Pornographer*, which suffered the same fate as *Orgazmo* at the hands of the MPAA. Although both films are set in the world of adult filmmaking, mine is a serious look at the topic. At issue in *The Pornographer* were two brief simulated sex scenes, in which the number of "pelvic thrusts" and "head bobs" were deemed excessive and ordered to be trimmed. David Rimawi, director of acquisitions for The Asylum, the company distributing my picture, indicated that the Rating Board members are "fairly consistent with their views of 'repeated incidents.' It is their belief that you have made your point after one or two examples of gunshots . . . or thrusts during sex."

When I expressed my mystification that both *Orgazmo* and *The Pornographer* got NC-17s—but *Boogie Nights*, which also deals with the adult movie arena, was released with an R,

Rimawi said "I doubt you'll see in *Boogie Nights* that [the thrusting] is done more than twice."

So I took another look at the R-rated version of *Boogie Nights*, and this is what I found: In addition to copious depictions of drug use, intercourse, masturbation, full frontal nudity, suicide, rape, and extreme violence, there are at least two scenes which seem to directly contradict the MPAA's standards of "no repeated incidents." During a montage of Mark Wahlberg's character's rise to porno stardom, there is a moment of simulated oral sex with a whopping 13 head bobs—almost double the number deemed excessive in the NC-17 version of *The Pornographer*. In another scene, the cuckold played by William H. Macy has a conversation with another actor at a party while his porn star wife has sex with a stranger behind him—and no fewer than 40 pelvic thrusts can be counted.

Neither NC-17 versions of *Orgazmo* nor *The Pornographer* has content that rises to the level of that in the R-rated version of *Boogie Nights*, a much bigger picture with name actors like Burt Reynolds. On the surface, this would seem like clear evidence of discrimination. But *Boogie Nights*' distributor, New Line, is not on the MPAA's board of directors—which weakens the case for conspiracy. So what gives?

Ray Greene, author, documentarian and former editor-in-chief of *Boxoffice* magazine, believes there are less troubling explanations for the perceived discrepancies between different films' ratings. "An independent film is going to tend to be—stylistically, thematically, and dramatically—different from a mainstream film," says Greene. "If anything, that is what might cause a different scale of judgment to be applied. I don't think there's a nefarious conspiracy to suppress independent films, but I do think that more daring material will run afoul even if it has the same content, because by being more daring it's going to make [the Rating Board] apprehensive and anxious; they'll wonder what's going on."

Having just completed a documentary chronicling the history of exploitation films in America, Greene has closely examined the history of film censorship and bristles at the suggestion that the MPAA is a "censoring body." The MPAA "is in the business of stopping censorship from happening." explains Greene. "When the ratings system came into existence, it actually opened up motion pictures, which contained all kinds of content that were completely proscribed prior to that time. When there was a production code there was a laundry list of things you could not do. Now you can do anything you want, but you have to accept the rating that's bestowed on your film."

The problem is that some moviemakers cannot "accept" the rating bestowed on their products because most distributors will not allow movies garnering NC-17 ratings to be released. That is because many mainstream newspapers, radio, and TV outlets will not run ads for NC-17 pictures, and some movie theatres and video stores will not carry the films. Despite the MPAA's efforts to destigmatize certain "adult-oriented" movies by creating the NC-17 some 10 years ago (thus replacing the uncopyrighted X rating), the NC-17 is still deemed by many consumers and retailers to be synonymous with pornography.

If the MPAA does not engage in direct censorship the way a government body would, its decisions do result in "de facto" censorship by forcing moviemakers to remove "objectionable" material from their films in order to get more favorable ratings. Studios routinely make filmmakers sign pledges that they will not deliver NC-17 films, thus resulting in one of the gravest artistic injustices of recent memory, the alteration of Stanley Kubrick's final film, *Eyes Wide Shut*, in order to earn it an R rating.

So the question remains: Do independent moviemakers receive the brunt of the MPAA's proscriptions when it comes to ratings? Rimawi at The Asylum did admit, "I'd be naive to think that the studios can't influence [the MPAA]—or any company with might that is willing to push them and really make them investigate every decision they make."

In the past, the MPAA does seem to have responded to pressure applied by well-known actors. Clint Eastwood successfully argued before the Ratings Appeals Board to change *Bridges of Madison County* from an R to a PG-13 rating. And when Kirk Douglas' *Diamonds* was initially given an R for scenes featuring prostitution and drug use, the actor issued a statement questioning the decision. The MPAA later changed its ruling and gave *Diamonds* a PG-13.

To many, one of the MPAA's most confounding lapses of judgment was the failure to award *Saving Private Ryan* an NC-17 for its horrific depiction of violent warfare and gore. In a statement on their website, MPAA president Jack Valenti claims that "contrary to popular notion, violence is not treated more leniently than any of the other material." But one wonders, in the case of *Ryan*, if the film's noble intentions of depicting the sacrifices made by D-Day soldiers didn't influence the board's decision. Would a smaller film by a lesser-known director haven gotten away with the same level of on-screen carnage?

Ray Greene speculates that "because the board members are representative of middle America, they're going to know *Saving Private Ryan* is made by Steven Spielberg. It doesn't have to be a conspiracy for them to feel, as so many do, some sense of generosity towards something by Spielberg, and give him the benefit of the doubt because of who he is."

Part of the problem in determining to what extent studios have influence over the board's determinations is the cloak of anonymity that covers the MPAA's decision-making process. According to the MPAA website, "There are 8 to 13 members of the Rating Board who serve for periods of varying length. There are no special qualifications for Board membership, except the members must have a shared parenthood experience, must be possessed of an intelligent maturity, and most of all have the capacity to put themselves in the role of most American parents." The problem is, we have no idea who these people are. Their identities are hidden. And without knowing the backgrounds, dispositions, and political leanings of these panelists, an attempt to determine bias becomes extremely complicated.

However, producer Eric Watson was given some insight into the makeup of the Ratings Appeal Board that upheld the NC-17 for *Requiem for a Dream* when he was told there were two priests on the jury. This calls into question not only the MPAA's assertion that jury members have a "shared parenthood experience," but also raises serious doubts about the board being representative of America as a whole.

Furthermore, the Rating Board seems to eschew any reliance upon precedent in making their determinations. Unlike the Supreme Court, which relies heavily on precedent, the Rating Board, whose members change from year to year, appear to rely more upon subjective gut reactions to what they're watching. When the NC-17 rating for James Toback's movie. *Black and White*, produced by Palm Pictures, was appealed last year, Palm production chief Hooman Majd was particularly upset by the Appeals Board's refusal to allow the filmmakers to refer to previously rated movies as precedents. Majd told *Daily Variety* that the whole process of recutting and resubmitting the film was "a huge waste of time and money."

I did talk to one independent moviemaker who was able to successfully use "precedent" to partially deter the MPAA from hamstringing his marketing efforts. Jerome Courshon wrote and produced the indie feature *God, Sex & Apple Pie*, which he will soon be four-walling in Chicago. He decided to have the film rated, because he was worried certain Chicago papers might not run ads for an unknown movie with such a provocative title. He was unaware, however, how far the MPAA's tentacles of influence would extend.

"When I began this process of having the movie rated, they faxed over paperwork." Courshon explains, "But they did not send me their little guideline brochure that everybody has to have in order to navigate their way through the MPAA waters." After Courshon's film was rated R, which cost him $2,500, he was then given the guidebook which explained that all advertising and publicity material must be "suitable for all audiences."

Realizing that his artwork, which featured a woman in a leather dominatrix outfit showing ample cleavage and sitting on top of a bare-chested man, might not be deemed "suitable for all audiences," Courshon quickly went about researching studio releases that had similar artwork. He discovered that the art for Paramount's *Sliver* featured Sharon Stone in a compromising position, not unlike the one depicted in his film's poster. Courshon also found other studio pictures with artwork featuring actresses with profound bustlines.

The result was a split decision. The MPAA forced Courshon to crop the image so you couldn't see how the woman was sitting on the man—but they did let the cleavage pass. "I have a gut feeling that, had I not done my research, they might not have approved the cleavage, and if they hadn't I couldn't have used anything in this shot." explains Courshon.

Making MPAA-ordered changes in a film or its artwork is costly, and this is one area where independent moviemakers are at a disadvantage. In the case of my film, we didn't go through the standard appeals process, because of the time and cost involved, but simply cut the film the way we were directed. It probably would have been a waste of money to appeal, because, as *Requiem* producer Eric Watson informed me, only one film in the history of the MPAA has ever been downgraded from an NC-17 to an R.

Perhaps what leads so many independent producers to determine that a double standard exists in the ratings of studio and nonstudio films are the other double standards that permeate the MPAA's decisions. The most obvious is the different treatment of sex and violence. Even in the current climate of Washington-led disapproval of violent cinema, sex is the culprit most often responsible for drawing an unfavorable rating. Despite the MPAA's assertion that violent films are just as frequently awarded NC-17s as sexually explicit pictures, a look at their website leads one to draw different conclusions. Of the NC-17 films listed which describe the objectionable material within each film that warranted the rating, only three of the movies cite violence as a contributing factor. All the others list sexual content.

When I examined the NC-17 cut of the controversial film *American Psycho*, I discovered that the level of violence in this version and the R-rated version was virtually the same. The key difference between the two versions was a sex scene between the psychotic main character and two prostitutes, which was amplified in the racier cut. And you only need to watch the recently R-rated Jennifer Lopez picture *The Cell*, in which a man's intestine is slowly pulled from his body, inch by agonizing inch, to question the role of violence in issuing NC-17 ratings.

The MPAA also appears to have a double standard when it comes to whose sexuality a movie examines. Colette Burson's first feature, *Coming Soon*, about "three 18-year-old girls in search of an orgasm," initially received an NC-17, despite the director's strong assertion that the film was less racy than the R-rated *American Pie*, which followed several male characters with the same goal. Burson told the *Boston Herald* of a phone conversation with an MPAA member who explained that because most American parents view female sexuality with a double standard, the board judges films with that same double standard in mind.

This seems to be a rare case of where the MPAA actually admitted to some of the strange criteria by which they judge films. Other than by offering some broadstroke standards, such as how they view use of the word "fuck" (one nonsexual use of the word will get you a PG-13, one sexual use commands an R), the MPAA's rating guidelines are murky, at best. Said Matt Stone, "The MPAA has no set rules. Things change from movie to movie. It makes no sense. In going through the notes we saw that they had no standards, so we decided these people are stupid and we'd just try to get it past them. If there was something they said couldn't stay in [*South Park*], we'd make it 10 times worse and five times as long. And they'd come back and say, 'OK, that's better.' "

Karl T. Hirsch, director of the indie feature *Green*, now works for The Asylum and spends a good deal of time maneuvering their movies through the MPAA obstacle course. Hirsch explains that "they do have a guidebook. But it really doesn't tell you anything. I was waiting for the handbook to say. 'In a blow-job scene, you can only have four or five head bobs.' But it's completely vague. I've asked them lots of questions, and they come back to me with 'Well just read the handbook.' And what that means is that it all depends on the subject matter and the film itself."

So is it just vagueness and inconsistency on the part of the MPAA that leads to the appearance of favoritism towards studio pictures? Because of the closed-door policy of the Rating Board, we can't be sure. We can only point to numerous instances of Hollywood movies which would seem to warrant an NC-17 when compared to their indie counterparts. My exercise comparing *Boogie Nights* to *Orgazmo* and *The Pornographer* can be performed with many films—and the appearance of contradictory rulings is what leads to the allegations of discrimination.

The MPAA damages its own credibility by being so reluctant to change its policies and procedures. Jack Valenti likes to cite studies that show a 74 percent approval rating amongst American parents as evidence that the system doesn't need fixing. But since when do "American parents" alone have the final say over the efficacy of a trade organization that is supposed to serve the needs of an entire film community? It's perfectly understandable that Valenti and company regard one of their primary duties as preventing government interference in the rating of motion pictures. But if a director is forced to cut material from his or her film to get a more favorable rating, does it really matter if it's the government or the MPAA ordering the changes?

It does not seem overly idealistic to demand a system that is both fair to filmmakers and accountable to parents. One solution, posed by Matt Stone in an editorial in *Daily Variety*, is to do away with the NC-17 rating altogether and strictly enforce the R. Right now, most kids can get access to any movie they want to see. But if we treated access to R-rated movies the same way we treat access to buying cigarettes, the need for a more draconian rating of NC-17 would, I hope, disappear—and with it the need for moviemakers to tamper with their work.

The DGA could also be instrumental in finding a solution by perhaps fighting to put an end to contractual obligations that force moviemakers to deliver films with certain ratings. Distributors could also refuse to do business with companies such as Hollywood Video and Blockbuster until they abandon their refusal to carry NC-17 titles.

But the real problem lies with the secretive, inconsistent and confusing manner in which the MPAA Rating Board assesses motion pictures. As long as these decisions are made in the dark by anonymous board members on the payroll of the studios, the independent moviemaker saddled with an unfavorable rating will always be left second-guessing the process.

If the MPAA doesn't change its system, moviemakers like *Requiem for a Dream* producer Eric Watson will continue to feel as he did when he recently told the *Hollywood Reporter* that "morally bankrupt studio films will continue to be released unscathed due to their financial and political muscle, while independent films dealing with powerful moral themes are going to be scapegoated."

GONE WITH THE WIND AND HOLLYWOOD'S RACIAL POLITICS

by Leonard J. Leff

Making Gone With the Wind, *David O. Selznick discovered, meant dealing with fierce criticism front black newspapers and public officials*

Throughout the late 1920s and early 1930s Margaret Mitchell, an Atlanta newspaperwoman, was writing a Civil War epic that she assumed no one would ever read. It had "precious little obscenity in it," she later told one correspondent, "no adultery and not a single degenerate, and I couldn't imagine a publisher being silly enough to buy it." Macmillan acquired the novel, however, and months before its publication, in 1936, the work was under consideration all over Hollywood. Opinion at Selznick International Pictures was divided: the story editor on the West Coast called the book "ponderous trash"; the story editor on the East Coast called it "absolutely magnificent." In the event, David O. Selznick bought *Gone With the Wind* for $50,000. The book, a commercial and cultural phenomenon, sold a million copies during its first month in print. The motion picture, which opened sixty years ago this month, remains a testament to the Technicolor glory of the Hollywood studio system.

Gone With the Wind had not gone easily to the screen. From the adaptation of the novel and the casting of Scarlett O'Hara to the heated negotiations with censors over small and not-so-small matters in the film, Selznick International faced one problem after another. David Selznick met—and solved—most of them. One persisted, though, and reasserted itself on February 29, 1940. Late in the afternoon of that day Hattie McDaniel was dressing for the Academy Awards banquet. A nominee for Best Supporting Actress, for her role as Mammy, she was apparently the first black actor ever to compete for an

Oscar. She may have been uneasy about protocol, for she was to dine at the Coconut Grove with her producer, Selznick, and the white stars of the picture, including Olivia de Havilland, also a nominee for Best Supporting Actress.

"We trust that discrimination and prejudice will be wiped away in the selection of the winner of this award," members of a national black sorority had written to Selznick International some weeks before, "for without Miss McDaniel, there would be no *Gone With the Wind.*" Selznick agreed—or so he told his correspondents. He nonetheless saw the letter as evidence that the disheartening, long-running debate on *Gone With the Wind* was not yet over.

Even before 1938, when Selznick International identified what it called a "Negro Problem," black Americans had taken a strong interest in *Gone With the Wind.* The black press was the most consistent and perhaps the most influential of the studio's advisers on racial issues; others included black actors, national black organizations, and the movie industry's notorious Hays Office. These people and institutions lacked common goals, and, as the historian Thomas Cripps has written, they rarely spoke with one voice. Some opposed production and release of the picture; others hailed it as a fine showcase for black actors. That lack of consensus not only complicated the production for David Selznick, whose liberal instincts warred with his intention of producing *his* story of the Old South *his* way, but also made *Gone With the Wind* a barometer of American race relations in the 1930s and 1940s.

In the fall of 1936, wringing his hands, Sidney Howard wondered why he had agreed to adapt *Gone With the Wind* for the screen. He had read and reread the novel, he wrote Selznick in early November, "and it is certainly quite a nut to crack." Two weeks later, from his home in rural Massachusetts, he wrote Margaret Mitchell that she had been too generous; her story was far more than he could compress into the two hours' screen time he was permitted. He would soldier on, of course, but he wanted her to read over his outline and to help out, especially with the black characters—"the best written darkies, I do believe, in all literature," he wrote. "They are the only ones I have ever read which seemed to come through uncolored by white patronising."

Like many northern whites, Howard looked to southern whites as authorities on "black psychology." Mitchell wanted to reinforce the notion of southern expertise, because to her, the Hollywood South often looked like a cartoon. In *Wonder Bar* (1934), for instance, Al Jolson had blacked up for a musical number staged in a fantasyland of pork chops and watermelons. Mitchell expected no better in *Gone With the Wind*: "Three hundred massed Negro singers," she wrote in a letter to Kay Brown, Selznick's New York representative, "standing on Miss Pittypat's lawn waving their arms and singing 'Swing low, sweet chariot, comin' for to carry me home,' while Rhett drives up with the wagon."

But some readers had found Mitchell's treatment of race less a cartoon than a nightmare. She had, for example, depicted her leading black characters as content with slavery, uninterested in freedom. They often seemed more like pets than people. When Scarlett and Big Sam were reunited after the war, "his watermelon-pink tongue lapped out, his whole body wiggled, and his joyful contortions were as ludicrous as the gambolings of a mastiff." The "good" black characters both loved and needed the whites. Though Mammy was one of the strongest characters in the novel, she could not manage Tara after the war without the guidance of her white masters. Her mind was too simple, not yet fully evolved, as readers could infer from a description of her as she looked at the once-grand plantation, her face "sad with the uncomprehending sadness of a monkey's face."

Lacking the protection and moral schooling of whites, the "bad" blacks were an unruly lot. Mammy and Big Sam called them "niggers." Mitchell called them "black apes" who committed "outrages on women." Reconstruction brought out the worst in these characters. Passing through Shantytown one evening, Scarlett was attacked by "a squat black negro with shoulders and chest like a gorilla." He was "so close that she could smell the rank odor of him" as he ripped open her bodice and "fumbled between her breasts." The Ku Klux Klan, according to *Gone With the Wind* was a "tragic necessity."

In treatments of the screenplay written throughout early 1937, Sidney Howard retained many of the incidents and much of the tone of Mitchell's southern romance. And in general, intent on fidelity to the novels he produced for the screen, Selznick was pleased. "One never knows what chemicals have gone to make up something that has appealed to millions of people," he wrote to Howard, or "how many seeming faults of construction have been part of the whole, and how much the balance would be offset by making changes . . . in our innocence, or even in our ability."

On reflection, though, Selznick knew that he could go too far in his faithfulness to Mitchell's text. "I, for one, have no desire to produce any anti-Negro film," he wrote in an exhaustive, exhausting memorandum to the screenwriter. "In our picture I think we have to be awfully careful that the Negroes come out decidedly on the right side of the ledger, which I do not think should be difficult." The screenplay needed only a deletion here, an elision there, starting, he told Howard, with references to the Ku Klux Klan. "A group of men can go out to 'get' the perpetrators of an attempted rape without having long white sheets over them and without having their membership in a society as a motive," Selznick wrote. About the words "darkies" and "niggers," which also appeared in the screenplay, the producer said nothing.

By the spring of 1937, spurred by memories of racism in *The Birth of a Nation*, black organizations on both coasts had written to Selznick International about *Gone With the Wind*. "We consider this work to be a glorification of the old rotten system of slavery, propaganda for race-hatreds and bigotry, and incitement of lynching," members of a Pittsburgh group wrote in a letter that, like other such correspondence, has rarely been cited, much less discussed, in popular histories of the picture. One studio official called such opinions "ridiculous," yet many blacks were convinced otherwise; they genuinely feared that what they saw as an "anti-Negro" novel would become an "anti-Negro" film. Selznick International meanwhile hastened to assure them that *no* movie company "intends to offer to the public material that is offensive or conducive to race prejudice."

Cautionary letters continued to arrive at the producer's Culver City offices well into 1938. An associate of the Conference of American Rabbis told Selznick that the novel, though it entertained readers, also excited a latent "anti-Negro antipathy." Selznick, the correspondent said, must not cater to the public's narrow-mindedness, in part because it was wrong and in part because he, David Selznick, like most of his Hollywood peers, was a Jew. Walter White, the secretary of the National Association for the Advancement of Colored People, also wrote to the producer. He offered to send along a packet of well-researched papers that demonstrated Mitchell's biased presentation of Reconstruction. Better still, he suggested, the studio should employ "a person, preferably a Negro, who is qualified to check on possible errors of fact or interpretation."

Selznick responded warmly. He, too, was a member of a persecuted race, he told White, and was sensitive to minority peoples' opinions. Moreover, he intended to hire "a Negro of high standing to watch the entire treatment of the Negroes, the casting of the actors for these roles, the dialect that they use, etcetera, throughout the picture." Among the candidates, he confided, was Hall Johnson.

Johnson, the leader of the Hall Johnson Choir, had been in and around Hollywood for several years. His music graced *The*

Green Pastures, and his singers, chained to oars, had sung and acted in *Slave Ship.* He was precisely what White feared: an insider, likely to endorse whatever portrait of slavery the studio conceived. White wrote Selznick that he hoped for a scholar, perhaps someone from Howard University. There, for the moment, the matter rested.

The casting of black roles in *Gone With the Wind* took place throughout late 1938. Selznick International scouted some actors by watching their previous films, others by attending their current onstage performances in Los Angeles. *The Pittsburgh Courier,* a black paper with national circulation, reported that one prominent actor (Clinton Rosamond) had not been considered because he was "too polished" for the parts. Others, according to a *Courier* correspondent, abased themselves during the auditions.

> Picture yourselves standing before Producer David O. Selznick, Director George Cukor, and 26 members of the production staff, all white, and reading [a] script which contains the word "Nigger" several times. Well, approximately one hundred Negro actors did just that in competing for coveted roles in the picture while all their years of racial pride [were] being wafted away on the wings of a gust of 'Wind.'

Like Eleanor Roosevelt, though, who engineered a screen test for her cook, most black actors saw *GWTW* as an opportunity for renown. Hattie McDaniel even auditioned in "Mammy rags" that may have been borrowed from the studio wardrobe department; she, Oscar Polk, Butterfly McQueen, and the other black actors chosen for *GWTW* were pleased to have work, especially in what promised to be a major picture.

As the principal photography began, in early 1939, scrutiny by the black press increased. Eight years before, *The Pittsburgh Courier* had acquired thousands of signatures on a petition to bar *Amos 'n' Andy* from the airwaves. The *Courier* hoped for even wider support on *Gone With the Wind.* Using the screenplay's racial epithets as a battle cry, the paper threatened a letter-writing offensive and, if necessary, a boycott of the finished picture. Selznick was nonplussed. The movie industry's censors had ruled only that "nigger" "should *not* be put in the mouth of *white people.* In this connection you might want to give some consideration to the use of the word 'darkies.'" For once, Selznick agreed with the Hays Office; certainly, he thought, the black characters could use "nigger" among themselves. But the *Courier* was not alone in its outrage.

The more strident *Los Angeles Sentinel* called for a boycott of "every other Selznick picture, present and future." "What's more," the paper continued, "let's start a campaign and find out whether or not some of those who oppose Hitler from a safe distance have courage enough to oppose race prejudice when it may hit them in their careers and in their pocketbooks." Again Selznick was baffled. Perhaps, he thought, he should hire a black agent as a public-relations liaison to the black community. Or perhaps he should simply have the legal department send harsh warning letters to reporters and others whose inflammatory comments threatened to injure the production.

Selznick had meanwhile chosen his technical advisers—both white. Aware of the potential for political backlash, he asked Kay Brown to assure Walter White that "the only liberties we have taken with the book have been liberties to improve the Negro position in the picture and that we have the greatest friendship toward them and their cause." Moreover, he promised that his advisers would not allow the studio to "turn out a Hollywood or NY conception of the Negro." Whether Selznick, Brown, or the studio consultants understood the "Negro position" was uncertain. Susan Myrick, a *Macon Telegraph* reporter and a dialect coach for *GWTW*, was convinced that the atmosphere of the picture belonged to the black characters; accordingly, she intended to teach the black actors to speak like "the middle Georgia Negro of befo-de-wah days." However accurate, that accent would connote the poverty and ignorance of black people—both the characters and, as White could easily have imagined, the actors who played them.

Kay Brown soon reported to Culver City on her meeting with Walter White. "Mr. White, honey chile, is a negro who by virtue of being white goes many places as a white," she wrote. "However, he does not sail under false colors and is well known in New York as a negro and promptly told me he was one during the first five minutes of the interview." Brown was charming, White was affable, and they parted friends; it was so merry a get-together that Brown hated to tell Selznick that White had asked for a copy of the screenplay.

White would have objected strenuously to "nigger," as Brown and Selznick must have known. Butterfly McQueen (Prissy) also apparently objected to the word, at least privately. "I was unhappy because it seemed so authentic," she later told a Georgia newspaper. The antecedents for "it" were presumably the clothes, the accent, the deference to the white characters, and above all the use in the screenplay of "nigger"—a word whose authenticity reminded her of a racial legacy she longed to forget. "I complained so much," she added, that Hattie McDaniel "warned me that Mr. Selznick would never give me another job." In fact McDaniel, too, had complained. According to *The Pittsburgh Courier,* she was "race-proud" and would never say the word "nigger." According to her biographer, Carlton Jackson, she also influenced her peers to make known their feelings about its use. Meanwhile, Joe Breen, the director of the Hays Office, was having second thoughts. A rerelease of *The Birth of a Nation* was pending; because of that and reports of theater riots over use of the word "nigger" in a 1934 picture, Breen urged that *Gone With the Wind* delete all racial epithets.

Selznick wanted to retain the "Negro flavor" of the picture—but to use "nigger" he would have to face down White, Breen, the black press, *and* his black actors. The actors, meeting privately with Victor Shapiro, the studio public-relations director, had expressed their anxiety over racial elements of the production yet agreed to play the slaves more or less as Margaret Mitchell and Sidney Howard had written them. In return, Shapiro vowed that they would not have to say "nigger." Selznick, with mixed feelings, honored Shapiro's promise. The words "darkies" and "inferiors" stayed in the screenplay—but not "nigger."

For some, the elimination of "nigger" temporarily halted the war against *Gone With the Wind.* "This admission marks a victory for the *Pittsburgh Courier,*" wrote the columnist Earl Morris, who had led the charge. Victory was sweet, too, as anyone could tell by the columnist's smile in the photograph taken of him at Selznick International; as a guest of the studio, he was shown looking over the revised script. No less eager to have friends in Hollywood, Walter White lent his name to a Selznick International form letter designed for blacks and others concerned about *GWTW*'s racial agenda. The text not only attributed the deletion of "nigger" to White but also touted the studio's portrayal of the chief black characters as "lovable, faithful, high-typed people—so picturized that they can leave no impression but a very nice one."

The atmosphere on the set appeared nice, very nice. One afternoon Hattie McDaniel entertained the cast and crew by humming and limp-stepping her way through "Old Folks at Home." As she turned and kicked and rolled her eyes, visitors to the set reportedly "laughed [them]selves sick." Even Butterfly McQueen, who still wanted to distance herself from her role, masked her resentment and occasionally played to white expectations. Watching McQueen take direction early on, Susan Myrick told Margaret Mitchell that the actress was " 'nigger' through and through."

Russell Birdwell, a Selznick International publicist, encouraged the "sepia players" (as the black press called them) to turn these cheerful faces to the public. The black actors of *Gone*

With the Wind, he told Selznick, "should do by-line stories, which we would plant in their papers throughout the country." The news releases not only would be good for the actors, Birdwell said, but also would help to counter any future attacks on the picture in the black press. Selznick agreed.

Oscar Polk, who played Pork, contributed to Birdwell's campaign. "As a race we should be proud that we have risen so far above the status of our enslaved ancestors," he wrote in a letter to the weekly *Chicago Defender.* Moreover, he and his fellow *GWTW* black actors "should be glad to portray ourselves as we once were because in no other way can we so strikingly demonstrate how far we have come in so few years." The *Defender* (which *The Pittsburgh Courier* once called the "Chicago Surrender, World's Greatest Weakly") printed the letter. The *Courier,* too, was ballyhooing the black actors, and gradually—again, for the moment—acclaim for McDaniel and others eclipsed the admonitions that had been hurled at the production.

By late spring of 1939, as Selznick started watching rough-cuts of important sequences in *Gone With the Wind,* his excitement increased; his accomplishment, he thought, would surpass even that of D. W. Griffith in *The Birth of a Nation.* The yoking of the two films was apposite, as a memorandum from Selznick to his assistant, Val Lewton, made clear.

> Increasingly I regret the loss of the better negroes being able to refer to themselves as niggers, and other uses of the word nigger by one negro talking about another. All the uses that I would have liked to have retained do nothing but glorify the negroes, and I can't believe that we were sound in having a blanket rule of this kind, nor can I believe that we would have offended any negroes if we had used the word 'nigger' with care; such as in references by Mammy, Pork, Big Sam, etc.

Lewton responded immediately. Yes, he conceded, the absence of the word "nigger" had cost the picture an ounce of dramatic punch and a pound of comic material. Since the company had promised the "negro societies" that the word would not be used, however, its restoration to the picture would cost Selznick his integrity. Selznick nonetheless continued to obsess over the question, as over much else in *Gone With the Wind.* He even ordered his script supervisor to comb the screenplay for places where Sidney Howard had used a line from Margaret Mitchell but had elided or employed a euphemism for "nigger."

Politics, not race, settled the question, as an examination of Hollywood archives shows. Selznick expected a tough fight with the censors over the word "damn" in Rhett Butler's curtain line. Concessions on "nigger," a word whose use Breen now adamantly opposed, might soften the Hays Office later on "damn"—or so Selznick apparently reasoned. "About the word, 'niggers,' " the producer wrote his assistant. "Okay, we'll forget it."

By late fall of 1939 *Gone With the Wind* had been shot, cut, and scored. "Frankly, my dear, I just don't care," Rhett Butler would say in prints of the film screened at previews. At the December 15 premiere in Atlanta, however, and at all screenings that followed, a Hays Office dispensation would allow him to curse. His "damn" would become news, as would the premiere itself; the free publicity it generated would help to build audiences—white and black—throughout the nation.

Black moviegoers' interest was high, as the studio could tell from the black press and even the daily mail. In November of 1939 a correspondent from Atlanta University had told Selznick that "your Negro Public" was just as eager as "your White Public" to receive the *GWTW* company. The writer hoped that Selznick would deny the "wholesale talk of forcing us to the back, during the parade so that we may not hinder other people who want to see their favorite Movie People." Among the favorites, perhaps chief among them, was "Hi-Hat

Hattie"—McDaniel's nickname on radio's *The Optimistic Do-Nuts Show.*

Selznick had planned to showcase the *GWTW* stars, black and white, who would arrive in Atlanta in style and appear briefly before or after the screening of the picture. He heard from a studio liaison in Georgia, however, that "Southerners would not care to have the Negro members of the cast" present. Selznick was caught. He wanted nothing—and certainly not racial tyranny—to harm the potentially "enormous Negro audience" for the picture. He was nonetheless wary of offending southern whites' racial sensibilities.

Polling studio employees from below the Mason-Dixon line, Selznick learned that southerners were second to none in their affection for Negroes "in what they regard as their proper place." Atlantans would warmly receive Hattie McDaniel and Oscar Polk and the others when they appeared on the stage of the Loew's Grand Theatre—but Atlantans would not dine with them, invite them to the Junior League Ball in honor of the other Hollywood visitors, or sit with them in an auditorium. And since the Grand was a whites-only theater, McDaniel and the other black "guests" would have no proper dressing rooms backstage, no proper places to enter and exit the theater, and no proper places to go to the bathroom. Selznick had lived with *Gone With the Wind* long enough to know a Lost Cause when he saw one. He acknowledged "the very delicate Southern attitude" toward black people and, regretfully, decided to feature only his white cast members in Atlanta.

To the astonishment of almost everyone, particularly Selznick, the interdiction of black actors had one more paragraph, until now a footnote to the history of *Gone With the Wind* and Jim Crow.

The printer's proof of the souvenir program for *Gone With the Wind* contained scene stills along with formal portraits of the stars of the film. On the front cover were pastel illustrations of Rhett Butler and Scarlett O'Hara, on the back studio portraits of other actors, including Hattie McDaniel, not in character but as themselves. Selznick, who already envisioned an Academy Award nomination for McDaniel, believed that the actor merited a place in the program because she "gives a performance that, if merit alone ruled, would entitle her practically to costarring."

When the Atlanta studio liaison saw the proof, however, he was wary. The program could include Mammy, the actor in costume, he said, but highlighting McDaniel "might cause comment and might be a handle that someone could seize and use as a club." Selznick was initially amused; the man was "nuts concerning use of Negroes" in the program. Southerners on the Culver City lot agreed—he was "completely cockeyed." Then again, Selznick thought, the studio was producing not only a $4 million epic but "the Greatest World Premiere in History!" Lest the latter harm the former, maybe he should "play it safe" and not, as his liaison had warned, provide "an opportunity for anyone else to make trouble." Less than a month before the premiere he ordered two editions of the program, one with McDaniel, one without. He brooded that the slight was unfair, putting him "on the spot of seeming ungrateful for what I honestly feel is one of the great supporting performances of all times."

The Atlanta premiere—from the separate telephone switchboard in the Selznicks' hotel suite to the rousing performance of the Ebenezer Baptist Church choir at the whites-only Junior League Ball—was nonpareil. So were the reviews that followed, as *Gone With the Wind* made its way to Los Angeles, New York, and other major cities across America. "Mightiest achievement in the history of the motion picture," the *Hollywood Reporter* concluded, and most metropolitan dailies concurred. Reaction in the black press was often as enthusiastic. Several critics praised Hattie McDaniel for the moral force she brought to the witty, sympathetic character she played; indeed, the portrayal of Mammy's grief on the death of the Butlers' daughter, filmed in an uncut shot as McDaniel climbed the stairs with De Havilland, was at once heartrending and authentic. Other critics thought that Hollywood's *GWTW* had tempered the novel's southern chauvinism and, as one prominent black magazine noted, "eliminated practically all the offensive scenes and dialogue."

Not everyone agreed, and certainly not those who, early on, had hoped for no mention of "darkies," for slaves in rebellion, for indictments of Ku Klux Klan activity and southern lynch mobs. Carlton Moss, writing in the *Daily Worker,* sternly condemned the picture. "Sugar-smeared and blurred by a boresome Hollywood love story," he told readers, *Gone With the Wind* offered up a motley collection of flat black characters that insulted the black audience. Hattie McDaniel's Mammy was especially loathsome in her love for a family, the O'Haras, "that has helped to keep her people enchained for centuries." The reviewer for the *Chicago Defender* called *GWTW* a "weapon of terror against black America."

Black activists responded with actions as well as words. As *Gone With the Wind* opened in American cities throughout the early 1940s, organized blacks made signs and walked picket lines in front of box offices. "YOU'D BE SWEET TOO UNDER A WHIP!" read one placard outside a Washington theater. "*Gone With the Wind* glorifies slavery" and "Negroes were never docile slaves," demonstrators shouted in Chicago. The police were on site, but the rally was peaceful. Not so in Brooklyn, where the line at the box office snaked around the Loew's Metropolitan. When the picketers began to weave in and out of the queue, the police moved them across the street from the theater. From there they continued to annoy the crowd. Eventually they stepped outside the blockade and started to bandy words with the police. According to the New York *Sun,* a seventeen-year-old black "swung like a cyclone" at a patrolman, "who took the gesture on the nose and in bad part." After the youth was arrested, his companions staged a "sit-down protest" to prolong their noisy demonstration against the picture.

Word of these incidents reached—and touched—David Selznick. "I like to think of myself as being a liberal," he told his business associate John Wharton in a long memorandum. Now, though, owing to the *Daily Worker* and those black papers whose censure had fostered the demonstrations, he feared that he would endure what D. W. Griffith had. Griffith had spent years trying to prove that he was not racist, and never succeeded. "I think that by our silence we may be giving the appearance of truth to the slanders," Selznick ruminated in that memorandum. He considered suing the *Worker,* but finally let Lillian Johnson and other black fans defend him. "I crossed a picket line," Johnson, a columnist, wrote in the *Gary American,* and "I wasn't sorry." Many other blacks followed her lead. By February of 1940, as the Academy Awards ceremony neared, even hostile voices in the black press had joined the rooting section for Hattie McDaniel.

On Oscar night, wearing an ermine stole over a blue gown, McDaniel arrived at the Ambassador Hotel and, like the other stars, entered to the cheers of movie fans black and white. For her and Selznick International the evening would be as radiant as the Oz of *The Wizard of Oz,* so magical that nothing could spoil it, not even a small band of demonstrators outside the hotel, protesting against the racism of *Gone With the Wind.* Inside the Coconut Grove, as McDaniel collected her Oscar, Clark Gable shook her hand and Vivien Leigh kissed her. At the podium, tearfully, she told the audience and newsreel cameras that she hoped to "always be a credit to my race." Black activists may have cringed.

By late winter of 1940, when *Gone With the Wind* was in general release, newspapers were teeming with reports of the war and predictions that America would eventually be drawn in.

Moviegoers attending *GWTW,* hearing the cannon fire approaching Atlanta, seeing the city burn and the fields go fallow, may have understood Ashley Wilkes's melancholy. Ashley never recovered from *his* war. Too much had been lost, he said near the end of the picture—not only lives but a way of life. Moviegoers sensitive to the advancement of the black cause no doubt bristled at Ashley's nostalgia for the days of "cavaliers and cotton fields" and, as Ashley says wistfully, "high, soft Negro laughter from the quarter." Soon, though, "Mammyism" would disappear from the screen and black performers like Dooley Wilson (*Casablanca*) and Leigh Whipper (*The Ox-Bow Incident*) would excel. A momentous era of civil-rights advances would follow. In retrospect the dialogue of African Americans and Selznick International over *Gone With the Wind* seems a notable early landmark.

"If my books had been any worse I would not have been invited to Hollywood. If they had been any better I would not have come."

—Raymond Chandler

WRITERS

THE SCREENPLAY IS a bastard form of literature. A script that's a "great read" may, in fact, be a lousy script for what is ultimately not read, but seen.

The vast majority of published screenplays are not the original screenplay at all, but a transcript of a finished film.

The writer's dissatisfaction with the motion picture process is extremely well documented. For one thing, they write about it. For another, the producers and executives have always treated the writer with suspicion mainly because it's unclear what they do. By that I mean that a writer sits down with nothing but a pencil (or typewriter or computer) and creates his product as if by magic.

Even worse for the writer, the movie is actually

made by the director. The same Joseph L. Mankiewicz that said, "Every screenwriter worthy of the name has already directed his film when he has written his script," also said, "I felt the urge to direct because I couldn't stomach what was being done with what I wrote. "

Being both a writer and director myself, I know the frustrations of both jobs on a film. A movie is a total collaboration between everyone who works on it. Unfortunately it does not matter how well written the speech is, or how beautiful the photography, sets or costumes are, if the actor stinks.

I was lucky enough to have had wonderful lunches with Alfred Hitchcock when we both had bungalows at Universal Studios. Framed on one wall in his office was a marvelous cartoon of two goats in a junkyard chewing on reels of film. One goat is saying to the other, "I liked the book better."

Russell Banks is a novelist who has had two of his novels made into films. He was fortunate to have as his directors Atom Egoyan and Paul Schrader. He writes knowingly about his own experience with novels and movies in *No, but I Saw the Movie.*

John Irving is another distinguished novelist who has had his books made into movies. He has written a lively book about *My Movie Business.* In this chapter, *The Twelve-Year-Old Girl,* he explains his motivation for *The Cider House Rules.*

David Leavitt discusses the Merchant Ivory adaptation of E. M. Forster's *Howard's End* in *Lost Among the Pinafores.* The producer/director team of Merchant Ivory has made a career of stately literary adaptations.

Daryl G. Nickens explains why he became a screenwriter in *The Great Escape—Or the First Time I Didn't Pay For It.* The metaphor of movies as escape is beautifully illustrated.

The reissue of Walter Bernstein's autobiographical *Inside Out: A Memoir of the Blacklist* gives me the chance to include here Bernstein's new Introduction and the last chapter of this wonderful and important book. The reprehensible way in which the Academy of Motion Picture Arts and Sciences, the Director's Guild, the

Writer's Guild and the Screen Actor's Guild, the media, the film and television, and radio business in general reacted to the hysteria in Washington is still disturbing. The revisionist right-wing justifications that are rattling around these days are warnings we should not ignore. Bernstein puts the human face on a difficult time.

John Landis

NO, BUT I SAW THE MOVIE

by Russell Banks

For many years, or maybe not so many—for some years, anyhow—I'd be out on the book-tour hustings and after a reading would be signing books at a table in the lobby, and a lovely thing would happen. A stranger, a total stranger, would appear in line and volunteer that he or she loved one of my books (one other than the book that I was at that moment signing, of course, and was now embellishing with endearments and fawning decantations of lifelong gratitude). There is, of course, nothing more satisfying to an author of serious literary fiction or poetry—which is to say, an author who does not write for money—than to be told by a stranger that one's work has entered that stranger's life.

And whenever a person told me that he or she had enjoyed *Affliction,* say, or *The Sweet Hereafter*, I assumed the reference was to my book, and I might say in a surprised way, for it was, after all, to me still somewhat surprising, "Oh? You read the book?" As if the reference were possibly to another affliction, like cholera or extreme poverty, or to a different Sweet Hereafter, a designer drug, maybe, or a chic new soul-food restaurant on Manhattan's Upper West Side. Inviting, I suppose, what usually followed, which was a description of the circumstances or conditions under which the book was read—a book club, my brother-in-law gave it to me for Christmas, a college course, I read it in prison, in the hospital, on a train/plane/slow boat to China, et cetera.

It's what we talk about when we talk about a book that one of us has written and the other has read. We're inevitably somewhat self-conscious, at a loss for the appropriate words, in a bit of a blush, both of us. Writing and reading literary fiction and poetry are activities almost too intimate to talk about. Literature is intimate behavior between strangers, possibly more intimate even than sex, and it occurs between *extreme* strangers, who sometimes do not even speak the same language and thus require the services of a translator. Sometimes one of the strangers (the writer, usually) has been dead for centuries; sometimes he or she is utterly unknown, anonymous, or someone, like Homer or the author of the Upanishads or the Song of Solomon, whose individual identity has been mythologized and absorbed by an entire people.

My point is simply that this activity of writing involves at its center the desire on the part of the writer to become intimate with strangers, to speak from one's secret, most vulnerable, truth-telling self directly to a stranger's same self. And it's so central to the impulse that it actually does not work when one's readers are *not* strangers, when one's readers are one's friends, lovers, or family members (it's well known, after all, that no writer takes pleasure from the praise of his mom or kid sister, and we're all conditioned from our apprenticeship on not to take seriously the critiques offered by our husbands and wives and best friends). Either way, people who know us personally have motives and knowledge that disqualify them as readers. No, it's only the kindness of strangers that counts, that shyly offered gift, "I have read your novel." (With the clear implication, of course, that it was not an unhappy or unrewarding experience.)

I know this, because I am a reader, too. I am other writers' intimate stranger, and I have sat next to an author at dinner and have felt the same odd, embarrassing need to declare, as if revealing a slightly illicit or inappropriate interest in baseball cards or negligee mail-order catalogs, that I have read his or her novel, and I know that, in saying so, I am confessing that I have traveled out-of-body deeply into that stranger's fictional world and have resided there, dreamed there, hallucinated there, and have been moved, comforted, and frightened, have laughed aloud there and maybe even wept. The author, I can always tell, is slightly embarrassed by my confession, but pleased nonetheless—the more so inasmuch as he or she and I have never met before and never will again, and he or she has never read anything of mine and, if the author wishes to preserve our beautiful relationship as it is, never will, either. Reader and writer from two different solar systems, our orbits intersect for a second, and we reflect back the flash of each other's light, take brief comfort from the actual physical existence of the other, and then speed on, safely back in our own imagined universe, as if the other were not circling far away in another universe, around a different, possibly brighter sun than ours.

In the last few years, however, there has been a subtle but important change for me in this exchange between writer and presumed reader. Nowadays, when at the book-signing table, I'm often approached by a person carrying a copy of *Affliction*, for example, the paperback with the picture of Nick Nolte and James Coburn on the cover, or maybe the Canadian edition of *The Sweet Hereafter* with Ian Holm and Sarah Polley staring mournfully out, and the person will say, "I loved *Affliction*," or, "*The Sweet Hereafter* meant a lot to me," and pleased an slightly embarrassed, as usual, I will say, "Oh? You read the book?" And the person will look at me somewhat quizzically and say, "Uh . . . no, but I saw the movie."

I honestly don't know how that makes me feel, how I *ought* to feel, or what I ought to say in response. What *do* we talk about when we talk about a book I wrote whose movie version you saw? Or a book I wrote that you know of solely because you heard about the movie and saw the clips on the Academy Awards television show? What is the relationship generally between literary fiction (that relatively esoteric art form) and film (the most popular and powerful art form of our time), and in particular between my literary fictions and their film adaptations?

These are not simple questions, and literary writers have historically been reluctant to discuss them, except in dismissive ways. Hemingway famously advised novelists to drive (*presumably* from the east) to the California-Nevada state line and toss the novel over the line, let the movie people toss the money back, then turn around and drive away as fast as possible. Which is what most novelists have done, and is what most producers, directors, screenwriters, and actors have wanted them to do. Let us buy your plot, they say, your characters, setting, themes, and language, and do whatever we please with them, that's what the money's *for*, Mr. Shakespeare, so we can leave dear old Lear happily ensconced at the Linger Longer Assisted-Living Facility in Naples, Florida, with his three daughters, Melanie, Gwyneth, and Julia, living together in adjoining condos nearby, heavily into Gulf Coast real estate, romance on the horizon, fadeout, and hit the credits soundtrack, "Stayin' Alive" by the Bee Gees, and let's get Newman for the old guy, and for his pal, whatzisname, the guy with glaucoma, get Jack—we'll keep the title, sort of, only we'll call it *Shakespeare in Retirement*.

Writers who didn't, or couldn't, afford to take Hemingway's advice almost always paid for it dearly with their pride, their integrity, often their reputations, and sometimes even their whole careers. The story is that Hollywood is like Las Vegas—if you have a weakness, they'll find it. Everyone knows Fitzgerald's sad tale of depression, booze, and crack-up, and there are dozens more. Faulkner seems to have managed only by staying solidly drunk from arrival to departure. Nelson Algren sold the film rights of *The Man with the Golden Arm* to Otto Preminger, contingent on Algren's being hired to write the screenplay; later, safely back in Chicago, he said, "I went out there for a thousand a week, and I worked Monday, and I got fired Wednesday. The guy that hired me was out of town on Tuesday." S. J. Perelman said of Hollywood, "It was a hideous and untenable place when I dwelt there, populated with few exceptions by Yahoos, and now that it has become the chief citadel of television, it's unspeakable." A native of Providence, Rhode Island, and a great writer about boxing and horse racing, you'd not think of Perelman as especially fastidious, but Hollywood he saw as "a dreary industrial town controlled by hoodlums of enormous wealth, the ethical sense of a pack of jackals, and taste so degraded that it befouled everything it touched." (Sort of the way I see Providence, now that I think of it.) More or less in the same vein, John Cheever said. "My principal feeling about Hollywood is suicide. If I could get out of bed and into the shower, I was all right. Since I never paid the bills, I'd reach for the phone and order the most elaborate breakfast I could think of, and then I'd try to make it to the shower before I hanged myself." Strong statements, but not at all atypical, when serious literary writers found themselves obliged to work in, for, and with the makers of movies. Ben Hecht put it in depressingly simple terms, "I'm a Hollywood writer; so I put on a sports jacket and take off my brain."

And yet, one is forced to ask, was that then and this now? And how do we account for the difference? Because, when one looks around today, one notices an awful lot of very respectable fiction writers having what appears to be a very good time in bed with Hollywood, both as authors of novels recently adapted to film, like Michael Ondaatje's *The English Patient*, Toni Morrison's *Beloved*, Peter Carey's *Oscar and Lucinda*, David Guterson's *Snow Falling on Cedars*, and Mona Simpson's *Anywhere but Here*, and as fiction writers turned screenwriters, like Richard Price, John Irving, Amy Tan, Jim Harrison, and Susan Minot, Paul Auster has even *directed* his first film and is planning to try a second. There are others waiting in the wings. And we're not talking about the Crichtons and the Clancys here, whose fiction seems written mainly to fit the template of blockbuster movies—a respectable line of work, but not one I myself identify with. No, we're talking about writers whose fiction aspires to the somewhat more Parnassian heights where literature resides, work composed without consideration of financial reward and meant to be compared, for better or worse, to the great literary works of the past. And there is a growing phalanx of such writers, whose often difficult, morally ambiguous novels, complexly layered books with unruly characters, have been eagerly sought out and adapted for film. I honestly can't remember a period like it. We could easily make a very long list of novelists and story writers, serious, literary writers, almost none of whom actually lives and works in Hollywood, as it happens (thanks to fax machine, modem, and e-mail), but all of whom are making a fairly good living from the film industry these days, a much better living, certainly, than they could make on the sales of their books alone or than many of them used to make teaching in university creative-writing programs.

I now must add my own name to that list, and confess that in the last few years, not only have I made a pretty good living from the movie business, I've had a heck of a good time doing it, too. And furthermore, I'm not ashamed or even slightly embarrassed by the movies that have been adapted from my novels. Well, that's not altogether true: there are a few moments in each that make me cringe and crouch low in my seat when I see them. But overall I am delighted to have been associated with the making of those two films, *Affliction* and *The Sweet Hereafter,* and am grateful to the people who made them and to the businesspeople who financed them. I think they are interesting, excellent films on their own terms, and I feel they honor the novels on which they are based. And I don't believe I'm alone in having had such a delightful experience—

most of the writers I listed earlier, if not all of them, feel the same about the films adapted from their works. Oh, Rick Moody might grumble about aspects of *The Ice Storm* and William Kennedy might quibble with some of the decisions made in the making of *Ironweed,* but unlike the Faulkners, Cheevers, Perelmans, and Hechts of previous generations, none of the writers mentioned here feels demeaned, exploited, or deceived. The contrast between my experience and that of so many of my colleagues on the one hand, and the experience of our predecessors on the other, is so great as to raise an interesting question. Simply, has the movie industry in the last ten or fifteen years, and especially in the last five years, become uncharacteristically hospitable to serious works of fiction, or have the sensibilities and needs of the writers of fiction been coarsened and dumbed-down to such a degree that they no longer feel offended by Hollywood?

Obviously—since, rightly or wrongly, I feel neither coarsened nor especially dumbed-down—I believe it's the former. It's Hollywood that's changed. And it's possible that my own experience there, since it hasn't been especially uncharacteristic, can illustrate how it has changed, if not suggest why. Although *Affliction* was not released until December 1998, and *The Sweet Hereafter* was released a year earlier, in December 1997, both movies were shot within weeks of each other between January and March of 1997. Both were filmed in Canada, *Affliction* in Quebec, less than two hours' drive from my home in upstate New York, and *The Sweet Hereafter* in Toronto and British Columbia. The most salient aspect of this (other than the fact that, because they were nearby, I got to hang around the sets a whole lot) is merely that neither movie was filmed in Los Angeles. A far more important fact, however, is that the director of *Affliction,* Paul Schrader, and the director of *The Sweet Hereafter,* Atom Egoyan, although a generation apart, are both auteur-style, independent filmmakers, serious cinematic artists with highly developed artistic imaginations.

Crucially, they are men with no studio affiliations, who finance their projects by hook and crook, pasting together support from half a dozen sources, foreign and domestic, risking their mortgages, their kids' college educations, and next summer's vacation every time out, in a game that for them is high stakes and personal, but leaves them with maximum control over what ends up on the screen. Final cut, in other words, all the way down the line. And this is only possible because of budget size. Paul Schrader likes to point out that somewhere around fourteen million dollars you have to put white hats on the good guys and black hats on the bad guys. It's practically an immutable law of filmmaking. Fourteen million dollars, adjusted to inflation, is the point where you're told by the person with the checkbook: no more shades of gray, no more contradictions, no more ambiguities. *Affliction* cost a little over six million dollars to make, *The Sweet Hereafter* cost about $4.7 million, and you can be sure that Nick Nolte, Sissy Spacek, James Coburn, Willem Dafoe, and Ian Holm did not receive their usual fees. These actors, movie stars who command salaries equal, in a couple of cases, to the entire budget of the movie, worked for far less because they admired the director and the other cast members and wanted to work with them, they were excited by the screenplay and the source material for the film, and they wanted to portray characters who were colored in shades of gray, wanted to inhabit lives made complex and believable by contradiction and ambiguity, dealing with serious conflicts that matter in the real world. They believed in film as an art form and in their craft and the abilities of their colleagues, and were trying for that rare thing, a collaborative, lasting work of art.

Two important factors, then, contributed mightily to getting these rather difficult and, some might say, depressing films made: the directors, both of them artists with strong personal visions of the world, were independent filmmakers free of studio affiliation, with track records that attract great actors; and both films were budgeted low enough to keep down the debt service, so that an investor could recoup his money and even make a profit without having to sell tickets to every fourteen-year-old boy and girl in America. Without, in other words, having to turn the movie into a theme park or a video game. Also, there may have been a third factor, which underlies both of these first two: technology. The technology of filmmaking has changed considerably in recent years. From the camera to the editing room, from the soundtrack to the production booth, filmmaking has gone digital. as they like to say, so that it's possible, for instance, as in *The Sweet Hereafter*, to send a school bus careening over a cliff and skidding across a frozen lake to where it stops, then slowly sinks below the ice, a horrifying sight—all composed in a few days in a darkroom in Toronto, pixels on a computer screen, a *virtual* school bus, cliff, frozen lake, et cetera, for one-tenth the price and in one-quarter the time it would have taken to stage and film in 35 millimeter an *actual* bus, cliff, lake, et cetera. The enormous and incredibly expensive technological resources and hardware available to a studio will soon be available to almost any kid with a credit card or an indulgent uncle, and that kid can set up shop with a laptop anywhere from SoHo to Montreal to Toronto to Seattle—and compete with the Lucases, Disneys, and Hensons of the world.

American independent filmmaking seems to be entering a truly brave new world, and it will create a transition comparable, perhaps, to the transition between silent films and talkies, one in which, thanks to technological change, the old controlling economic structures undergo seismic shifts and rearrangements, with the result that the prevailing aesthetic and thematic conventions will have to give way. The boom in recent years of independent moviemaking is just the beginning. The trend toward multinational corporate bloat and gigantism will no doubt continue, if for no other reason than, thanks to that same technological change put to other uses, it *can*—unifying theme parks, professional sports, retailing, and gambling under one all-season stadium roof, so that the distinction between shopping and entertainment eventually disappears altogether, and Las Vegas and Orlando become our national cultural capitals, the twenty-first-century Model Cities of America. But at the same time, thanks to the very same technology, the equivalent of a cinematic *samizdat* is beginning to evolve right alongside it. This is where the real filmmaking is being done; the rest is little more than consumer advertising, tie-ins, and product placement. And this is where we'll see the bright young directors, screenwriters, cinematographers, and actors going to work. The Atom Egoyans and Paul Schraders of the future will be making their films rapidly and cheaply, editing them as fast as they're shot, and releasing them as independently as they're made, by the Internet or on video and DVD. Films like *The Blair Witch Project* and *Being John Malkovitch* and *The Celebration* and the recently released *Last Night*—inventive, unconventionally structured, freshly and bravely imagined movies, are not anomalies in today's film world, although five years ago they would have been. Five years ago they probably would not have been made at all. Nor, for that matter, would *Affliction* and *The Sweet Hereafter.*

This is why I think you're seeing so many serious novelists hanging around the filmmakers these days. They sense there's something marvelous happening here, and, if it doesn't take too much time away from their fiction writing and pays reasonably well, they'd like to be a part of it. Just consider the writing itself—until fairly recently, the conventions of screenwriting were, from a late-twentieth century novelist's perspective, moribund, stuck in linear time, glued to the old Aristotelian unities of place, time, and character, a three-act tale as anachronistic and predictable as . . . well, as a late-nineteenth century novel. What self-respecting postmodernist fiction writer would want to work in a form so limited and so inappropriate to our times? Yet for the writers of screenplays, until recently, it was as if, five generations after Faulkner, Joyce, and

Woolf, modernism never existed, or if it did, that it had no relevance to narrative except between the covers of a book. No wonder Ben Hecht felt he had to take his brain off when he went to work in Hollywood. No wonder Hemingway couldn't be bothered even to cross the state line. And no wonder there was such a fuss a few years ago when Quentin Tarantino in *Pulp Fiction* pushed the envelope a little and played with narrative time and point of view. At the time, it was a radical move for a screenwriter, perhaps, but all he was doing was employing a few of the tools that practically every second-year fiction-writing student keeps at the ready, switchback and replay, and a *Rashomon* split point of view.

Consider, again, our two examples, *The Sweet Hereafter* and *Affliction*, not just how those screenplays were written, but the (to me) amazing fact that the novels got adapted for film at all. Never mind the subject matter—although it is amusing to imagine pitching the stories to an old-time studio executive. "Mr. Warner, I've got this very dark story that starts with a school-bus accident in a small north-country town, and a large number of the children of the town are killed, and the movie is about the reaction of the village to this mind-numbing event." Or this: "An alcoholic, violent, forty-five-year-old small-town cop tries and fails to overcome the psychological and moral disfigurement inflicted on him as a child by his alcoholic, violent father." The door, Mr. Banks, is over there.

Let's look at just the narrative form and structure of the two novels. *The Sweet Hereafter* is told from four separate, linked points of view, four different characters, each of whom picks up the story where the previous narrator left off and continues for seventy-five or so pages before handing it off in the process remembering and recounting his and her past, offering reflections, ruminations, observations, and grief for the lost children. *Affliction* is told from the point of view of an apparently minor character who is gradually, indirectly, revealed to be an unreliable narrator and thus by the tale's end has become the central figure in the story, displacing the person we *thought* the story was about. Neither form lends itself to a conventional three-act screenplay with the usual plot points and fixed unities of time, place, and point of view, and if for no other reason than that (never mind subject matter), I was amazed that anyone even wanted to *try* to make a movie from them. Happily, both Atom Egoyan and Paul Schrader did, and they both felt free to invite me into the process of adaptation from the start and allowed me to look over their shoulders, as it were, all the way through to the editing room and beyond. It was fascinating and very instructive to see the liberties they took, not with the books, but with the old conventions of filmmaking, from screenplay to casting to camera placement to editing and sound.

For instance, to preserve the multiple points of view of *The Sweet Hereafter*—in the novel one can think of them as being structured vertically, like four columns of type, or four members of a mile relay team, which in the "real-time" constraints of a movie (as opposed to the more interactive "mental-time" freedoms of fiction) would have resulted in four separate, consecutive, thirty-minute movies—Egoyan essentially tipped the story onto its side, ran the several points of view horizontally, as it were, almost simultaneously, the relay runners running four abreast instead of sequentially, so that the story moves back and forth in time and from place to place with unapologetic ease. Egoyan trusts his viewer to reconstruct time and place and reunify point of view oh his or her own, just as one does when reading a modern novel. No big deal. Similarly, Schrader with *Affliction* felt no compunctions against letting the narrator of the novel, a minor character, it seems, one outside the action, function in the film as the witness and recapitulator of his older brother's deeds and misdeeds. This is the character who would surely have been eliminated at once from a studio production of this film, but Schrader makes him slowly, subtly, become the center of the story, using voice-over to establish his presence at every crucial juncture and giving us explicit, dramatized inconsistencies, conflicting versions of events, to establish his unreliability, so that Willem Dafoe's voice-over at the end, "Only I remain . . . ," can be heard and felt with a terrible chill of recognition by all of us in the audience, we who—unlike poor Wade Whitehouse, the ostensible and long-gone hero of our story—*also* remain. And in that way, the story of *Affliction* becomes our story, Wade's affliction becomes our culture's affliction.

Working closely with Egoyan and Schrader, I received a crash course in filmmaking, and what I learned *can't* be done in film was just as interesting and instructive to me, the fiction writer, as what I learned *can* be done in film was interesting and instructive to me the neophyte screenwriter. A particularly useful, and typical, insight, for instance, came to me early on in the writing of *The Sweet Hereafter* screenplay. Egoyan had told me that one of the aspects of the novel that most excited him was the final scene, a demolition derby. We even drove to the Essex County fair in upstate New York and videotaped one. It was the most cinematic scene in the book, Atom said. But when it came time to write it into the screenplay, he just couldn't. It was too big, too loud, crowded, too crammed with action. What to do? He asked me. "What's the underlying function of the scene in the *novel*?" I explained that it served as a social rite, a familiar but strange, rigidly structured ritual that could embrace, embellish, and reconfigure the roles of the various members of the community. With the devices and artifices of fiction available to me, I could keep the noise down, thin out the crowd, slow down the speed—distancing the demolition derby, so that it could function in the novel as an emblem for everything else in the story. He got this. Also, all along I'd told him that, to me, the novel only *seemed* realistic; that actually it was supposed to be experienced as a moral fable about the loss of the children in our culture, an elaboration on a medieval fairy tale. That's when he proposed cutting into the film the whole of the Browning poem "The Pied Piper of Hamelin," inserting a literal reading of the book. At first I said no way, too literary. There's barely a mention of it in the book, one or two passing allusions, maybe. But the more I thought about it, the more I realized—too literary for a *novel,* maybe, but not for a film. Just as the demolition-derby scene was too cinematic for a film, maybe, but not for a novel. Film, I was discovering, is in your face; fiction is in your head.

Here's a further example: something I learned a full year after *The Sweet Hereafter* was released. In Toronto one night, Atom and I gave a presentation to benefit a small theater group there and decided that I would read scenes from the novel, and he would show clips of the film version of the same scenes, and then we'd discuss why we'd each done our respective work the way we did. One of these scenes was the incest scene, which a number of people who had, and some who hadn't, read the book complained about in the film. "It was like a dream," and "I thought maybe I'd imagined it," the fourteen-year-old Nichole tells us over and over in the novel—distancing us from the actual act, the incest, by placing her account of her *response* to it between it and us, so that we simultaneously imagine the act and the girl in two different time frames, both during and after. Egoyan tried to find a cinematic way to show that from Nichole's point of view it was like a dream, maybe something she imagined, et cetera, and as a result he presented it as if it *were* a dream, i.e., dreamy, with candles, music, a father who almost seems to be her boyfriend, which has the effect, not of distancing the incest and allowing us to pity the victim and fear for her in an appropriate way, but of romanticizing it, making the victim seem way too complicit and fear and pity nearly impossible.

These lessons don't suggest to me that fiction is in any way superior to film. Merely different, in fascinating and challenging ways. Furthermore, the freedom to make movies this way, to be inventive, imaginative, and complex in the formal and structural aspects of the screenplay, and to deal with life-and-death issues that affect us all in our day-to-day lives, this is what attracts novelists like Paul Auster, Peter Carey, John Irving, and so many others like them to the movie business. It's not, as in the past, merely the business of the movie business that attracts; it's the movies that can be made there. It's certainly what has attracted me. And as a direct result of my experience with *The Sweet Hereafter* and *Affliction,* in the last few years I've become a screenwriter myself. I'm a dues-paying member of the Screenwriters Guild of America, having adapted two of my novels: *Rule of the Bone,* for Chris Noonan to direct, with Chris, his partner Barry Mendel, and me to produce; and *Continental Drift,* with Willem Dafoe and me to produce. I am also now at work on an adaptation of a novel by a different novelist, *On the Road,* by Jack Kerouac, for Francis Coppola, and am planning soon to write an original screenplay, too. And the people I'm working with, the directors, actors, producers, even the agents, are smart, and they are exceedingly skilled at what they do. They know all kinds of things that I don't, and in no way do they make me feel that, to work with them, I've got to put on a sports jacket and take off my brain. Quite the opposite.

Eudora Welty once said, "The novel is something that never was before and will not be again." That is the reason why we write them. When it begins to appear that a film can also be that new, that uniquely itself, then, believe me, men and women who otherwise would be writing novels will want to make films, too. We are fast approaching that point. Oh, sure, it is a lot of fun to hobnob with movie stars and go to Cannes and Sundance and ride to the Oscars in a limo the likes of which you haven't seen since your senior prom, but the thrill fades faster than cheap cologne. The thrill of becoming intricately and intimately involved in the process of making a true work of narrative art, however, and the chance to make that work of art collaboratively in the most powerful medium known to man, that's as thrilling as it gets; at least for this old storyteller it is. And, too, as Peter DeVries once said, "I love being a writer. What I can't stand is the paperwork."

But I don't want to leave the mistaken impression that I or any of the other novelists I've mentioned, my blessed colleagues, is likely to give up writing fiction to devote him- or herself to film. Despite the paperwork. That's inconceivable to me. These dalliances with film—however thrilling, remunerative, and instructive they are—can't replace the deep, life-shaping, life-*changing* response one gets from creating a fictional world, living in that world for years at a time, then sending it out to strangers. *Perfect* strangers. A novel, like a marriage, can change your life for the rest of your life; I'm not so sure that can be said of a movie, any more than it can of a love affair.

What, then, *do* I say to the very kind stranger who tell me, "No, but I saw the movie"? I can answer, "Ah, but that was in another country, friend, and in a different time. If you read the book, you will now and then be reminded of that country, perhaps, and that time, but only dimly and incidentally." For when we open a novel, we bring to it everything that we bring to a film—our memories and fears and our longings and dreams (our secrets, even the ones we keep from ourselves)—all of which the film either displaces or simply disregards as it unspools in the dark before us. All of which—our memories, fears, longings, and dreams—the novel engages and utilizes wholly as it takes us out of our lives into another that's as much of our own making as it is of the novelist's. That intimacy, that secret sharing among strangers, is what no novelist and no reader can give up. No matter how remarkable it is, a film is what it is, regardless of our presence or absence before it. The darkened theater can be empty, and it won't affect the essential nature of the film bring shown there. But a novel simply does not exist until it's read, and each time it's read, even if it's read a second time by the same person, or a third, even if it's read a thousand years after it was written, it's just as Eudora Welty said, it is "something that never was before and will not be again."

THE TWELVE-YEAR-OLD GIRL

by John Irving

There is no language in a screenplay. (For me, dialogue doesn't count as language.) What passes for language in a screenplay is rudimentary, like the directions for assembling a complicated children's toy. The only aesthetic is to be clear. Even the act of reading a screenplay is incomplete. A screenplay, as a piece of writing, is merely the scaffolding for a building someone else is going to build. The director is the builder.

A novelist controls the pace of the book; in part, pace is also a function of language, but pace in a novel *and* in a film can be aided by the emotional investment the reader (or the audience) has in the characters. In a movie, however, the screenwriter is not in control of the pace; that kind of control doesn't get exerted until the editing process.

As for what novelists call "tone," the cinematography may provide a close equivalent to a novel's tone, but no matter how evocative of a book's narrative voice the camera is, it isn't the same as language.

However many months I spend writing a screenplay, I never

feel as if I've been *writing* at all. I've been constructing a story—that's true—but without language. It's like building a castle (and the characters who inhabit and/or attack the castle) with blocks. The scenes are the blocks. I always write a lot of letters when I'm working on a screenplay, doubtless because I miss using language. When I'm writing a novel, I write very few letters; my language is all used up.

The moments that matter most to me in a novel are all moments of language. Here are two examples from *The Cider House Rules,* for which there are no equivalents in the screenplay. (If, in the finished film, equivalents exist, they are solely the magic of Oliver Stapleton with his camera. I had nothing to do with them.)

The first moment is a description of Senior Worthington, Wally's father—"only a tangential victim of alcoholism and a nearly complete victim of Alzheimer's disease." Senior has Alzheimer's before anyone has identified the disease.

> There are things that the societies of towns know about you, and things that they miss. Senior Worthington was baffled by his own deterioration, which he also believed to be the result of the evils of drink. When he drank less—and still couldn't remember in the morning what he'd said or done the evening before; still saw no relenting of his remarkably speeded-up process of aging; still hopped from one activity to the next, leaving a jacket in one place, a hat in another, his car keys in the lost jacket—when he drank less and *still* behaved like a fool, this bewildered him to such an extreme that he began to drink more. In the end, he would be a victim of both Alzheimer's disease *and* alcoholism; a happy drunk, with unexplained plunges of mood. In a better, and better-informed, world, he would have been cared for like the nearly faultless patient that he was.
>
> In this one respect Heart's Haven and Heart's Rock resembled St. Cloud's: there was no saving Senior Worthington from what was wrong with him, as surely as there had been no saving Fuzzy Stone.

The second moment is a description of the cider house after Mr. Rose's death, when the men are picking up their few things and getting ready to leave.

> At the end of the harvest, on a gray morning with a wild wind blowing in from the ocean, the overhead bulb that hung in the cider house kitchen blinked twice and burned out; the spatter of apple mash on the far wall, near the press and grinder, was cast so somberly in shadows that the dark clots of pomace looked like black leaves that had blown indoors and stuck against the wall in a storm.

Most of my friends who are novelists have told me that they never know the end of their novels when they start writing them; they find it peculiar that for my novels I need to know, and I need to know not just the ending, but every significant event in the main characters' lives. When I finally write the first sentence, I want to know everything that happens, so that I am not inventing the story as I write it; rather, I am remembering a story that has already happened. The invention is over by the time I begin. All I want to be thinking of is the language—the sentence I am writing, and the sentence that follows it. Just the language.

In the case of adapting a novel for the screen, the screenwriter *usually* writes with this kind of foreknowledge. One already knows the ending; one moves the story toward it. This is the only aspect of screenwriting that resembles writing a novel for me. I know the ending before I begin; I know where the blocks go. At least that much of the storytelling process is familiar.

I must know the structure of the story I'm telling, whether I'm writing a novel or a screenplay. But there the comparison begins and ends.

The movie script of *The Cider House Rules* is a play in three acts. Act I, which details Homer's relationship with Dr. Larch and his entrapped life at the orphanage hospital, ends when Homer leaves St. Cloud's with Wally and Candy. Homer breaks free of the orphanage and, momentarily, of Larch's moral authority.

Act II introduces Homer's new life at the Ocean View apple orchards: his acceptance by the picking crew of black migrants (and by Wally's mother, Olive); his falling in love with Candy; his subsequent refusal to return to St. Cloud's and become Dr. Larch's replacement.

Act III begins with the concurrent news that Mr. Rose has got his daughter pregnant—Rose Rose wants an abortion—and that Wally is returning from the war, paralyzed. Simultaneously, Candy chooses Wally over Homer, and Homer accepts that, as a consequence of his medical training, he has an obligation to give Rose Rose an abortion. Once Homer acknowledges her need for that procedure, he must resign himself to a broader role: he goes back to the orphanage hospital at St. Cloud's, exactly as Dr. Larch intended.

The last scene in the screenplay had to show Homer Wells not merely accepting but embracing the role of Dr. Larch's replacement. In the course of the film, we have seen both Larch and Homer reading to the boys in the bunk room—always from Dickens, and at least once from *David Copperfield,* the first sentence of which ("Whether I shall turn out to be the hero of my own life. . . . ") Homer finally fulfills.

I knew I wanted to have Homer reading to the boys from *David Copperfield* at the end, but there was something more important—unique to Dr. Larch. I wanted Homer to imitate Larch's blessing to the boys, his nightly benediction. That was the last scene; it shone like a beacon on some distant shore. Wherever the story took Homer, I knew where he was going to end up. In that sense, it is the most important scene in the movie; it underwent the largest number of revisions, accordingly. (Most of them concerned which passage from *David Copperfield* Homer should read.)

But there were two earlier scenes, both of which emphasize Larch's possessive love of Homer, and they were equally important to me. They required very little in the way of revision, but if (for any reason) I had been unable to be on the set for most of the shooting of the film, I would have at least made sure that I was on hand for these two scenes.

It was not until I'd seen both of these scenes shot, as I had written them, that I felt certain of the film's essential fidelity to the novel.

One morning at the orphanage, one of the orphans finds a twelve-year-old girl sleeping on the ground near the incinerator—she's not an orphan. The next we see of the girl, she's in the operating room; Edna, Homer, and Dr. Larch are attending to her. It's too late. The girl is going to die. But before she dies, she will inspire the most direct confrontation between Homer and Dr. Larch on the abortion issue.

Jane Alexander (Edna) told me that it was the abortion politics of *The Cider House Rules* that had made her want to be a part of the movie; this is the most political scene in the film.

71 INT. OPERATING ROOM—MORNING

(*Edna is holding the head of the frightened young girl. The girl is feverishly hot and whimpering; she keeps looking at her feet in the stirrups as if she's an animal caught in a trap. Larch and Homer stand on either side of her.*)

EDNA Her temperature is a hundred and four.

LARCH (*very gently*) How old are you, dear? Thirteen?

(*The girl shakes her head. The pain stabs her again.*)

LARCH (*cont.*) Twelve? Are you twelve, dear? (*the girl nods*) You have to tell me how long you've been pregnant. (*the girl freezes*) Three months?

(*Another stab of pain contorts the girl.*)

LARCH (*cont.*) Are you *four* months pregnant?

(*The girl holds her breath while he examines her abdomen; Homer examines the girl's abdomen, too.*)

HOMER (*whispers to Larch*) She's at least *five.*

(*The girl goes rigid as Larch bends into position.*)

LARCH Dear child, it won't hurt when I look. I'm just going to *look.*

(*Homer assists Larch with the speculum.*)

LARCH (*cont.*) Tell me: you haven't done something to yourself, have you?

TWELVE-YEAR-OLD It wasn't me!

LARCH Did you go to someone else?

TWELVE-YEAR-OLD He said he was a doctor. I would never have stuck that inside me!

HOMER Stuck *what* inside you?

TWELVE-YEAR-OLD It wasn't me!

(*Homer holds the girl still—she is babbling on and on while Larch is examining her.*)

TWELVE-YEAR-OLD (*cont.*) It wasn't me! I would never do no such thing! I wouldn't stick that inside me! It wasn't me!

(*Larch, his wild eye peering into the speculum, makes an audible gasp from the shock of what he sees inside the girl. Larch tells Homer to have a look. As Homer bends to the speculum, Larch whispers something to Edna. She brings the ether bottle and cone quickly; she puts the cone in place, over the nose and mouth of the frightened girl. Larch drips the ether from the bottle to the cone.*)

LARCH (*to the twelve-year-old*) Listen, you've been very brave. I'm going to put you to sleep—you won't feel it anymore. You've been brave enough.

(*Homer stares into the speculum; he closes his eyes. The girl is resisting the ether, but her eyelids flutter closed.*)

EDNA That's a heavy sedation.

LARCH You *bet* it's a heavy sedation! The fetus is unexpelled, her uterus is punctured, she has acute peritonitis, and there's a foreign object. I think it's a crochet hook.

(*Homer has pulled off his surgical mask. He leans over the scrub sink, splashing cold water on his face.*)

LARCH (*cont.*) (*to Homer*) If she'd come to you four months ago and asked you for a simple D and C, what would you have decided to do? *Nothing*? *This* is what doing nothing gets you, Homer. It means that someone else is going to do the job—some moron who doesn't know *how*!

(*Homer, furious, leaves the operating room. Edna lifts the girl's eyelids for Larch so that he can see how well under the ether she is.*)

LARCH (*cont.*) I wish you'd come to *me,* dear child. You should have come to me, instead.

The word *tweak* is an important one in the movie business. Scenes are always getting "tweaked"; dialogue gets "tweaked" most of all. In this scene—indeed, in *most* scenes—we changed some dialogue. Edna and Larch *don't* talk about "a heavy sedation"; Larch says instead to "make it deep." In the editing process, Lasse also chose to lose the dialogue at the front of the scene—about the girl's exact age, and how many months pregnant she is—because he wanted to get to Larch's lines "It won't hurt when I look" and "I'm just going to *look*" as quickly as possible.

Of course Larch's most important lines are: "*This* is what doing nothing gets you, Homer. It means that someone else is going to do the job—some moron who doesn't know *how*!" I thought that the camera should be on Larch when he delivers those lines, but Lasse wanted the camera on Homer's face, on his reaction. A better choice.

The girl who played the twelve-year-old was actually twelve herself. Her mother was on the set. I talked to the mother between takes. Michael talked to the girl much in the manner that Dr. Larch might have. The girl's mother told me that her daughter "understood absolutely everything" about the scene. Yet one of the wanna-be producers who'd been involved with the making of *The Cider House Rules* when Phillip Borsos was still alive insisted that this scene had to go; at the very least, the girl should be of "legal age," he said. It's hard to imagine how someone who felt that way ever convinced himself that he wanted to produce *The Cider House Rules* in the first place.

Politically speaking, if I were to make a list of people who should see *The Cider House Rules*, two groups would go to the top of the list: politicians who call themselves pro-life (meaning anti-abortion) and twelve-year-old girls.

LOST AMONG THE PINAFORES
E.M. FORSTER AS COSTUME-DRAMA FODDER

by David Leavitt

"It will be generally admitted that Beethoven's Fifth Symphony is the most sublime noise that has ever penetrated into the ear of man." So begins chapter five of E. M. Forster's *Howards End,* along with Proust's account of the Vinteuil septet one of the most beautiful meditations on music to be found in modern literature. Six people, related in various ways and loosely comprising a family, are sitting in the Queen's Hall in London, listening to a performance of the Fifth Symphony. (Numbers matter to Forster; it is no coincidence that the Fifth Symphony is played in chapter 5.) With acuity and fleetness, he gives us their responses:

> Whether you are like Mrs. Munt, and tap surreptitiously when the tunes come—of course, not so as to disturb the others; or like Helen, who can see heroes and shipwrecks in the music's flood; or like Margaret, who can only see the music; or like Tibby, who is profoundly versed in counterpoint, and holds the full score open on his knee; or like their cousin, Freulein Mosebach, who remembers all the time that Beethoven is "echt Deutsch"; or like Fréulein Mosebach's young

> man, who can remember nothing but Fréulein Mosebach: in any case, the passion of your life becomes more vivid, and you are bound to admit that such a noise is cheap at two shillings.

The concert progresses, and as it does, very little happens outside the characters' minds. But within their minds—what reactions! As Helen observes, "How interesting that row of people was! What diverse influences had gone into the making!" Later, in a moment of abstracted panic, she flees the theater, bearing with her the umbrella of the young man sitting next to her, a clerk called Leonard Bast whose voice will soon join the others, turning the sextet into a septet like Vinteuil's. This inadvertent act of theft will prove to be the fulcrum on which the novel turns, leading Leonard to seek out the Schlegels, who will involve him with the Wilcoxes, who will seal his fate.

How to translate such a scene into cinema? That was the question I asked myself about a decade ago, when I learned that the famous team of Merchant, Ivory, and Jhabvala was going to be making a film version of *Howards End.* After all, bringing to cinematic life an episode in which very few words are spoken, and no one moves, is no mean feat. For the language of cinema, as I learned from the director John Schlesinger the one time I tried to write a screenplay, is essentially gestural. "Too much talk!" was always his complaint about the script I was working on for him. Coincidentally, the scene in the screenplay that he liked best had no dialogue; it was a study of faces, during which the two principal characters watched a performance of Dido and Aeneas at Carnegie Hall. And how else but through gesture could one get across the import of a passage like this one?

> "No; look out for the part where you think you have done with the goblins and they come back," breathed Helen, as the music started with a goblin walking quietly over the universe, from end to end. Others fol-

> lowed him. They were not aggressive creatures; it was that that made them so terrible to Helen. They merely observed in passing that there was no such thing as splendour or heroism in the world. After the interlude of elephants dancing, they returned and made the observation for the second time. Helen could not contradict them, for, once at all events, she had felt the same, and had seen the reliable walls of youth collapse. Panic and emptiness! Panic and emptiness! The goblins were right.

This passage is crucial to the novel in that it explains Helen, investing with motive the recklessness that will soon become her leitmotif. A few paragraphs later "that tense, wounding excitement that had made her a terror in their nursery days" provokes her to leave the Queen's Hall.

> Helen pushed her way out during the applause. She desired to be alone. The music summed up to her all that had happened or could happen in her career. She read it as a tangible statement, which could never be superseded. The notes meant this and that to her, and they could have no other meaning, and life could have no other meaning. She pushed right out of the building, and walked slowly down the outside staircase, breathing the autumnal air, and then she strolled home.

Such a sequence would pose a challenge to any filmmaker. How would Merchant, Ivory, and Jhabvala handle it? I wondered. Would they render the concert, á la Schlesinger, without words? Would they use voice-overs? Or would they surprise me by finding a means of translation so clever and so unexpected as to astonish?

Well, in the end, they did surprise me, though not in a remotely positive way.

Here, then, is how Merchant, Ivory and Jhabvala have rendered chapter five in the film version of *Howards End.*

We are in a small concert hall—smaller than the Queen's Hall. There is no orchestra. Instead, at a piano, sit an uncredited Simon Callow and a woman with large quantities of black-gray hair; they are playing a four-hand transcription of the opening movement of Beethoven's Fifth Symphony. In the audience Helen sits next to Leonard. Helen alone. No Margaret, Tibby, Aunt Juley, Fréulein Mosebach, or Fréulein Mosebach's young man, as in the novel.

After a few seconds the pianists stop playing, and Simon Callow, rising from his bench, gives a speech:

> It will, I think, be generally admitted that Beethoven's Fifth Symphony is the most sublime noise ever to have penetrated the ear of man. But what does it mean? One can hardly fail to recognize in this music a mighty drama, the struggle of a hero beset by perils riding to magnificent victory and ultimate triumph. That's described in the development section of the first movement. What I want to draw your attention to now is the third movement. We no longer hear the hero but a goblin. Thank you. Mother. . . .

This speech bears careful analysis. In essence, it cobbles together bits and pieces from the concert scene, beginning with an almost verbatim transcription of the opening line and ending with the appearance of a goblin. And yet much more is altered than left alone! Forster's account of the symphony's first movement—"Gusts of splendour, gods and demi-gods contending with vast swords, colour and fragrance broadcast on the field of battle, magnificent victory, magnificent death!"—becomes the rather banal "struggle of a hero beset by perils riding to magnificent victory and ultimate triumph," while Helen's subtle distinction between the "heroes and shipwrecks of the first movement" and the "heroes and goblins of the third" becomes the lecturer's "We no longer hear a hero but a goblin." Most distressingly, given the allergy to cliché that is such a hallmark of Forster's prose, the two halves are glued together by the leaden "But what does it mean?"

Why is this? My guess is that by replacing the orchestral

concert with a lecture, Jhabvala had hoped to find a dramatic means of incorporating some of Forster's verbal ideas into the screenplay. (Not incidentally, a lecture would also have been substantially less expensive to film.) And yet the decision to give these words to a pompous speechifier has a corrosive effect on them.

Consider, for instance, the opening line. In the written version, a hint of the vernacular ("noise" instead of "music") softens the impact of what might otherwise seem merely a piece of grandstanding. Moreover, the sentence echoes the opening line of *Pride and Prejudice*—"It is a truth universally acknowledged, that a single man in possession of a large fortune must be in want of a wife." Austen, as it happens, was Forster's favorite writer, and it is her modest voice that we hear at this moment in the book: a far cry from Simon Callow's booming, Scotch-accented baritone.

Even more injurious to the novel is the heedlessness with which Jhabvala fuses ideas that in the novel belong to distinctly different characters. It was one of Forster's most noteworthy strategies to draw back periodically from the action at hand in order to offer commentary of his own; this is certainly the case with the opening paragraph of chapter 5, in which the six auditors are observed, as it were, from on high. And yet later on the narrative is handed—almost literally—to Helen:

> For the Andante had begun—very beautiful, but bearing a family likeness to all the other beautiful Andantes that Beethoven had written, and, to Helen's mind, rather disconnecting the heroes and shipwrecks of the first movement from the heroes and goblins of the third.

With three words—"to Helen's mind"—Forster indicates a clear transition from omniscient narration to a single character's intimate point of view. In the film version, on the other hand, both the "sublime noise" and the shipwrecks come from Simon Callow. More importantly, the "heroes and goblins" that belong to and in a certain key sense define Helen's imagination are taken away from her. For Helen's decision to flee the auditorium, if it is to make sense at all, must owe entirely to her reaction to the music. In the film, by contrast, she leaves because she is bored; to make the point vivid, Ivory has her check her watch not once, but twice.

So now Helen is checking her watch, and Simon Callow's mother is playing a passage from the symphony's third movement, and Callow is pacing the stage and talking. "A single, solitary goblin walking across the universe again and again," he pontificates, as the camera fixes on Helen, looking unconvinced, and Leonard, looking blank. All at once she picks up his umbrella and leaves. At first Leonard doesn't notice. An old man with a white beard raises his hand to ask a question.

> Questioner: Why a goblin?
> Speechifier: I beg your pardon?
> Questioner: Why a goblin?
> Speechifier: It's obvious. A goblin signifies the spirit of negation.
> Questioner: But why specifically a goblin?
> Speechifier: Panic and emptiness. This is what a goblin signifies, you see. . . .

"Panic and emptiness—a crucial phrase that recurs on several occasions throughout the novel—is here grafted onto a windbag's stodgy nonanswer, made part and parcel of the "spirit of negation" to which Callow—unequal to his elderly interrogator—must lamely resort. Even Helen herself seems to dismiss the goblin and all it implies as unworthy of her attention.

It is at this point that the film moves beyond mere misguidedness and begins to manifest a real contempt for Forster's vision. All at once Leonard realizes that Helen has made off with his umbrella. As he gets up to follow her, she disappears into the rain, to the accompaniment of a booming fragment of the Fifth Symphony. Yet no sooner has she arrived at Wickham Place, and a sopping Leonard stepped through the door to beg restitution of his umbrella, than she is demanding his opinion of the lecture, the title of which, we learn, was "Music and Meaning":

What did you think of the lecture? I don't agree about the goblins—do you?—but I do about the heroes and shipwrecks. You see, I'd always imagined a trio of elephants dancing at that point—but he obviously didn't.

While this speech is effective to the extent that it dramatizes how much the Schlegel sisters, with their flow of talk, flummox poor Leonard, it is also insidiously slanderous of Helen—even more so than Callow's callow lecture, since in this case the words come out of her own mouth. That she "disagrees about the goblins"—her own goblins—only brings home the point that this Helen is a flustered and muddle-headed child, not the visionary, undisciplined rebel that she is in the novel, and that she will grow into (to be fair to Jhabvala) as the film progresses. And yet how much is lost as a consequence! For in the novel, the scene in Queen's Hall serves as nothing less than a précis of the grand themes that will carry *Howards End* to its inevitable and tragic denouement: the clash between intellect and instinct; the impotence of talk; the grave matter, in Lionel Trilling's words, of "who shall inherit England." In the film, on the other hand, music—the art Forster cherished above all others—becomes merely the occasion for a slight and basically unfunny set piece: an opportunity, for Helen and Leonard, in the parlance of Hollywood, to "meet cute."

Why have I chosen to focus here on only this one episode from *Howards End?* Many other aspects of the film are deft and feeling. Several of the actors, most notably Emma Thompson as Meg and Adrian Ross Magenty as Tibby, give wonderful performances, and a few scenes—Jacky and Leonard's intrusion upon Evie's wedding, the final reconciliation between Meg and Mr. Wilcox—make for cinema of a high order. And yet something is deeply wrong here. For the sort of misrendering that mars the concert scene cannot be written off as an erroneous slip, or blamed merely on obtuseness. On the contrary, it seems to have been part of a conscious strategy, the intention of which was to muffle Forster's voice and blunt his vision, leaving us with the impression that this most intimate of authors is as decorative, touchy, and faintly ridiculous as Simon Callow nattering on about the spirit of negation. Alas, the only spirit negated here is Forster's own.

It is not my intention, here, simply to condemn the film of *Howards End,* nor to argue that the filmed adaptation of great novels is a priori a doomed enterprise; indeed, one need only recall John Huston's film of Flannery O'Connor's *Wise Blood* or, more to the point, Charles Sturridge's delicate and sincere film of *Where Angels Fear to Tread* to realize that great novels can be made into good films. And yet if a director or screenwriter is going to succeed in translating a novel into such a radically different medium—and often a medium that came into being only after the novel was written—he or she must first of all express a genuine respect and, if possible, fondness for the writing. And this is what I miss in most of Merchant Ivory's films: fondness. I never got the feeling that any member of the team really liked *Howards End,* or *A Room with a View,* or *The Remains of the Day.* Instead these books merely provide a period backdrop for mannered British actors to emote against. As Americans, we have the same appetite for them that we have for Britcom night on PBS, for *Keeping Up Appearances, To the Manor Born,* and *Waiting for God,* shows which in effect tell us that there'll always be an England, and not the England of *Trainspotting,* or even *The Full Monty;* instead this is a world where Miss Marple pours out, and Hyacinth Bucket (pronounced Bouquet) mans the white-elephant table at the church "Bring and Buy." How ironic that Forster—England's most trenchant critic and prophet—should of all writers have become fodder for such a voyeuristic and distinctly American fetish.

THE GREAT ESCAPE—OR THE FIRST TIME I DIDN'T PAY FOR IT

by Daryl G. Nickens

The first time I snuck into a movie theater was the summer after my grandfather was killed. As a young man, he had been a Pullman porter, a prestigious and lucrative job in the segregated world of that time—so much so that it was not unheard of for black men with professional degrees to prefer it to the struggles of practicing their erstwhile professions; but upon marriage to my grandmother, my grandfather settled into the quiescent drudgery typically available to black men of his generation: He shined shoes, dug ditches, slung hash—anything for an honest dollar—until, in a stroke of luck late in his life, he landed a cushy government job as the night watchman at a minor federal building on the outskirts of Capitol Hill. One night, while on duty, he was murdered by intruders with his own gun. In early 1963, such an event was still rare enough that the mystery of his death and the whereabouts of the murder weapon headlined the *Star* and *Times-Herald,* and even merited a small front-page column in the then normally local-news-adverse *Post*. The D.C. Police, assisted by the FBI, vigorously pursued the case. Within a week, his assailants were apprehended: two boys barely in their teens—boys my age—who confessed to accidentally shooting him, after hiding in a bathroom until after closing to steal the gun from an old man they figured wouldn't put up much of a fight. No one had intended it to happen. It was a random tragedy without an author.

My grandfather's death, like all such unexpected renders in the fabric of normal life, had unforeseen consequences. When my parents fought—which they did frequently—I would sometimes come across him in the pantry, the calm in the eye of the storm, quietly advising my father on how to weather the latest squall that, like the certainty of typhoons in the tropics, he accepted as the inevitable consequence of life with someone who was, in his understated summation of my mother's character; "a little high strung." He had been the ballast of our home. Without his steadying influence, my parents' marriage floundered on the shoals of their inability to live together, and slowly and painfully went to pieces. Whenever I had money, I jumped ship for a few hours, escaping into the place that had always been there for me whenever anything went bad: the movies.

Mostly, I paid to get in with my own money, which I earned by collecting bottles for deposit refunds or by carrying, groceries for overloaded shoppers coming out of the neighborhood Safeway. Occasionally, my parents paid. When my grandfather was alive, I could always ask him if all else failed; and for the price of a lecture on the virtues of self-sufficiency—which I ordinarily tried to embody—I was in. That summer, though, there was no money. It wasn't just that his funeral expenses ate up his meager death benefits and then some, but, as I figured out much later, he had helped keep our household afloat financially as well as emotionally. Having seven mouths to feed, my father took a second job, as much to be away, I suspect, as for the money. With the dog days of summer settling in, my mother, resentful of being alone, fell into a loud and angry depression, which, without the buffer of my grandfather or my father, fell upon my four younger sisters and me like a hurricane upon little houses on an exposed shore. There was nothing to do but ride out the gale as best we could. I would take refuge whenever I could in one of my storm cellars: the Lincoln, the Republic, and the Booker T., the three movie theaters on U Street, the Pennsylvania Avenue of black Washington. But, more and more frequently, I would spend my money on ice cream from the alcoholic Good Humor man whose otherwise unpredictable appearances were somehow synchronized to the days my mother would spend her last dime on a fountain

Coke for herself—which she'd make me run to the drugstore to buy—convinced that Coke syrup soothed the ulcers my sisters and I were giving her. The two littlest of my sisters would cry because they couldn't have ice cream. My mother would yell at them for crying. And I would buy them ice cream with my money because they generally kept their promises to shut up if I did.

But, as predictably as some no-account lover in one of my grandfather's Bessie Smith records, the day I most needed my money, it was gone: a day when I was awakened by my mother screaming at my father for not leaving her enough money to even buy a fountain Coke; a day the Good Humor man, of course, showed up like some mocking angel of financial death, and caused my sisters to cry without relief; a day I needed the shelter of a movie. I scoured the neighborhood for bottles to little avail. And Saturday, the big shopping day at Safeway, was a distant shore, and eternity away. As I stood in front of the Lincoln, the big-screen flagship of the three theaters, I was certain of two things: that the title on the marquee spoke to my deepest desire, and that there was only one way I was going to see the *Great Escape*—I'd have to sneak into the theater.

Waiting by the alley door, I little appreciated the irony of breaking into the movies to watch a breakout from the Stalag Luft III because my heart was pounding so hard I was certain the heaving of my chest would betray me to the usher, as he let out the patrons from the previous show. But when the door opened with a sudden, ominous creak, an attractive woman was first out. The usher's eyes zeroed in on her rear end like a Tex Avery wolf's, and I knew I had suddenly become invisible. When I got inside, I snagged a ticket stub off the floor, just to be on the safe side. But I did not feel truly safe until the lights went down, and, enveloped in the cool darkness, I was transported to another world. I didn't know then that it was a world created by a screenwriter, anymore then I could know that I would grow up to be one, or that this day would be one of the reasons why. What I knew was that it was a world that made sense, where tragic deaths only came in the service of noble causes. And though I also knew that was a lie, it somehow made the truth bearable. I saw the movie twice.

INSIDE OUT: A MEMOIR OF THE BLACKLIST

by Walter Bernstein

Some time ago, after I had been cleared from the blacklist and could work again under my own name, I wrote a movie about this period—*The Front,* which starred Woody Allen and Zero Mostel. The film continues to be shown at various colleges and I have been invited to speak about it to students. It is always a moment of mutual amazement, the students amazed that there could have been a witch hunt on so large a scale so recently in America, and I amazed at their amazement. They knew more about Oliver Cromwell (the history majors, anyway) than they did about Joe McCarthy. A few had heard about the senator in a class or two. Some had known about a blacklist. They found it all hard to believe. Not like that. Not in America.

And yet the subject refuses to die. It is like a sore that will not heal. Even those now claiming that McCarthy wasn't all bad (it was his means, not his goal) testify to its continuing interest. When the Motion Picture Academy recently decided to give Elia Kazan its Lifetime Achievement Award, the outcry that arose was unexpected in its range and intensity. It came not only from those who had been blacklisted—that was both expected and insignificant—but from many others who objected to the industry's highest award being given to an informer. It inspired commentary from France to Australia. The blacklist period will not go away, which is the only good thing about it.

This book is an account of one man's life during that shameful time, although it is also an account of what brought him here, what he believed, and what got him blacklisted. It is history as seen through the eyes of a participant on a particular side, one that was considered subversive and even treasonous. A memoir is always history, whatever its intentions, no matter how subjective. We are formed by history and conditioned by politics, whether we like it or not.

Still, looking back, as Lot's wife unhappily discovered, is dangerous. The past can be deceptive and untrustworthy, particularly if you are writing about yourself. The temptation to cop a plea is enormous. Secretly, you want to be taken as the true self you know you are: brave, sensitive, modest, generous, always ready to speak truth to power regardless of the risk. It gets worse when you are writing about politics, about your involvement in what happened a half-century before. Then you are dealing not only with your own elusive memory, but what has happened since then, and the temptation here is to let yourself off as easily as you can, to align yourself now, however unconsciously, with the side that won. If you are not careful, you can be turned into a pillar of the community.

There was nothing heroic about being blacklisted. There was fear and anger and pain. But there was also the constant support of friends; and looking back, for all its perils, has been a chance to revisit them, to see Zero painting with delicate fury in his studio because he cannot work as an actor, to find myself with him and the ostracized others, feeling again the consoling warmth, the shared utopian hopes. We were loyal to a cause and blind to many of its defects, but we believed in its promise. In our present age of barbarism, it may seem ridiculously naive to think, as we did then, that it was possible to make a better world. But it was what we felt and what we acted on. We settle now for less; against the odds, we continue to hope. And there is always something worth fighting for.

Can it happen again? the students invariably ask. Of course it can, I answer. Maybe not right away; you need a powerful external enemy and we don't have one yet. But our prosperity and strength have never saved us from the damage we inflict on ourselves because of our fears and the political profit that can be made from them.

Hindsight cannot change history. The past is what it was, open only to interpretation. This book concerns the blacklist, but it is also about war and the movies. I have been shaped by them all. It is one man's story during one period of his life. Perhaps it can also stand as part of the larger, darker history of our country.

New York City
2000

INSIDE OUT

by Walter Bernstein

The New York *Times* had just published extracts from a secret speech that Premier Khrushchev made to the congress. What he had said was shattering—a detailed attack on the dead Stalin as despot and dictator, a full and crushing account of his crimes: the purges, the trials, the frame-ups, the executions, all that our enemies had been saying about him. The effect was devastating. What had we believed all these years? Did it come down only to the tyranny of a paranoid dictator? Was it a man or the system that had failed? Was it Marxism itself? For more than a hundred years people all over the world had been inspired by the ideal of socialism. They had fought and suffered and died for this ideal. And for half a century the battle for socialism had become above all else the need to support and preserve the Soviet Union, the workers' state, the country of "already existing socialism." Had it all been for a lie? I would not accept this, would not relinquish what had inspired so much of my life, the socialism in which I still believed, however corrupted it may have become. For we all accepted, without question, the truth of these revelations. That was another revelation. We did not doubt it for a moment. Perhaps we had been predisposed. Soviet anti-Semitism, the phony treason trials in Eastern Europe, everything that had created doubt but not defection, had prepared us for this. Now our questions had been answered.

We discussed all this in Party meetings and at one another's houses, and we were still discussing when the Russians invaded Hungary. The people of Hungary had risen up against their own already existing socialism, calling for more freedom, more democracy, and Russia had sent in its tanks and rolled over them and crushed the rebellion. That was it for me. Doubt solidified into conviction. This was no longer a Party I wanted to belong to. I left; so did all my friends. There were no speeches or denunciations, no rending of garments. We left quietly, some with sadness, some with relief, without announcement. I simply stopped going to meetings. So did most of the others in my branch until the only ones left were those who still worshipped Stalin and the undercover FBI agents, although it was difficult to tell which was which. No one tried to urge me back. The Party was imploding. Two-thirds of its membership left within the year. I felt both sadness and relief. I would miss the connection to decent and committed people who believed as I did and were willing to risk much on those beliefs. No one I knew had ever been treasonous. Those who were friends would remain friends. The others would drop out of my life. I would not miss the dogma or the unthinking obedience to the Soviet Union. I reread those writings of Marx that had stirred me the most, looking, I suppose, to bolster my faith, and found they held the same powerful truths for me. I had left the Party but not the idea of socialism, the possibility that there could be a system not based on inequality and exploitation.

The immediate, nagging problem, though, was the fronts. Once again I didn't have one. Leslie was happily ensconced in City Hall, Leo was deeply involved in production, Howard had moved to Los Angeles, and I couldn't find anyone else. There were jobs to be had but no way I could take them. A story editor I knew visited me at home (he was more paranoid than I about phones being tapped) to say that his producer wanted me to write for his new dramatic series on NBC. I said I would when I found a front. Time passed and I still hadn't found anyone and he called again. I said I was sorrier than he was and would let him know as soon as I found someone. He called again a week later. He said his producer was furious with me.

"He thinks you're stalling," he said.

"Why should I be stalling?" I said. "I need the work. I just haven't found a front yet."

"He says he knows that you have."

In fact, he went on, the producer had been told by another producer that someone was roaming the halls of NBC claiming to be my front, available for assignments.

I did not know whether to be flattered or enraged. Had I achieved such eminence that someone could get work simply by claiming to be me? Suppose he did get a job? What could I do about it? The producer didn't believe me and I could tell from the story editor's face that he didn't, either. Maybe I should just find this person and see if he would really front for me. I would forgive his transgression; like the rest of us, he was just trying to make a buck. But suppose he wouldn't? After all, this way he was keeping 100 percent instead of the measly 10 or 20 he would get fronting. Who needed me? Who was I, anyway? Could there be another me somewhere, a doppelgänger ready to take my place? Why not? I had just seen *Invasion of the Body Snatchers*. Who knew?

I watched television, waiting to see if a show came up with my name on it. None ever did. Knowing my predicament, both Leslie and Leo volunteered one more time. I chose Leo as the safer choice for both of us and wrote a script that mollified the producer. My impostor was not heard from again, but I was sure he still lurked in the shadows, waiting his chance. Maybe there was more than one of him; after all, this was America, land of opportunity. My problems remained the same, although the atmosphere seemed to be improving. The FBI stopped accosting me but still telephoned once a month. The same man always called, first carefully giving his name, Special Agent Graubard. He would ask if I was ready to talk and I would say no and he would thank me and hang up. I tried to picture him at his desk, going down his list of subversives, hoping someone would talk to him. He would be in his suit and tie, since Mr. Hoover insisted his agents be jacketed at all times. A few other agents would also be on phones, but the lucky ones would be going out into the field for the daring face-to-face work. Possibly, like me, Graubard hated wearing a tie.

I began to feel sorry for him. He was always polite, even apologetic for disturbing me, and after a while he started calling me Walter. It turned out he was Walter, too. We had a good chuckle over that. He said that his friends called him Wally. I said I never allowed anyone to call me Wally. Well, maybe Sidney Lumet. He knew I knew Sidney. He knew everyone I knew. I said that was unfair, that I knew nothing about him, and he told me he was married and had two children, a boy and a girl, and they were thinking of having another but were not sure they could afford it. I said I, too, had a boy and a girl. He knew that, of course, but it cemented our relationship even further.

The cold war continued, but at a less hysterical pace. Joseph McCarthy died, but he had done his work. Fear became internalized and a pall of conformity settled on the land. Public discourse became bland and timid. There was some agitation about the atom bomb, but little critical evaluation of anything else. The colleges were quiet. The scientists kept their mouths shut. Intellectuals stopped questioning society and stuck to questioning one another, except those doing piecework for the CIA. The movies settled for Cinerama and costume pictures and musicals and stories about great men. There was *The Glenn Miller Story, The Eddy Duchin Story, The Monte Stratton Story.* The studios had always done biographies. They had done Thomas Edison and Alexander Graham Bell and Stephen Foster and Lou Gehrig and Jesse James and, naturally, Abraham Lincoln. They had also done Juárez and Zola and Louis Pasteur. The new biographies were different from the old ones. For one thing, all the men seemed to have been married to June Allyson. For another, they achieved a stupefying dullness that the old movies rarely approached, although many came close.

The various witch-hunting committees were also starting to run low on witches. There were fewer and fewer Communists to go after and the liberals had either been purged or cleansed themselves with an acceptable anticommunism. The committees had also been rocked by some unexpected Supreme Court decisions—unexpected because it was considered a conservative court, headed by the former Republican governor Earl Warren. In two of the decisions the Court supported the First Amendment positions of men fired from their jobs or denied admission to the California bar for past activities such as supporting causes like Loyalist Spain. In another, the Court ordered the acquittal of five Communist Party officials convicted under the Smith Act, saying the evidence was insufficient. In a third, the Court asserted that Congress was not a "law enforcement or trial agency" and could not expose for the sake of exposure in the areas of ideas protected by the First Amendment.

There were other decisions, all stressing the right to academic freedom and political liberty. They asserted that the Court would not uphold contempt citations based only on an investigator's idea of what was un-American. The committees continued to function, continued doing their damage with informers and intimidation. If you refused to cooperate, you lost your job even if it was harder now to jail you for contempt. But now they were restricted to more stringent rules of evidence. There were rumors that the blacklist was breaking up. The director-producer Otto Preminger was said to have hired Dalton Trumbo to write a script for him under his own name. Preminger was an interesting contradiction, a Nazi on the set and a kind, generous, cultivated man in private life. When FBI agents had come to question him about his hiring practices, Preminger had thrown them out of his office. He was also a shrewd businessman, and if he had hired Trumbo, it was because he knew he could get away with it. These were all hopeful signs. Maybe the ice was melting. We were wary, not yet willing to trade hope for belief, but our gatherings now had a kind of pleasant giddiness. Our jokes were less bitter. For the first time we allowed ourselves a cautious optimism.

The first of my friends to get work openly was Martin Ritt. He was hired by David Susskind to direct a movie called *Edge of the City.* It had been done initially as a television show called *A Man Is Ten Feet Tall,* written by Robert Alan Aurthur, who had also written the screenplay. It had received excellent reviews and its success had enabled Susskind, the producer, to make a movie deal with MGM. Certain he would have a fight on his hands, he had proposed Marty as the director, but no one at the studio objected. They were too busy fighting off a takeover attempt and had no time for politics. Their only concern was that Marty was a first-time movie director and Susskind should keep close watch to see that he didn't go over budget.

We had a party to celebrate. Everyone was happy for Marty.

There was a little envy, but not much. We all felt it was a harbinger of good news for all of us. There were also no smoke signals from Syracuse. Perhaps the tide was turning, the networks getting bolder, the movie studios sensing where more money could now be made. Marty directed the movie without incident. Word spread that it was good and he was offered a job by NBC in Hollywood. We celebrated again; first the movie walls, then the television walls were tumbling down. *Edge of the City* opened to laudatory reviews and Marty climbed up another rung. Twentieth Century-Fox offered him a directing job. The studio had a stable of young actors that included Joanne Woodward, Tony Randall, and Anthony Franciosa and a script for a movie called *No Down Payment* about young suburban marrieds, and it wanted Marty, another young comer, to direct. No one knew that the script, attributed to Philip Yordan, had actually been written by Ben Maddow. Even Marty did not know. He signed a contract—and Spyros Skouras, the head of Fox, received a call from Ward Bond asking what did Skouras think he was doing, hiring a Communist?

Bond was part of an extreme-right-wing Hollywood group that included Adolphe Menjou, John Wayne, Robert Taylor, Victor McLaglen and several other actors and directors. McLaglen financed his own private troop of cavalry which he trained for use in case the Communists started anything. Menjou had testified as a friendly witness before the House committee and urgently asked them what it was doing about the thousands of Communists pouring across the Mexican border disguised as farm laborers. They were a nutty, rabid group, but power had been ceded to them by the studios and their word was often law. Bond, in particular, was a bully. He was also a good actor and a fixture in John Ford movies. When he died, Ford closed production on the movie he was making and went to his funeral. His cast was lined up waiting for him when he returned. They knew Ford's long connection to Bond and expected a few heartfelt words. Ford did not disappoint them.

Stepping out of his car, he turned to Andy Devine and said, "Now you're the biggest shit I know."

Bond's call to Skouras got the attention he wanted, if not the result. Marty was summoned to New York for ten days of private meetings between him, his lawyer, his agent, Skouras and other Fox executives. Marty's lawyer, Sidney Cohn, was known for having represented the writer-director Carl Foreman before the House committee. Foreman did not intend to be a friendly witness, but taking the Fifth Amendment, refusing to answer because the answer might incriminate him, would make him unemployable. Cohn had come up with a solution that became known as the Diminished Fifth. Foreman partially answered some questions about himself and did not name anyone else. That he got away with it was an indication of changing times. Joseph McCarthy was dead along with the worst excesses of his time. The cold war had simmered down. Foreman's success was also an indication to some people that maybe there had been a little hanky-panky. His movies had been highly profitable for Columbia Pictures and it wanted to keep him working. Possibly money had changed hands. There was no proof of this, only supposition. In any case, what had worked for Foreman now worked for Marty. He signed a statement for Fox disavowing any present Communist ties. He gave no names. His statement was enough for Skouras to stand up to Bond, and Marty was finally, unconditionally, free to work.

But we were unaccustomed to anyone's being cleared without informing. There were mutterings that maybe Marty had given names; no one really knew what went on in those meetings. When he and his wife returned to California, old friends came around, and while no one asked directly, there were subtle probings. I knew Marty and knew he would stay blacklisted forever rather than inform. I also knew he would deck anyone who suggested he might. I thought there might be some envy involved here. Marty was working under his own name. He was acceptable again, back in society's bosom. The rest of us were still outside, noses pressed against the glass.

Dalton Trumbo was indeed openly hired by Otto Preminger to write *Exodus* and then by Kirk Douglas to write *Spartacus*. Some blacklisted actors were hired under their own names. Their parts were smaller than those they had gotten before being blacklisted, their pay was less, and they either received no billing or a mention low down in the credits, as though the producers didn't want to call attention to what they had done, but their faces were up on the screen again and it still took a certain courage to hire them.

And I got a call from Sidney Lumet. He had been hired by Carlo Ponti, husband of Sophia Loren, to direct a movie with her. Sophia had just done her first Hollywood film with Cary Grant and now she was to do her next in New York. Paramount had bought a World War Two short story about a kept woman who falls in love with a young soldier waiting to go overseas. It sounded like *Shopworn Angel*, made first with Nancy Carroll and Gary Cooper and then remade with Margaret Sullavan and James Stewart. Those had been about World War One, but any war would do when it came to kept women and virginal soldiers. The story had worked then and there seemed no reason why it shouldn't work now.

Ponti had asked Sidney to suggest a writer and he had suggested me. He said he had worked with me in television, I had been in the war and knew soldiers, if not kept women, and he thought I would be perfect for this script. He said nothing about the blacklist and Ponti didn't ask. He hired me. I waited for the other shoe to drop. Paramount had the same screening procedures as other studios. It submitted names to clearing agencies. It was sure to have the same list as my friend Special Agent Wally Graubard and it would find my name there and that would be that. But nothing happened. Irwin Shaw spoke to his agent, Irving Lazar, who agreed to represent me, and he negotiated my deal with Ponti.

I was working again. As myself. After eight years I was no longer blacklisted. At least in movies. On the East Coast. For the moment. I could not let myself believe it was really true or would really last. But there it was: a job under my own name.

Then why didn't I feel any different? I had money; I could pay some bills; I didn't need a front anymore. There could be other jobs after this; I might even have a future. I could have a career. People would answer my phone calls. They would not cross the street to avoid me. Al Levy saw me in a restaurant and called afterward to say I looked different. He said I had walked in as though I owned the place. I thought I had slunk in as usual. Maybe I did look different. I didn't feel different. Sidney and I were working together, as we had done before; there was no change in that. Wally Graubard still called. He didn't mention my new job and I didn't tell him. Maybe the FBI didn't know everything. My friends, my politics, my apartment, my life remained the same. So did my anger. So did my feelings for the people who had gone through this with me. Love and kinship had helped sustain me in those years, opened my heart. The time had not been entirely wasted. I tried to feel guilty at having been cleared while others weren't but couldn't quite manage it. They would be next and it wouldn't be too long. My clearance would be the first of many. The ice was truly melting. Not only that; now I could really strike a blow for the cause. I could be a front.

Neither Polonsky nor Manoff had been cleared and Manoff had written a charming script on his own. He had shown it to Marty Ritt, who liked it and thought he might get it produced. Paul Newman would play the lead and Marty would direct. But Arnie needed a front. He and Abe and I discussed the problem in Steinberg's while Max hovered with the dreaded protose steak. The solution was obvious. It made us laugh. It had a satisfying, joyful sense of completion. It even had irony, a quality we cherished. I would be Arnie's front. I sent back the healthy soybean and ordered a triple portion of the Steinberg Special

Platter of smoked salmon, whitefish, and sturgeon with coleslaw, potato salad, olives, radishes, sliced tomato, and Bermuda onion. We ordered extra onion rolls along with the toasted bagels. We spurned the regular cream cheese and ordered cream cheese with chives, knowing the chives were really scallions, but no matter, this was no time to quibble. The sky was the limit. The decision was so natural it seemed like no decision at all. My name had been purified. It carried weight; it was free of entangling alliances. It could be used.

That was when I felt different: when I saw my name on the cover of Arnie's script. Maybe it was seeing it from the other side of the looking glass. Blacklisted, I had needed a front, a person; the name was taken as a matter of course. But now I saw the name was everything. Your name was who you were and how you used it told what you were. No wonder we despised the informers. Not only for turning in friends, for profiting from their misfortune, but for turning over their own names and thus giving sanction to what was contemptible. The power I now had was not only that I could compete equally on the open market. It was the power to give my name.

The script for Sophia Loren was called *That Kind of Woman* and Ponti decided I should write it in Hollywood, where he and his partner, Marcello Girosi, had their offices. He was going back to Italy, but Girosi would be there to keep an eye on me. I was reluctant to leave my children, but they could come on holidays and for the summer if I stayed out there that long. The idea of living permanently in Hollywood did not occur to me, partly from predilection and also because I was still waiting for the other shoe to drop. But I lent my apartment to a friend and flew out and rented a car and a little house in Beverly Hills from which you could see both the ocean and the mountains across the valley. The house was the pool house belonging to an estate and I had privacy and the use of the pool. There were worse ways of returning to Hollywood. Girosi was an affable, cosmopolitan man who urged me not to work too hard, just do my three pages a day and everything would be fine. But when I turned in my first several pages, he became apprehensive. I had written them with only the dialogue and indications of the action and he was worried I did not know how to write a movie. I was worried I was going to be fired and consulted my friend Bob Parrish, who by then had become a director. He told me not to worry, just to write in shots and camera angles and Girosi would think I knew what I was doing.

"The director won't pay any attention to them, anyway," he said consolingly.

I did what he said, inserting long shots and close-ups and reverse angles, and as Bob had predicted, Girusi was happy and impressed with how soon I had learned film technique. He consulted Ponti in Italy and they offered me a contract to continue writing other scripts for them after this one. Again, Irving Lazar was to make the deal, this time directly with Paramount, which was putting up the money for Sophia's movies. I was having a very good time. I missed Abe and Arnie and Steinberg's, but there were close friends like the Ritts, the Parrishes, and Charley Russell, who was hanging on by his teeth. Marty and I were able to play more tennis than we'd ever dreamed of. There were always courts available and they were free. I would pick him up early in the morning (he was ready at six, but I refused to appear before eight) and first he would buy the *Racing Form* and then we would find one of the many public courts. Success had mellowed Marty and he rarely threw his racket anymore, making our games somewhat less interesting.

I made other friends, male and female. The blacklist was behind me. Its pain was in the past, remembered but unfelt, pain's only blessing. I knew something was missing, had left my life a little emptier, but I thought it was only New York. I missed the city, my city, missed its energy, its hipness, missed walking. If you walked at night in Beverly Hills, you would be stopped by cops in a patrol car, who would ask you politely where you lived and then politely drive you there. The Beverly

Hills cops were more polite even than the FBI, but you had the feeling that if you refused their kind offer of a lift, they would just as politely shoot you dead on the spot. So, in the evenings when I was alone and longing for sidewalks, I would drive into Hollywood and walk along real streets, feeling the comfort of solid pavement under my feet. I would buy a magazine at the out-of-town newspaper stand and go to Don the Beachcomber and read in the dim light designed for lovers and drink navy grogs and eat egg rolls and spareribs and feel pleasantly content.

Then the other shoe dropped. Lazar called. "Paramount's not signing your contract," he said. I asked why not. "Because," he said, "they know the committee's got a subpoena out for you."

"How do they know that?"

"How do they know?" he asked rhetorically. He sounded irritated. "They know. And they won't sign your contract until you do something about it."

I knew what that something was. I would have to go and be a friendly witness. No one was offering me any other kind of deal. If I did not do that, if I took the Fifth Amendment or otherwise defied the committee, I was back to being blacklisted.

I was not sure if I would take the Fifth. It was an honorable position, but I had felt for some time that it was not for me. I don't know why. Perhaps some ego-driven need for self-revelation or a misguided belief that I could show the committee what we patriotic Commies were really like. Or maybe a masochistic urge to go to jail, the ultimate in being blacklisted. I was prepared to tell the committee about myself but not about anyone else. At any rate, that is what I thought I would do. The hard truth was that refusing to tell about anyone else meant a contempt citation, and even with the recent Supreme Court decisions, it still could mean a year in prison. The goal was not to testify at all. I thanked Lazar and packed my bags and called Girosi to tell him I had to return home temporarily on urgent family business and would continue writing there. He was puzzled but sympathetic. Then I went on the lam. I flew to New York but stayed with friends instead of going back to my apartment. I consulted a lawyer friend, Leonard Boudin, who had represented other people before the committee, and he checked with its chief investigator and reported back that it was true. A federal marshal was out with a subpoena, summoning me to present myself before the House Committee on Un-American Activities.

I needed a place where I could live and work and not be found. It had to be close to New York so I could consult with Sidney on the script. It had to be secret. I was not the first to have had this problem and there were Party members and ex-members and sympathizers who could be called on to help. I ended up in Little Compton, Rhode Island, a guest of Harvey and Jesse O'Connor. Harvey was a journalist who had written several muckraking books about the oil and steel industries and the financier Andrew Mellon. He had now pretty much retired, but both he and Jesse were active in progressive causes. Jesse came from Chicago money and they lived in a large Victorian house overlooking the ocean, the kind of house called a cottage across the bay in Newport. They were a close-knit couple, sharp-tongued and affectionate with each other, finding it a little hard to get around now, but spry in heart and mind. They also owned a tiny two-room shack along the water, which they offered me for as long as I wanted. There would be no charge, of course. They never asked why I needed it and I never told them. They were involved enough as it was. All they knew was that a friend had told them he had another friend who needed a place to stay for a while. That was enough for them. They took helping for granted and accepted the risk as natural and familiar.

The shack was notable for having been put together out of thirty-two doors from houses that no longer needed them. Windows were cut in at random. The effect was disconcerting.

Nothing quite fitted together, and when the doors were not warping, they were sagging. It was a little like the set for *The Cabinet of Dr. Caligari.* But the weather was warm and there were large rocks outside encrusted with mussels that I could pick and bring back to steam and eat on the rickety porch. Harvey gave me an open invitation for cocktails and occasionally, at the end of the workday, I would walk down the beach and join him on his spacious veranda, where he sat with a pair of binoculars and a pitcher of martinis and we would drink and take turns looking out to sea.

I stayed in Little Compton for about six weeks, finishing the script, taking occasional trips into New York to consult with Sidney. The House committee held its hearings without me. All the unfriendly witnesses took the Fifth Amendment and I wondered if out of solidarity, I would have done the same. I was glad not to have had to make the decision. These hearings lacked the brio of the previous ones. They had a tired air and went quickly, by rote, as if everyone just wanted to get them over with. The Hearst papers obediently put them on the front page, but below the fold. No further hearings were scheduled, not even executive sessions, and I figured I was home free. There was no reason to serve me with a subpoena if there was no place for me to testify. Leaving Little Compton, though, was not easy. It had been an unexpected paradise, a one-man artist's colony, a retreat where I had had day after peaceful day to work and read and listen to music and eat uncounted mussels. A pool house in Hollywood didn't even come close.

I said a sad farewell to the O'Connors, thanking them as best I could, wanting them to know how much they had done for me, and headed back to New York. Production had started on *That Kind of Woman* with Tab Hunter playing the young soldier Sophia improbably falls in love with. Not improbably because she was leaving her rich benefactor for the doomed boy; in the movies the improbable would have been if she hadn't left him. Doom was one of film's great aphrodisiacs. But

Tab, sweet and shy, with the weak good looks of many young leading men in the fifties, was just not in her league. He might hold his own with Sandra Dee; he was no match for Sophia. If they married, you knew who would carry whom over the threshold.

But Sidney thought he could make a sexual attraction work and the atmosphere on the set was jolly and optimistic. During the lunch break we would send out for hero sandwiches and bottles of Soave. Every so often, if a stranger appeared, I would feel caught out, as if I should be hiding in another room, but the feeling disappeared after a while. Sidney wore funny hats and had a mania for bringing in his films under schedule so that the shooting moved crisply along. He was full of talent and nervous energy, always on the move. Ideas did not interest him as much as action. Like Marty Ritt, coming from the same background, Sidney loved actors and they responded to him. With Sophia, he was supportive and encouraging. She was friendly and nervous. Her English was not fluent and she missed Ponti. He had found her when she was only sixteen; he was tutor and protector as well as husband. She felt lost without him there but at the same time excited by the freedom. She worked hard and took direction willingly. She had no airs. Everyone liked her.

Paramount still refused to sign my contract. Lazar told me this in his hotel room; he had come to New York on other business. The studio said it didn't care that the hearings were over; I would still have to go before the committee. So far as it was concerned, the subpoena was still up and running. I said that was crazy. Lazar agreed. It was a disgrace. He said he wouldn't stand for it and picked up the phone and called a high executive at Paramount. He was genuinely angry as he got the man and started berating him. I listened with pleasure; for the first time someone was openly fighting on my behalf. Lazar was a fighter. I remembered when I had first met him. Back in 1947 I would spend Sundays at Irwin Shaw's beach house in Malibu. There would be other guests and we would play ball on the beach and swim and then have a long, delicious lunch with a great deal of wine. Irwin also had a rubber life raft and we would take it out beyond the breakers and ride the waves back in. The surf was very heavy and the raft always pitched over and sometimes you would get picked up and whirled around by a wave and slammed down hard on the seafloor. You had to be in pretty good shape, but we were young and still fit from the war. Lazar came out a few Sundays, small and bald and older and unathletic, and would insist on going out on the raft with us. This meant searching for him after the raft overturned. We usually found him facedown in the shallows and had to pump the water out of him. But he would bound up briskly and insist on going out again. He had nerve and I watched him now, yelling at the Paramount executive, and felt a glow of trust.

"He doesn't have to go!" he shouted at the man. "There's no reason! I'm not going to let him, you hear me? I'm telling you! He doesn't have to go!"

He went on like this for a while, full of fight and fury, and then stopped as the executive replied. I couldn't hear what he said, but Lazar listened for a long time. Then he hung up the phone and turned to me with a shrug.

"You have to go," he said.

His anger was gone. He had made his pitch and it hadn't worked. The executive had set him straight. If I wanted to work, I would have to go. That was the end of it as far as Lazar was concerned. I wasn't going and I told Lazar that. He shrugged again. He knew where the power was. I thanked him for trying and left.

Carlo Ponti returned from Europe for the and of shooting on *That Kind of Woman* and wanted to know what was going on. We met in a conference room at Paramount's New York office. Ponti and an interpreter sat on one side of a long table; Ponti was not yet fluent in English. Leonard Boudin and I sat across from them. Ponti was a short, stocky, balding man, cultivated and intelligent. He resembled a more sophisticated Harry Cohn. He had a commanding presence, and when he wanted to, he could be charming. Leonard spoke first. He told about the subpoena, what it meant and what I would do if I had to testify, the bottom line being that I would not give names. The interpreter translated for Ponti, who listened impatiently, then rattled off a long stream of Italian. The interpreter then turned to us and said, "Mr. Ponti would like to know who has to be fixed and for how much."

"Is politics," Ponti said, waving his hands dismissively. "Is politics."

He could not understand why such a fuss was being made. It was just getting in the way of what was infinitely more important, making a movie. If politics was involved, someone certainly could be bribed. Politicians were politicians, whether Italian or American. Grease a few palms and get on with what had to be done. He had a Renaissance grasp of knavery. But like most producers, he regarded putting up his own money as a mortal sin and was not about to hire me himself. He was sympathetic, he wanted me to work for him, he regarded the Red scare as a bad American joke, product of a frightened, provincial people, but basically I was out of luck.

I needed a job. Marty was getting nowhere with the Manoff script, but that wasn't for me, anyhow. I was only the front. We worried that my name on that script would now be a liability and decided not to send it around for a while. Marty was also planning to produce a remake of the Japanese film *Seven Samurai* that Yul Brynner was going to direct for United Artists. This would be Yul's first film to direct and he was excited at the prospect. He said he wanted to get out of acting and into something that used his brains. He and Marty had asked me to write the script, now called *The Magnificent Seven,* but I was then involved with Ponti and Girosi. Now I was uninvolved, but the job had since gone to Bob Aurthur. Even if it were open, I was not sure any studio would hire me now that Paramount wouldn't. Lazar confirmed this. He said he couldn't get me work since word had spread about my subpoena and other studios were taking the same position as Paramount. I was blacklisted all over again. The dressing room lunches with sandwiches and white wine were finished. It was back to Steinberg's and the protose steak. Abe and Arnie would be there, ready with tart comfort. Max, the waiter, would bring us glasses of tea. We would laugh and make plans and help each other. We would discuss possible fronts. I would be back where I belonged, ready to bleed again.

Then Marty called from Hollywood. Bob Aurthur had withdrawn from *The Magnificent Seven* so that I could get the job. He had told Marty that he could easily get another movie, he already had several offers, and he knew what had happened with me and Paramount and thought I needed the job more than he did. He knew I had been offered the movie first and he thought it only fair.

Once again I was overwhelmed by someone's generosity. I knew Aurthur only slightly. Maybe he had other offers or maybe he didn't; the gesture was selfless. He was not just being fair. I called him up and thanked him, and he insisted his other offers were real, he could get another job tomorrow. He would not accept that he had done anything much. Now I had to be approved by United Artists. UA was a small, independent company with a rich history. Started by Chaplin, Pickford, Fairbanks, and Griffith when they decided they didn't need the established studios, it had shrunk over the years until now it was owned by a small group of New York lawyers headed by Arthur Krim. It had been very successful bankrolling stars like Burt Lancaster and Frank Sinatra, who had their own production companies.

By Hollywood standards, UA was suspiciously liberal. Krim himself was a leading Democrat and friend of Lyndon Johnson's. If I had a chance anywhere, it was there. Marty and Yul pleaded my case, but it was not really necessary. Krim and his colleagues had no use for the blacklist but had of necessity gone along when it was most virulent, looking the other way when they knew Lancaster and Belafonte were using blacklisted writers under other names. They were ready to take advantage of the fact that the times were changing. Their attitude was that officially they knew nothing of any subpoena. They were not about to force anyone to testify. I was simply a writer like any other writer and should be considered on my merits.

So we lifted our glasses of tea to my luck and I flew back to my little pool house. I screened *Seven Samurai* a few times and then tried to forget it. Kurosawa's movie was a masterpiece. All I could try to do was a pastiche set in our cowboy West. I wrote a first draft and was in the middle of script conferences with Marty and Yul when Lazar called. Paramount had called him. It had heard I was working for United Artists and, urged by Ponti and Girosi, wondered if I would come in and meet with the head of Paramount. Possibly an agreement might be reached.

The head of Paramount was a tall, courtly southerner named Y. Frank Freeman. I never did find out what the Y stood for; no one else seemed to know, either, or else people weren't telling. All I knew about him was that he came from the business side and his politics were somewhat to the right of Ward Bond. I had no great hopes but figured there was nothing to lose.

When I entered his office, Freeman stood up and gravely shook my hand. He asked if I wanted something to drink. When I declined, he said nothing for a moment, then sighed and remarked upon how difficult the times were, so many good people hurt, so much damage done. He talked about a recent strike of technicians against the studios. The strike had been lengthy and vicious. The Paramount strikers, most of whom he had known for years, loyal employees of the studio, were picketing right out in front of his office window. Freeman knew he could bring them back in, settle the strike just by talking to them, they were his boys, after all, but when he tried a few times, went out to make the attempt, Russian-looking men kept interfering. He shook his head sadly. He was not joking. He said he liked helping people in my unfortunate position and named a few he had helped. They all turned out to be informers. Then he asked if I minded answering a few questions. He had a file on his desk. It turned out to be my complete political dossier. It went all the way back to Dartmouth and the YCL. It included the trouble I had at Fort Benning when I was discovered living off the post. It had information about my Red aunt Sara. It would have been silly to ask him where it came from. I could only admire its thoroughness.

Freeman thought he would start from the top and ask me if these associations were true and, if so, what I thought of them now. Or, if organizations still existed, if I still belonged to them. If I didn't mind. His courtesy never flagged. He was consistently polite, not as polite as the Beverly Hills cops but probably just as deadly. I said I wouldn't mind at all. I really didn't. There was not much more the studios could do to me than what had already been done. They could continue to blacklist me, but I had survived that once and knew I would again. The thought made me light-headed, as though I could float, released from some self-imposed restraint. A movie contract was, after all, only a movie contract. I wanted it, but there was another life out there that I had felt good living, that had nothing to do with movie contracts, even if it was all tied up with movies. Y. Frank Freeman, the courtly southern gentleman, was giving me a choice. I could celebrate that life or lie about it or just keep my mouth shut. It was up to me.

I told him to ask his questions and I would answer. He went down the list carefully, making notes as he went. I felt like the star guest of *This Is Your Life.* When we came to Yugoslavia, Marshal Tito would bound out from the wings, grinning at my amazement. The audience would applaud. The causes rolled by, bearing their load of nostalgia. How noble this one was, how misguided that one, how could this other one be both noble *and* misguided? How stupid I was to join this, how lucky to have been part of that! These causes were what had shaped my life, given it purpose, enriched it, impeded it, gotten me blacklisted for eight years. They belonged to a time when I had hope and belief in what they represented. Most of them had ended in defeat and some in corruption, but there were many that I still believed in, would join their equivalents again if they existed, even if they were thought subversive, even if I knew their time had not yet come.

I told Freeman that and, when he had finished, he thanked me for being frank. He said he would take the matter up with a friend who advised him on such things, a man named O'Neill, head of the American Legion. I would hear from Paramount. He appreciated my coming in. We shook hands again and he walked me to the door and asked what I would do if I had to testify before the committee. I told him I might or might not take the Fifth Amendment, but I wouldn't give names.

"Then don't go," he said.

His answer surprised me since Paramount had been the one insisting I go. But he was serious. He said there was no point going if that was my position. I would only be making more trouble for myself. He may have been idiotic about the "Russian-looking men," but he was shrewd about the committee. Either go and be friendly or don't go at all. He seemed concerned for me, as he had been about his boys, the strikers. I thanked him for the advice and left.

Two weeks later I got a call from Lazar. "Whatever you did, it worked," he said. "They'll make the deal with Ponti. You're cleared, kid."

I went outside and stood by the pool and looked out across the valley. I was cleared, finally cleared—this time, it seemed, for keeps. My mind tried to fasten on what this meant, but all I could feel was an emptiness, an absence of something undefined but precious. I had felt like this when the war ended and the staff of *Yank* had dispersed. My friends would still be my friends, but we were no longer held together by the cement of repression. We were no longer a community. I had broken out, but at a price, the loss of the bonding, the group support, the liberating affection. The absence I felt was the absence of love.

But I had what I wanted. I was working again in movies, a cooperative enterprise. I would find a community there. I still lived in a country where there was no shortage of injustice and inequality, and so there would be people to join with to fight against this. Repression had not been our only bond. We had also been bound together by a common cause, our friendships built on the belief that there was a better world to be made. I was only as alone as I wanted to be.

Tomorrow morning, first thing, I would apply for a passport. I would get it now. The American Legion had certified me as no longer unclean. When the Legion spoke, committees listened. I could go anywhere, work anywhere, subject only to the vagaries of the marketplace, welcomed back to the world of dog-eat-dog. The trick now was not to act like a dog.

The mountains shimmered in the distance. The air was still, without fragrance, the silence soothing, broken only by the occasional soft hum of tires as a car swept by on the road below. Here, you could really rest in peace. I stripped down and dived naked into the pool, swimming back and forth under water, holding my breath until life forced me to the surface.

I sit on the set of a movie about to start shooting. The name of the movie is *The Front*. Woody Allen has the title role. Martin Ritt will direct and I have written the script. The movie is a comedy. It is the only way this studio, Columbia Pictures, will do a picture about the blacklist. It has also insisted on a star and suggests Robert Redford or Warren Beatty but has agreed to our choice of Woody. He is not a star of their magnitude, but he is on the way.

I feel calm, but my face is dotted with bits of Kleenex where I have cut myself shaving. I look like someone to be avoided.

On the set Marty talks quietly with Woody. Zero Mostel is also in the cast and he walks arm in arm with the lovely Andrea Marcovicci. He is singing softly to her, an aria from *Don Giovanni*. *"Là ci darem la mano,"* he sings, a song of seduction. Take my hand. You will say yes. I marvel again at Zero's grace, his dancer's movements. We have cast him because he is right for the part and because he had been blacklisted. We have cast all the parts we could that way, deliberately. It is our revenge.

I watch Zero and Joshua Shelley, who came to our touch football games in his camouflage suit, and Lloyd Gough, who used to play the concertina and sing at cause parties, and Herschel Bernardi, whose sister, the cabdriver, came in to sing at Berkowitz's restaurant. They all were blacklisted, but they have survived, however well, and now they are working again. I have trouble seeing them clearly; something is in my eye. The first assistant goes up to Marty and whispers in his ear. Marty nods and pats Woody on the shoulder. Woody does not like to be touched, but he accepts this. The actors take their places. Marty comes back to where I sit. We look at each other.

"Well?" he says.

I nod. There is nothing to say. We have come a long way for this and now it is time to do the work. Marty turns back to the set. The cast and crew are waiting. I can see clearly now, everything in focus.

"Action!" Marty calls.

The movie begins.

4

"If you can't imitate him,

don't copy him."

—Yogi Berra

DIRECTORS

LARRY KASDAN'S PIECE POV could have been in the Writers Chapter, but since he is also a director and would be the one shooting his script I've placed it here.

Stanley Kubrick has left us an extraordinary body of work and a marvelous mystique. *Dr. Strangelove, A Clockwork Orange, Barry Lyndon, Paths of Glory,* just an astonishing list of films. 2001, *A Space Odyssey* remains a seminal motion picture and arguably the most beautiful science fiction film ever made. Kubrick, like Hitchcock, was a master both at filmmaking and self-promotion. Here are an interview with the man himself done at the time of the first theatrical release of *2001,* and an excerpt from Michael Herr's book, *Kubrick.*

Most of what is written about the movie business and filmmakers in the newspapers and magazines is either fluff or inaccurate. Rick Lyman's article *Whoa, Trigger! Auteur Alert!* was the first (and the best), in his continuing series of columns about watching a movie with a director. Quentin Tarantino's passion for movies is refreshing and inspiring.

Rebecca Mead's piece on my friend Sam Raimi is here mainly because of my belief that Sam is one of the most influential modern filmmakers. His *Evil Dead* films have had a tremendous impact on contemporary filmmakers in Hong Kong, here, and in Europe.

During one of my lunches with Hitchcock, the conversation turned to a recent movie that was made by a younger director famous for "Hitchcockian" pictures. Hitch was pretty ungenerous in his opinion of the movie and its director. "But Hitch," I protested, "I'm sure it is meant as an homage," (the French pronunciation). He replied, "You mean fromage."

Natalie Zemon Davis's new book *Slaves on Screen* examines both the historical and cinematic subject of slaves and slavery in five movies: *Spartacus, Burn!, The Last Supper, Amistad,* and *Beloved.*

I first met Gillo Pontecorvo when I was a Juror at the Venice Film Festival, which he was running at that time. Aside from being the director of the magnificent *Battle of Algiers*, he is a lovely and funny man. Gillo's politics are easily explainable he says, by the simple fact that he was born in Pisa. So, of course, he leans to the left.

Davis writes about Gillo's film *Burn!* which features a terrific performance from Marlon Brando.

The documentary film director faces a daunting task. Not only is their job to tell a story, but to do so without the benefit of artifice. David Geffner's article *People Who Need People* talks about the unique and often difficult relationship between the documentary directors and their subjects.

Just quickly before you start this chapter about directors, one more quote from the Master, Alfred Hitchcock:

"There is no terror in a bang, only in the anticipation of it."

John Landis

POV

by Lawrence Kasdan

Three years ago Professor Nicholas Delbanco asked me if I'd give the Hopwood Lecture that year. I was very flattered, but I was in the middle of writing a screenplay. When I declined, Mr. Delbanco asked if I would give the lecture sometime soon. "Of course," I said quickly. But I hoped I wouldn't have to. I was dreading it.

It's true that I had delivered the commencement address here to the LS&A class of 1990. That was easier, even though there were sixteen thousand people in Crisler Arena. I knew every one would be feeling good. I had underestimated the number of graduates who would be stoned, but that only made it easier. I was like a bag of potato chips to those folks.

But the Hopwood Lecture is a different matter! It's a little intimidating. What could a screenwriter add to the tradition of the Hopwood Lecture?

Here are some examples of what you see when you look at Mr. Delbanco's book of collected Hopwood Lectures:

1961—Saul Bellow on "The Future of Fiction"

1933—Max Eastman on "Literature in the Age of Science"

1951—Mark Van Doren on "The Possible Importance of Poetry"

Norman Mailer, Alfred Kazin, Archibald MacLeish. . . . In 1974 W. D. Snodgrass ruminated on *A Midsummer Night's Dream* at some length—it's quite wonderful to read—but from the looks of it, it must have taken two hours to deliver. In those days, I think, they must have given out the money *after* the lecture.

Then about a year ago, Mr. Delbanco asked again. I had no

The Hopwood Lecture, The University of Michigan, April 20, 1999 good excuse, so I agreed. And for a year I haven't known what to talk about. To be the last Hopwood Lecturer of the century! I thought it would come to me. But it didn't come to me this whole last year, while I was writing and directing my new movie, which is called *Mumford*.

I should mention one other factor here. A few months before he called, I had been writing a screenplay for this new movie. I was adding a character, a psychiatrist in the small town of Mumford. Stumped for a name for the character, I did what I often do—let my eyes lazily scan the spines of the books on the shelves by my desk. . . . I saw Nick's book of Hopwood Lectures and stole his last name for the shrink. You can see the character in the movie when it comes out in September. Please. Anyway, I felt I owed him one.

When I had finished that movie, finally, at the end of March, I sat down at my computer and focused.

From March 30th until April 13th, a week ago, I sat at my computer and tried to write this speech. I worked really hard. But it wouldn't come. I couldn't figure out what it should be. What tone should it have? Who was it aimed at?

I must tell you, my problems do not have to do with public speaking. I enjoy that. But what I like to do is Questions and Answers. I've often done that and I've never had to prepare. Q and A's play into all my strengths—glibness, superficiality, the appearance of wit—what I call my faux wit. In Q and A's I have a certain lighthearted breeziness that eludes me in my actual life. I just let the audience do the work—ask questions and set the agenda—then I go on and on, mesmerizing myself with my insightful, humorous responses.

I worry that I have a heavy step in life. I take things too seriously. I am envious and admiring of people who seem to tread more lightly, with more natural joy, through their days. I would like to be more like that. I would like to have a lighthearted breeziness in more of my life.

But when I read the Hopwood Lectures in Nick's book,

Burt Lancaster **PHOTOFEST**

Barbara Payton **PHOTOFEST**

Larry Fine, Jermoe "Curly" Howard, Moe Howard; The Three Stooges **PHOTOFEST**

Anne Baxter and Bette Davis in Joseph L. Mankiewicz's *All About Eve* (1950) **PHOTOFEST**

Charlie Gemora in makeup
for *The Monster and the Girl*
COURTESY BOB BURNS

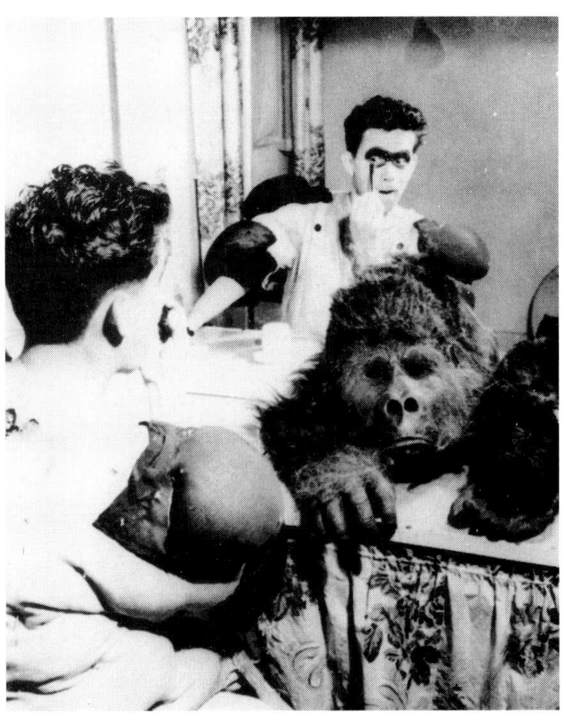

Charlie Gemora as the gorilla in a scene from *The Monster and the Girl* COURTESY BOB BURNS

Christian Bale in Mary Harron's screen adaptation of Bret Easton Ellis' *American Psycho* (2000)
PHOTOFEST

Vivien Leigh and Hattie McDaniel in David O Selznick's screen adaptation of Margaret Mitchell's *Gone With the Wind* (1939) PHOTOFEST

Nick Nolte, James Coburn, Willem Dafoe, and Sissy Spacek in Paul Schrader's screen adaptation of Russell Banks' *Affliction* (1998) **PHOTOFEST**

Michael Caine and Tobey Maguire in Lasse Hallstrom's screen adaptation of John Irving's *The Cider House Rules* (1999) **PHOTOFEST**

Anthony Hopkins and Emma Thompson in the Merchant Ivory screen adaptation of E.M. Forster's *Howard's End* (1992) **PHOTOFEST**

Zero Mostel and Woody Allen in *The Front*, directed by Martin Ritt from a screenplay by Walter Bernstein (1976) **PHOTOFEST**

Steve Mc Queen in John Sturges' *The Great Escape* (1963)
PHOTOFEST

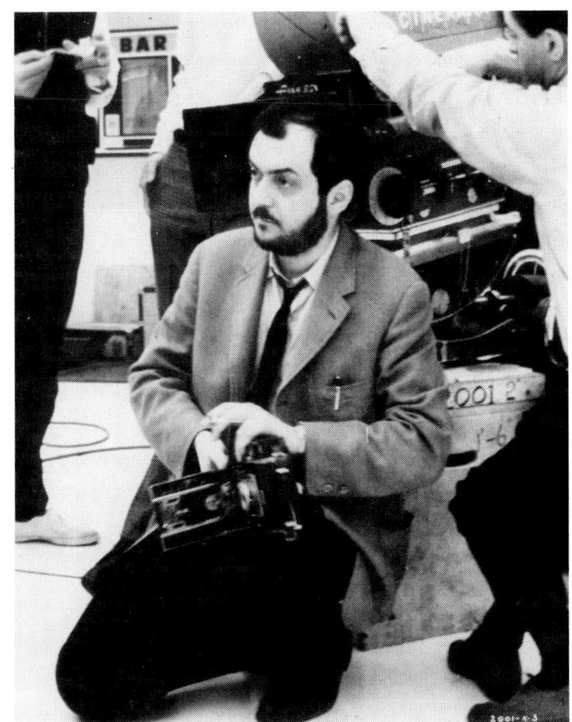

Stanley Kubrick on the set of *2001: A Space Odyssey* (1968)
PHOTOFEST

Jobeth Williams, Tom Berenger, Glenn Close, Kevin Kline, Mary Kay Place, William Hurt, Meg Tilley, and Jeff Goldblum in Lawrence Kasdan's *The Big Chill* (1983) **PHOTOFEST**

Roy Rogers and Trigger
PHOTOFEST

Gary Lockwood and Kier Dulleau in Stanley Kubrick's *2001: A Space Odyssey* (1968)
PHOTOFEST

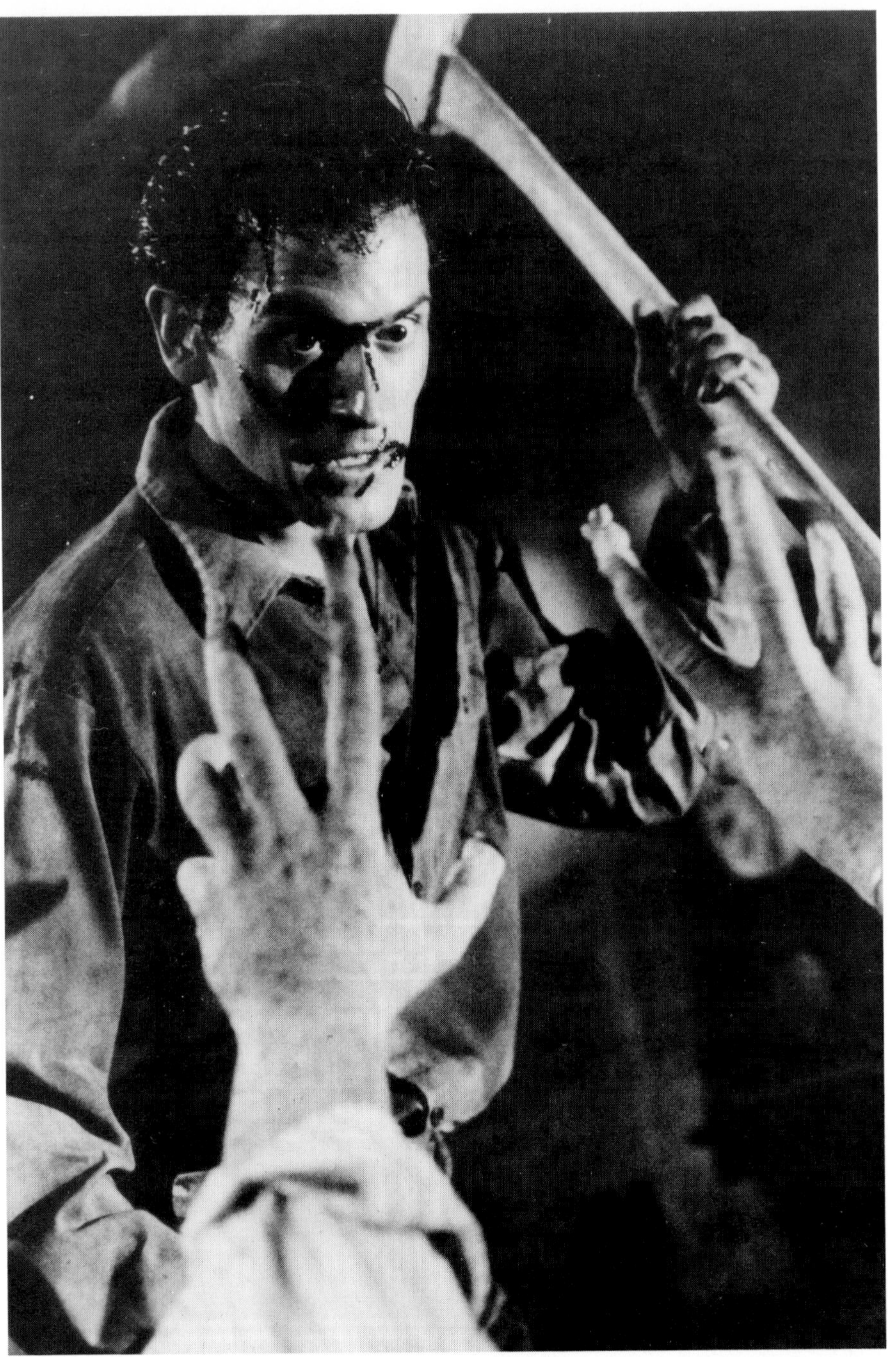

Bruce Campbell in Sam Raimi's *Evil Dead II* (1987) **PHOTOFEST**

Marlon Brando in Gillo Pontecorvo's *Burn* (1969) **PHOTOFEST**

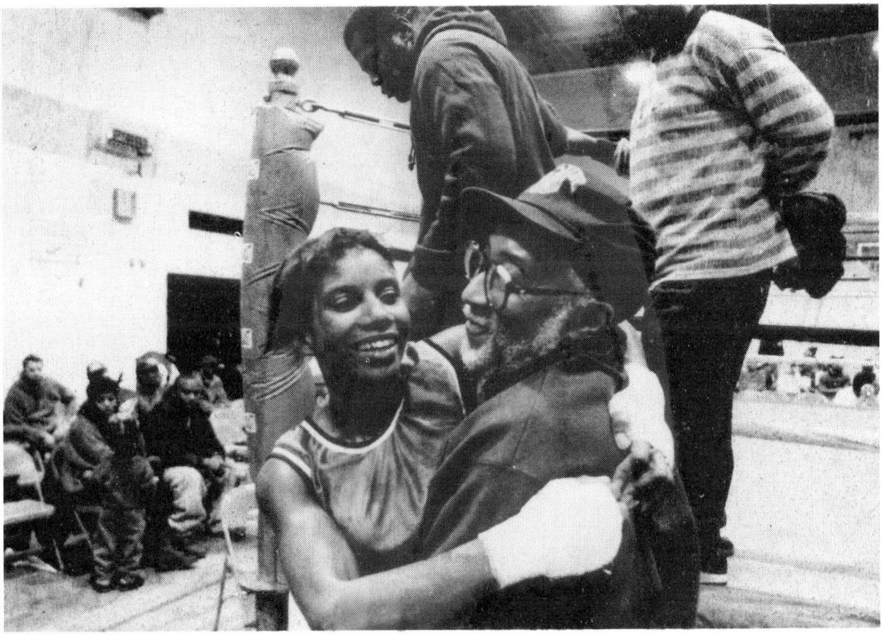

On the Ropes, a documentary by Nanette Burstein and Brett Morgen (1999) **PHOTOFEST**

Grace Quek, the subject and star of Gough Lewis' documentary *Sex: The Annabel Chong Story* (1999) **PHOTOFEST**

Zero Mostel, Kenneth Mars, and Gene Wilder in Mel Brooks' *The Producers* (1967) PHOTOFEST

Ray Harryhausen with Medusa puppet from *Clash of the Titans* (1981) PHOTOFEST

The Sopranos l-r: Dominic Chianese, Tony Sirico, Vincent Pastore, Steve Van Zandt, James Gandolfini PHOTOFEST

Al Pacino, Marlon Brando, James Caan, and John Cazale in Francis Ford Coppola's screen adaptation of Mario Puzo's *The Godfather* (1972) PHOTOFEST

Anne Parillaud, David Proval and Robert Loggia in *Innocent Blood,* directed by John Landis from a screenplay by Michael Wolk (1992) **PHOTOFEST**

Rosalind Russell, Cary Grant, Billy Gilbert and Porter Hall in Howard Hawks' *His Girl Friday* (1940) **PHOTOFEST**

Brad Pitt as Heinrich Harrer in Jean-Jacques Arnaud's *Seven Years in Tibet* (1997) **PHOTOFEST**

John Howard, Ronald Coleman and Edward Everett Horton in Frank Capra's screen adaptation of James Hilton's *Lost Horizon* (1937) **PHOTOFEST**

which appropriately is called *Speaking of Writing*, I find that very few of the distinguished authors have a light step. No matter how funny a few of these speeches are, almost none of them could be called lighthearted. When you read them in bulk, you understand that most authors spend so much time inside their heads—or as we used to say in West Virginia, "down in the mine"—away from the company or thoughts of others, away from social intercourse, that they have become just a bit deranged. They go on and on about things that obviously weigh heavily on them but may not mean much to anyone else. I'm relieved to see that. Because even a screenwriter, that most collaborative sort of writer, spends entirely too much time alone, and goes a little crazy too.

Last week I did a newspaper interview about my visit to campus. And the writer mentioned that when Pauline Kael gave the Hopwood Lecture, she did a Q and A. I got very excited. But when we called to get a transcript, we were told that there is no record of the event and that Ms. Kael was asked to make a speech, said she would, then spoke for five minutes and opened the floor up to questions. This had been viewed as a most unhappy development for everyone but Pauline.

I didn't want to behave like Pauline. So, with some disappointment, I turned away from that particular scam and did the thing I find most difficult—I got to work.

I grew up in a house where writing was seen as a legitimate undertaking. That was a blessing. My father died when I was fourteen. After he was gone my mother started saying that he had wanted to be a playwright when he was studying at Brown and that not writing was one of many frustrations in his short life. There was no evidence of this, no writing, no old plays. But here, I think, the mythology was more important than the fact. Maybe, I thought, it was in my genes.

My mother too was a writer in her youth. She said she had studied with Sinclair Lewis at the University of Wisconsin before she had to drop out and help support her family during the war. I've always believed this, but last week I decided to just do a little checking. I looked up Sinclair Lewis on the Internet and found myself on the Sinclair Lewis Homepage, which put me in reach of the Sinclair Lewis Society. I zipped off an E-missive to Professor Sally Parry at Illinois State, and she replied that indeed Lewis had taught at Wisconsin around 1940. I was delighted to hear my mother's story was possible. But here was the best part, from my point of view—according to Lewis's biographer, he taught only five sessions, then quit, saying the students had learned everything they could from him. I like this because it proves that Lewis, like certain other writers I know, was either incredibly lazy, or irascible, or easily bored. My mother says he was kicked out for living with an undergraduate girl. I like that too.

In the fifties, my mother sold some stories to what were called "confession magazines." After that, she did not continue her writing. But to this day she sees herself as a writer. She believed in writing and she preached the religion. She taught me that everything in life could be transmuted into art, that everything was grist for the mill, though I wasn't sure what grist was or what kind of mill you take it to.

My mother never learned to drive and therefore we spent a lot of time on both city and Greyhound buses. I can't remember a time when I rode with her that she didn't engage the nearest stranger in conversation, drawing from them, usually, quite a bit of their personal history or current troubles. When I would question her about it, she'd say, "Oh, I'll use it all someday in a story. People just love to talk, you know, if someone will just listen."

"But it embarrasses me," I'd say.

"That's silly," she'd laugh. "It's what writers have to do."

"I don't like it," I'd grumble.

"Why, Larry," she'd say, "it's all grist for the mill."

While I was growing up in West Virginia, my mother occupied herself with another activity. Here's how it went:

She would send away for self-help books, and get them in the mail on a ten-day free trial basis. Titles like *Think and Grow Rich, How to Win Friends and Influence People, Three Weeks to a Happier Life, Twenty-two Minutes to Total Success* . . . that kind of thing. I remember one was called *You Are Not the Target,* which she used to quote to me in the middle of our horrendous fights, in order to explain that it wasn't really me she was yelling at. (*Think and Grow Rich* is a classic in this field, written by a man named Napoleon Hill. His name carried as much weight in our house as Ernest Hemingway or Harold Robbins. Harold Robbins was my mother's favorite example of someone who had gotten rich writing, without any talent.)

My mother did not keep any of these mail-order books. We had, after all, very little money. (Obviously . . . I don't think rich people were sending away for books like that.) What she would do is copy out huge sections of the books on her typewriter (there was no Xerox then), typing away faster than I have ever seen anyone type. Reams and reams of material, whole chapters at a time. And then, when she had mined them for all they were worth, she'd send them back to the publishers.

She said that this was all just research for the ultimate, all-encompassing self-help book she herself was going to write. This was going to be the mother of all self-help books . . . by my mother.

Even as a very young person, someone who didn't understand much of the world, this behavior seemed strange to me. I'll admit, right here, that there have been many times when I've thought my mother's conduct was neither rational nor productive. (I would say, in fact, that we've had our troubles . . . in the same way that in Ireland the Catholics and the Protestants have had theirs.)

But looking back on it now, I wonder if maybe I owe her everything. Whether by nature or nurture, I became a writer.

I remember watching her at work in the little room she used as her study. Every surface was stacked high with her typed pages and visiting books, magazine clippings, and yellowing newspapers, plus helter-skelter heaps of family documents—insurance policies, tax forms, wills, and bills. She sat in the valley between these mountains of non-fileable, non-discardable material at her huge Royal typewriter. Her fingers blurred across the keyboard so fast I expected them to turn to butter like the tigers in my favorite children's story. Copying some new book, just out of its cardboard mailer. Copying and copying.

The pages would fly out of the machine like the mops in *Fantasia,* multiplying and swirling wildly in the air. It seemed crazy, yes, but also magical. And even though I knew that wasn't writing going on there, it was something very close to it. It smelled like writing. I loved the way the typewriter chattered, like a machine gun, and I liked the way her translucent, onion-skin paper would fill with thick black typescript. I knew I didn't want to copy books for a living. But I liked all the rest of it.

Early in 1963, my brother and I rode a bus for ninety blocks down Miami Beach to see David Leans film *Lawrence of Arabia* on the Lincoln Road Mall. When we arrived at the theatre, we were told we were welcome to go in, but the movie had started two minutes earlier. My brother refused to enter. He said this movie was too good to "come in in the middle." As I endured that long wait, I thought my brother was crazy, but I worshipped him. We loitered in the streets for six hours so we could see the movie properly at the evening show, right from the start. When it began, I realized that my brother had been right.

There was not a wasted second in more than three hours of film. The first images of the movie were as important as the last. Each frame had been painstakingly composed to create an enormous, seamless tapestry. When we came out of the theatre into the balmy Florida evening, I knew that I had to make movies. But I had no idea how to go about it.

The idea that movies were written had never been considered in the town where we lived. In West Virginia in the fifties, nobody thought much about how movies were made. It was assumed they just happened, and the actors made up the dialogue. My brother, home from Harvard, taught me otherwise. I began to think perhaps writing could be the path to the movies for me.

When it came time to apply to college in 1966, a friend told me that the University of Michigan had the richest college writing contest in the country. The great playwright Arthur Miller had won the award, and it helped pay his way through school. Also, incredibly, his playwriting teacher, a man named Kenneth Rowe, was still teaching there. I had no money myself and I determined to follow in Miller's footsteps.

I was so overwhelmed by the size of the place my freshman year, I could barely get myself to class, much less write something for the contest. But a year later, getting myself to classes didn't seem terribly important. What mattered was this—I had talked my way into Kenneth Rowe's drama class and was writing all the time. All the time, that is, when I wasn't going to the movies. I entered the Hopwood contest in both fiction and drama.

I don't want to spend much time telling you this next thing, so I'll assume everybody can quickly understand just how unformed a person can feel at nineteen years old. It was true that I was passionate about writing. But I had no idea if that was just a fantasy my mother had created in my mind. My classmates at Morgantown High thought I was a pretty good writer, but I had a feeling their critical standards weren't too rigorous.

When I received the letter telling me that I had won Hopwood Awards in both fiction and drama, my life changed forever. It was the first sign the real world, the outside world, the big-time world, had given me that this was not just a hopeless dream. Confirmation, validation, encouragement. And money. I was working two jobs at that time and borrowing to pay for school. This Hopwood money seemed enormous to me. It *was* enormous.

It's odd how simple it is. You get this award that says someone thinks you're for real. And that's all you need to hear. Even though I had many discouraging years after that, there was never a day after I received that letter that I doubted I would be able to make my way as a writer. For that, I will be eternally grateful to the Hopwood Awards.

By the time I was a junior, I was taking perhaps my third class with Kenneth Rowe. He was a sweet, gentle, reserved man, a great teacher . . . by 1969 very slow and fragile, in his fortieth year of teaching at Michigan. He was very tolerant of me, for he had figured out very quickly what I was up to. After writing plays for about a year, I began applying everything he was teaching me to my real pursuit, which was writing for film.

Writing screenplays is a weird kind of writing. It doesn't look like any other kind of writing. The form is unique and rigid. Contained within it are paragraphs of prose description that might be mistaken for fiction. And bursts of neatly spaced dialogue that might be mistaken for drama. There are big, heavy, capitalized headings that could be mistaken for girders holding up the script. These slug lines, as they're called, give you the time and place of the scenes:

INT. RACKHAM AUDITORIUM—DAY

But it's not prose or theatre or structural engineering. It's screenwriting. Which means it's a little bit of all those things. At its worst, it's a miserable waste of everybody's time and talent. But at its best . . . well, at its best, it could be mistaken for poetry. Let me give you an example:

Robert Bolt's screenplay for *Lawrence of Arabia** is among the greatest ever written. It's a true story about a British military officer, T. E. Lawrence, who was obsessed with the desert and the Bedouin people who lived there. He became a hero for

*Note: Michael Wilson, a blacklisted screenwriter, was the first writer on the project. His claim to shared credit was upheld in 1963 by the British Screen Writers' Guild, but the Writers Guild of America continues to list the matter as "open." See "Who Wrote *Lawrence of Arabia*?" by Joel Hodson in *the Journal* (of the Writers Guild of America, West), vol. 8, no. 3 (March 1995).

his leadership of those forces during World War I. Lawrence was an outsider in his native England and an outsider among the Arabs, whom he dearly loved. The film concerns his efforts to figure out his identity against the stirring backdrop of desert warfare. It is full of wonderful scenes, but the one that haunts me is this, in the middle of the film—

Lawrence has led an Arab force in an unexpected victory over the Turks at Aqaba. But now, in this scene, having crossed the Sinai desert with just two faithful boy servants, he emerges on foot. His crossing has cost the life of one of the boys. The surviving boy coaxes the nearly catatonic Lawrence up onto their single camel. Three tracking shots bring them to desolate civilization, signalled first by barbed wire, then by the bombed-out ruins of an outpost. The only sounds: the wind, the banging of doors, a whisper of musical score.

The boy runs ahead through the rubble, then returns excitedly to Lawrence. But Lawrence sits on the camel, his face and robes so caked with dust that he appears finally to have become one with the desert, to have become, as he hoped, a Bedouin. But the transformation seems to have sapped the last life from him.

The frightened boy throws water in Lawrence's face, washing away half his Arab countenance. His white English skin forms the other half of the mask.

Gently, he tells the boy, "It's all right."

They move through the ruins and we cut ahead. As they approach another banging door, we hear the largest sound . . . the horn of a ship? Here in the desert? Lawrence and the boy come through the door and stop. After a beat, we see what they see—there is a steamship plowing through the sand dunes, a mirage-like clash of Lawrence's two worlds.

Lawrence and the boy appear over a rise. The great music swells. We cut to their point of view—the Suez Canal, steamship now in the distance. Lawrence and the boy stare at the sight. Then a long shot of a lone motorcyclist riding along the opposite shore of the canal. The boy starts yelling at the cyclist, a British soldier. We cut to a medium shot of the soldier as he stops, cups his hand to his mouth and shouts at them. What he shouts is this: "Who . . . are . . . you?"

Finally, only now, do we cut to a close shot of Lawrence's face. And once again, over his face, do we hear the shouted question which has been at the center of this epic film since its first frame. A question which Lawrence does not know how to answer.

"Who . . . are . . . you?'

And that's what great screenwriting is about.

When you've finished writing a poem or a short story or an essay, you have the thing in your hand. Good, bad, or indifferent, you have done the job and created the thing. But in screenwriting, when you're done, what you've created is the plan for a movie.

It's your best idea of what should be shown, in what order and from what point of view. What the characters should say, when and where they should say it and who should be around while they're saying it.

Screenwriters often compare themselves to architects. They create the plans, but someone else has to construct the building. It's not an empowering attitude. John Gregory Dunne once wrote, "Wanting to be a screenwriter is like wanting to be a co-pilot."

While there can scarcely be any form of writing that doesn't employ an implicit or unspoken point of view, in screenwriting Point Of View—POV in capital letters—is an explicit, mechanical direction, as explicit as "insert scalpel between second and third ribs" or "this file cannot be opened because its application could not be found."

One of the delights of screenwriting is that the writer and then the filmmaker can jump the POV around (and usually do) with enormous freedom and never lose the audience, which has been trained since the beginning of cinema to quickly and easily accept the shifts.

For the screenwriter it means the story can be told from any and all angles imaginable: the leading character's . . . the waiter's serving his lunch . . . the sandwich on his plate . . . the bird outside the window. When I was making my first film, *Body Heat*, twenty years ago, there was a pivotal moment when the lead couple commit to their life-changing, nefarious scheme. I wanted the camera to start very low, looking up at their passionate embrace (and the office ceiling above them), to rise up past their faces and continue up, up through where we knew the ceiling should be, tilting down to hold their frantic grappling in view the whole time.

My cameraman, an older veteran of many Hollywood movies, objected. Exasperated by the discussion, he finally said, "But whose point of view is it?" I didn't know exactly, but I answered immediately, with authority, the way threatened beginners often do—"God. It's God's POV, obviously."

If you're lucky enough to make your own movies, the second level of fun comes when you figure out how you will physically, technically, literally get into each designated point of view. That's where you have the energetic company of your crew, skilled craftspeople who only want to help you figure it out. And it can be exhilarating.

The truth is almost everything about making movies is exhilarating, except for getting up very early in the morning and, sometimes, the finished product.

Even when you're writing or making a bad movie, you almost never think that. As each problem gets solved, each detail finished and delivered, there's a continual sense of triumph. That's why filmmakers are always so shocked when people hate their movie. Personally, I want to shout at the movie critic, or callous, overheard, amateur critic—"But don't you think I wrote that one scene great? Wasn't that a marvelous solution?

Didn't you gasp at the surprise of that line of dialogue, the wit of that staging? Don't you realize how hard it was to get the trucks into that location?" I mean . . . cut me some slack here!"

Ever since I was playing guard on the sixth grade basketball team at Edgington Lane Elementary School, I've been outraged by this fact of life—my accomplishments are limited by my abilities. Since I've made a life in the movies, I'm amazed that people aren't more sympathetic to the fact that my achievements have been somewhat limited by my talent.

If you write screenplays, you become a jack of many trades, but perhaps, master of none. It requires a combination of skills that aren't necessarily related. Among them:

—a sense of structure and narrative;

—a visual approach to the world—the story should be told, wherever possible, in images rather than words . . . and yet, you must have . . .

—a certain talent with dialogue, either naturalistic or stylized, but in either case with the goal of creating something that can sound true to the audience;

—finally, a sense of character: can you add anything to the general understanding of things, that complex web of motivation and passion, purpose and reflex? Do you have the imaginative generosity to create real, flawed characters and engage an audience in their adventures?

When I'm asked how I start a screenplay—with a story? a setting? an image I want to photograph?—I always give it a moment, hoping the answer has changed . . . but it never has. I always start with character. There's some behavior, some peculiarity, some way of thinking or talking or *proceeding*, that I want to explore.

Sometimes it's frustrating. Sometimes Hollywood movies seem stupidly resistant to the fascinating unpredictability of human beings. It's considered bad for business. A writer I know was in a meeting once with a studio executive who said with exasperation, "These characters are way too complicated for a movie this expensive."

The truth is, one of the strengths of American movies is that they have been, for the most part, about action first . . . then character, as revealed through action. My favorite movies work that way. When the actions the characters take perfectly elucidate their personalities, that's when movies are at their best.

When your strengths are in character, rather than story, you always feel a little out of the stream of American film. I was talking once to a screenwriter named Alvin Sargent, who wrote *Julia* and many other terrific movies: We were commiserating, agreeing that for us inspiration always arrived in the form of character, never story. He said, "Here's what it will say on my tombstone—'Finally, a plot!' "

I think the thing that has made screenwriting so irresistible to me is its ability to do anything. It is, in some ways, the freest, most unbounded writing. And the kind of writing most appealing to a control freak. You, the screenwriter and filmmaker, decide every image you will use to tell your story, every picture your audience will see, every sound they will hear. You control it all, every piece of the puzzle. (You have no control how each viewer receives that information, what button it pushes in their own memory bank, what connotations it holds for them. But you do get to impose the stimuli you wish on them . . . in a dark, cool place, where your light is the only light, where they sit, receptive, with others who share their anticipation and high hopes.)

A novelist allows each reader to decide exactly what the people and places look like, supplying only as much information as he chooses. A playwright and his director try to focus the attention of the audience on that slice of the stage that is most important at that moment. A poet hopes his words will lift the reader into the same airstream that inspired the poem.

But a filmmaker *demands* that you accept his version of

these characters, their appearance and inflections, their clothes and body language. He directs your attention to whatever detail, no matter how small, he wants you to notice. He focuses your attention on whomever he wishes during the scene, perhaps on a listener across the room, far from the nominal action, perhaps on the ticking time bomb in the basement, or across town or across the continent.

While I believe that screenwriting at its best can reach the highest level of writing, one of the great things about it is . . . no one ever expects it to. It's always a pleasant surprise when a movie is well-written. Even good movies have luxuriated in their low-rent status. A movie is a diversion, an entertainment. It is, after all, "just a movie."

Abraham Polonsky, a screenwriter who was blacklisted in the fifties after writing the scripts for *Body and Soul* and *Force of Evil*, and then came back to write some more good movies, said recently, "For me, movies are irrevocably and richly rooted in kitsch, in childhood, in storytelling, in the rubbish of paperbacks and sitting under street lights. . . . "

I find that idea liberating and inspiring. My experience is that high art often starts in low places. I know those words conjure up for me some of what makes movies so sexy and exciting.

Screenwriting may be the most fun of all writing, and almost everybody thinks they can do it. (In Los Angeles it's hard to find anyone who hasn't given it a try.) Here's how it works:

INT. RACKHAM AUDITORIUM—DAY

LAWRENCE KASDAN addresses a restless audience at the Hopwood Awards presentation. His wife, son, and in-laws are seated among the crowd of Hopwood winners, professors, and interested parties. Some people have simply wandered into the cozy auditorium looking for a place to sleep: They seem annoyed by the drone emanating from the podium.

Cut to CLOSE ON one of these fellows, SMITTY, as he is wakened by the MODEST LAUGHTER one of Kasdan's comments provokes.

SMITTY

[muttering to himself]

Who the hell is this guy? What's he going on about? And what's wrong with his voice?

Cut to Kasdan at the podium. There is a *lighthearted breeziness* to his delivery. He seems relaxed, smiling as he talks, apparently having a good time. Picking up his speech in the middle—

LAWRENCE KASDAN

. . . From March 30th to April 13th, I sat at my computer and tried to write this speech. . . .

His voice becomes distant and echoey as we PUSH IN TIGHTER on his face and come around the side of his head. There is a drop of sweat slowly rolling down his neck from behind his ear toward his Armani shirt collar. The muscles in his neck are tight. We begin to hear HIS THOUGHTS VOICE-OVER, while his actual speech continues under—

LAWRENCE KASDAN (VO)

I don't think this is going very well. I shouldn't tell them how hard it was to come up with this. They're going to wonder, how hard could it be to come up with crap like this?

INT. KASDAN'S OFFICE (LOS ANGELES)—NIGHT

The calendar on the wall shows it's April llth. Kasdan sits in front of his computer, but he is not writing. His feet are up on the desk and he has turned his chair so that he can watch the Los Angeles Lakers play the Seattle Supersonics on the television across the room. Cut back to:

INT. RACKHAM AUDITORIUM—DAY

LAWRENCE KASDAN (VO)

I should have let Meg read this first. She would have stopped me. . . .

Kasdan turns his head slightly and we RACK FOCUS from his sweaty neck to the portion of the audience visible beyond him, then PUSH PAST HIS NOSE toward a tighter shot of his wife, MEG KASDAN. We hear her thoughts VOICE-OVER.

MEG KASDAN (VO)

This is so embarrassing. I bet they don't ask a screenwriter to do this again any day soon. Why didn't he let me read his speech, like I usually do?

Her thoughts FADE as we PAN TO HER LEFT to find Kasdan's son, JON, sitting beside his mother. We hear his thoughts—

JON KASDAN (VO)

Wow, I really feel for Dad. I guess these people aren't as stoned as those kids at commencement. . . . Man, that girl in the third row is a real fox. Maybe I should have gone to school here instead of NYU. . . . I wonder what time I'll get back to Manhattan tonight. . . .

We hear some more of Kasdan's actual speech over Jon's face, then SMASH CUT TO an EXTREME CLOSE-UP of Lawrence Kasdan's mouth. It's apparent that, out of vanity, he's had some bonding work done on his two front teeth: His speech continues—

LAWRENCE KASDAN

> . . . My mother too was a writer in her youth. She said she had studied with Sinclair Lewis at the University of Wisconsin. . . .

The MUSIC GROWS LOUDER as Kasdan's speech fades into the distance. We cut to A SERIES OF SHOTS:

UNIVERSITY OF WISCONSIN CAMPUS, 1941. Sinclair Lewis comes running down a grassy slope, cuts through some bushes and winds up on a pathway, where a PRETTY UNDERGRADUATE GIRL waits for him. They embrace, then hurry off. A moment later, Lawrence Kasdan's mother, SYLVIA, in her early twenties, comes hurrying up from the other direction, short story clutched in hand, looking for Lewis. She stops, frustrated, moving into a MEDIUM SHOT. Suddenly her image MORPHS into an older version of herself, as we cut to—

WHEELING, W. VA., 1956. Lawrence Kasdan's mother is listening to the Mailman, who is obviously telling her some intimate detail of his life. She nods sympathetically, her arms full of newly delivered mail-order books. Cut to—

HER OFFICE, stacks of papers everywhere. She props a new book up next to her big Royal typewriter and begins to type. The CAMERA DRIFTS OFF her, over the stacks of paper to the doorway where it arrives at the same time as LITTLE LARRY KASDAN, seven years old, sweaty and dirty, holding a basketball. He leans against the doorjamb and watches his mother with wondering eyes. The typewriter's CHATTER RISES to drown out the MUSIC; it sounds like a machine gun.

LITTLE LARRY'S POV: Between the mountains of paper, he can just barely see his mother pounding away at a furious pace. But she's disappearing fast in a *whirlwind of onionskin typing paper*. It swirls magically around her, rising up and growing in density until Larry's mother is completely obscured . . . *and disappears*. [Note: Special effect to be done by Industrial Light and Magic.] We begin to hear Kasdan's Hopwood speech again and we are back—

INT. RACKHAM AUDITORIUM—DAY

CLOSE ON NICHOLAS DELBANCO watching Kasdan on the stage.

LAWRENCE KASDAN

. . . When I'm asked how I start a screenplay. . . .

We hear Delbanco's thoughts VOICE-OVER—

PROF. DELBANCO (VO)

He used my last name in his new movie without even asking me! I wonder if I can sue him?

We FLASH PAN down the row to where this year's winner of the Kasdan Award sits clutching his envelope—

KASDAN AWARD WINNER (VO)

Why doesn't he talk about the money? How can you talk about screenwriting and not talk about the money?

Cut to an ANGLE from behind Kasdan on the stage to include the audience.

LAWRENCE KASDAN

. . . Finally, I'd just like to say. . . .

On the word "Finally" a noticeable wave of relief sweeps across the entire audience: We begin a series of VERY QUICK CUTS—

MEG KASDAN (VO)

Thank god!

JON KASDAN (VO)

All right!

PROF. DELBANCO (VO)

I'm definitely suing him.

KASDAN AWARD WINNER (VO)

Maybe I could get a discount fare to Vegas this weekend and turn this into some real money.

And last, we cut to CLOSE ON Smitty, from the first scene, VOICE-OVER.

SMITTY (VO)

Finally . . . it's about time! Now maybe I can get some sleep—

He is interrupted by the echoey VOICE-OVER of Lawrence Kasdan.

LAWRENCE KASDAN (VO)

Hey! Who asked you? You don't like it, I'll cut you out of this scene.

SMITTY (VO)
(freaked out, looking around)

Who is this? Is this Freddy Krueger? How'd you get in my thoughts?

LAWRENCE KASDAN (VO)

This is my script. So long, sucker. . . .

Smitty vanishes from his seat. Only ONE STUDENT near the back notices, and looks on in mystification. (The role of the Student is played as a favor to me by Leonardo DiCaprio.)

Cut back to Lawrence Kasdan at the podium, *feeling good now*. The Hopwood Lecture is finally behind him, and he can get back to procrastinating on his next script. But what he says is—

LAWRENCE KASDAN

So you see, that's how it's done. It looks easy and it pays well. No wonder so many people want to do it. The truth is, it's the world's best job. Thank you for appearing in my screenplay: And thank you very much for having me here. Goodbye.

FADE OUT.

FROM *KUBRICK*

by Michael Herr

> *Somehow or other we get into this rather heavy rap—about* death, *and* infinity, *and the origin of* time—you know the sort of thing.
>
> Terry Southern

Stanley Kubrick was a friend of mine, insofar as people like Stanley have friends and as if there *are* any people like Stanley now. Famously reclusive, as I'm sure you've heard, he was in fact a complete failure as a recluse, unless you believe that a recluse is simply someone who seldom leaves his house. Stanley saw a lot of people. Sometimes he even went out to see people, but not often, very rarely, hardly ever. Still, he was one of the most gregarious men I ever knew, and it didn't change anything that most of this conviviality went on over the phone. He viewed the telephone the way Mao viewed warfare, as the instrument of a protracted offensive where control of the ground was critical and timing crucial, while time itself was meaningless, except as something to be kept on your side. An hour was nothing, mere overture, or opening move, or gambit, a small taste of his virtuosity. The writer Gustav Hasford claimed that he and Stanley were once on the phone for seven hours, and I went over three with him many times. I've been hearing about all the people who say they talked to Stanley on the last day of his life, and however many of them there were, I believe them all.

Somebody who knew him forty-five years ago when he was starting out said, "Stanley always acted like he knew something you didn't know," but honestly, he didn't have to act. Not only that, by the time he was through having what he called, in quite another context, "strenuous intercourse" with you, he knew most of what you knew as well. Hasford called him an earwig; he'd go in one ear and not come out the other until he'd eaten clean through your head.

He had the endearing and certainly seductive habit when he talked to you of slipping your name in every few sentences, particularly in the punch line, and there was always a punch line. He had an especially fraternal temperament anyway, but I know quite a few women who found him extremely charming. A few of theme were even actresses.

Some Americans move to London and in three weeks they're talking like Denholm Elliott. Stanley picked up the odd English locution, but it didn't take Henry Higgins to place him as pure, almost stainless Bronx. Stanley's voice was very fluent, melodious even. In spite of the Bronx nasal-caustic, perhaps the shadow of some adenoidal trauma long ago, it was as close to the condition of music as speech can get and still be speech, like a very well-read jazz musician talking, with a pleasing and graceful Groucho-like rushing and ebbing of inflection for emphasis, suggested quotation marks and even inverted commas to convey amused disdain, overenunciating phrases that struck him as fabulously banal, with lots of *innuendo*, and lots of latent sarcasm, and some not so latent, lively tempi, brilliant timing, eloquent silences; and always, masterful, seamless segues, "Lemme change the subject for just a minute," or, "What were we into before we got into *this*?" I never heard him try to do other voices, or dialects, every when he was telling Jewish jokes. Stanley quoted other people all the time, people in "the industry" whom he'd spoken to that afternoon (Steven and Mike, Warren and Jack, Tom and Nicole), or people who died a thousand years ago, but it was always Stanley speaking.

When I met him in 1980, I was not just a subscriber to the Stanley legend, I was frankly susceptible to it. He'd heard that I was living in London from a mutual friend, David Cornwell (b.k.a. John le Carré), and invited us for dinner and a movie. The movie was a screening of *The Shining* at Shepperton Studios a few weeks before its American release, followed by dinner at Childwick Bury, the 120-acre estate near St. Albans, an hour north of London, that Stanley and his family and their dogs and cats had just moved into. Stanley wanted to meet me because he'd liked my book about Vietnam. It was the first thing he said to me when we met. The second thing he said to me was that he didn't want to make a movie of it. He meant this as a compliment, sort of, but he also wanted to make sure I wasn't getting any ideas. He'd read the book several times looking for the story in it, and quoted bits of it, some of them quite long, from memory during dinner. And since I'd loved his movies for something like twenty-five years by this time, I was touched, flattered, and very happy to meet him, because I was of course fairly aware that it was unusual to meet him. Stanley wasn't someone you ran into at a party and struck up a relationship with.

He was thinking about making a war movie next, but he wasn't sure which war, and in fact, now that he mentioned it, not even so sure he wanted to make a war movie at all.

He called me a couple of nights later to ask me if I'd read any Jung. I had. Was I familiar with the concept of the Shadow, our hidden dark side? I assured him that I has. We did half an hour on the Shadow, and how he really wanted to get it into his war picture. And oh, did I know of any good Vietnam books, "You know, Michael, something with a *story*?" I didn't. I told him that after seven years working on a Vietnam book and nearly two more on *Apocalypse Now*, it was almost the last thing in the world I was interested in. He thanked me for my honesty, my "almost blunt candor," and said that, probably, what he most wanted to make was a film about the Holocaust, but good luck putting all of *that* into a two-hour movie. And then there was this other book he was fascinated by, he was fairly sure I'd never heard of it, Arthur Schnitzler's 1926 novella *Traumnovelle*, which translates as *Dream Novel*, meaninglessly called *Rhapsody* in the only English edition available at that time. He'd read it more than twenty years before, and bought rights to it in the early seventies (it's the book that *Eyes Wide Shut* is based on), and the reason I'd probably never heard of it (he started to laugh) was that he'd bought up every single existing copy of it. Maybe he'd send me one. I could read it and tell him what I thought.

"You know, just read it and we'll talk, I'm interested to know what you think. And Michael, ask around among your friends from the war, maybe *they* know a good Vietnam story. You know, like at the next American Legion meeting? Oh, and Michael. . . . Do me a favor will you?"

"Sure."

"Don't tell anybody what we've been talking about. . . . "

The next afternoon, a copy of the Schnitzler book arrived, along with the paperback edition of Raul Hilberg's enormous *The Destruction of the European Jews*, delivered by Stanley's driver, Emilio, who whether I realized it or not was about to become my new best friend.

I read the Schnitzler right away and that's when I had my early inkling of how smart Stanley really was. *Traumnovelle*, published in Vienna in 1926, is the full, excruciating flowering of a voluptuous and self-consciously decadent time and place, a shocking and dangerous story about sex and sexual obsession and the suffering of sex. In its pitiless view of love, marriage, and desire, made all the more disturbing by the suggestion that either all of it, or maybe some of it, or possibly none of it is a dream, it intrudes on the concealed roots of Western erotic life like a laser, suggesting discreetly, from behind its dream cover, things that are seldom even privately acknowledged, and *never* spoken of in daylight. Stanley thought it would be perfect for Steve Martin. He'd loved *The Jerk*.

He'd talked about this book with a lot of people, David Cornwell and Diane Johnson among them, and since David and Diane and I later talked about it among ourselves (and out of Stanley's hearing, I think), I know that his idea for it in those days was always as a sex comedy, but with a wild and somber streak running through it. This didn't make a lot of sense to us, we were just responding to the text as a work of literary art, and not a very funny one. Maybe *Traumnovelle* is a comedy in the sense that *Don Giovanni* is: attempted rape and compulsive pathetic list-keeping, implied impotence and the Don dragged down into hell forever, the old sex machine ignorant and defiant to the end. A pretty severe and upsetting comedy, not very *giocoso*, and not the essence of *Traumnovelle*, which more than anything else was sinister. The way we writers saw it; it was as frightening as *The Shining*. Now I think we were all too square to imagine what Stanley saw in Steve Martin, because this was not *The Jerk*. This could have turned out to be another one of those stories you heard so many times about him, usually from cameramen and other high-echelon crew, *Stanley said we should try to do it this way and I said it's never been done this way, and it can't be done this way, the wrong stops on the wrong lens on the wrong camera, and he did it anyway, and he was right.*

We talked about it for years, starting that afternoon, because I don't think Emilio could have made it back to St. Albans before Stanley called, "Didja read it? What do you think?" After about an hour, he asked if I'd had a chance to look at the Hilberg book yet. I reminded him that I'd only just gotten it.

When he sent you a book, he wanted you to read it, and not just read it, but to drop everything and get *into* it. John Calley, who was probably Stanley's closest friend, told me that when he was head of production at Warner Bros. in the seventies and first working with him, Stanley sent him a set of *The Golden Bough,* unabridged, and then bugged him every couple of weeks for a year about reading it. Finally, Calley said, "Stanley, I've got a studio to run. I don't have time to read mythology." "It isn't mythology, John." Stanley said. "It's your *life*."

I picked up the Hilberg many times and laid it down again. I finally read it only a few years ago, when I knew there was no possibility that Stanley would ever use it for a film and I could see why Stanley was so absorbed by it. It was a forbidding volume, densely laid out in a two-column format, nearly eight hundred pages long, small print, heavily footnoted, so minutely detailed that one would have to be more committed than I was at the moment to its inconceivably dreadful subject. I could see that it was exhaustive; it certainly *looked* like hard work, and it read like a complete log of the Final Solution. And every couple of weeks, Stanley would call and ask me if I'd read it yet, "You should read it; Michael, it's *monumental*!" This went on for months.

Finally I said, "Stanley. I can't make it."

"Why not?"

"I don't know. I guess right now I just don't want to read a book called *The Destruction of the European Jews*."

"No, Michael," he said. "The book you don't want to read right now is *The Destruction of the European Jews,* Part Two."

You know, Michael, it's not absolutely true in every case that nobody likes a smart-ass," Stanley was saying.

I once described 1980–1983 as a single phone call lasting three years with interruptions. This serial call had many of the characteristics of the college bull session, long free-form late-night intellectual inquiries, discursions, conversations, displays, like talking to a very smart kid in a dorm room until three in the morning, and I'd think, *Doesn't this guy get tired?* But then Stanley never went to college; he was only a stunningly accomplished autodidact, one of those people we may hear about but rarely meet, the almost but not quite legendary Man On Whom Nothing Is Lost.

"Hey Michael, didja ever read *Herodotus*? The Father of *Lies*?" or, "Frankly, I've never understood why Schopenhauer is considered so pessimistic. *I* never thought he was pessimistic, did *you*, Michael?," laughing at the four or five things he found so funny in this, with a winsome touch of self-deprecation, half-apologetic, *It's not* my *fault I'm so smart*. And I'd think, *Doesn't he have anything else to* do? But this *is* what he did. These calls were about information. They were about Stanley's work.

We'd be talking about something, like why "most war movies always look so phony," or why we thought this movie or that book was such a hit, and we'd be suddenly off across two thousand years of Western culture, "from Plato to NATO." He was just au old-fashioned social Darwinist (seemingly), with layer upon layer of the old, now vanishing, liberal humanism, disappointed but undimmed, and without contradiction; if he made no distinctions between Art and Commerce, or Poetry and Technology, or even Personal and Professional, why should he make them between "Politics" and Philosophy?

Stanley had views on everything, but I wouldn't exactly call them political. ("Hey Michael, what's the definition of a neo-conservative? . . . A liberal who's just been *mugged*, ha ha ha ha.") His views on democracy were those of most people I know, neither left nor right, not exactly brimming with belief, a noble failed experiment along our evolutionary way, brought low by base instincts, money and self-interest and stupidity. (If a novelist expresses this view he's a visionary, seemingly, but if a movie director does, he's a misanthrope.) He thought the best system might be under a benign despot, although he had little belief that such a man could be found. He wasn't exactly a cynic, but he could easily have passed for one. He was certainly a capitalist. He believed himself to be a realist. He was known to be a tough guy. The way I see him, essentially, he was an artist to his fingertips, and he needed a lot of cover, and a lot of control.

For the most part we talked about writers, usually dead and white and Euro-American, hardly the current curriculum: Stendhal (half an hour), Balzac (two hours), Conrad, Crane. Hemingway (hours and hours—"Do you think it was true that he was drunk all the time, even when he wrote? Yeah? Well, I'll have to find out what he was drinking and send a case to all my writers."), Céline ("My favorite anti-Semite."), and Kafka, who he thought was the greatest writer of the century, and the most misread: People who used the word "Kafkaesque" had probably never read Kafka. I'd read *The Golden Bough* and didn't have to go through that again, but he urged me to check out Machiavelli, and *The Art of War* (years before Michael Ovitz slipped him a copy), and Veblen's *The Theory of the Leisure Class.* He had a taste and a gift for the creative-subversive, and he dug Swift and Malaparte and William Burroughs, and was interested to know that Burroughs was a friend of mine. I got him to read Faulkner, *Absalom, Absalom!*; he thought it was incredibly beautiful, but "there's no movie in it. I mean, where's the *weenie,* Michael?" Then he'd be into something else, the "inevitable" fiscal and social disaster lurking in the burgeoning mutual funds market, or how he'd like to make a movie about doctors because "everybody hates doctors" (his father was a doctor), or the savage abiding mystery of Mother Russia, or why opera was "quite possibly the greatest art form" except, oh yeah, maybe for the movies. Then he'd dish about the movies.

"Always thinking, huh Stanley?" I said after one of those exhausting (for me) rooftop-to-rooftop riffs of his. I felt that these calls were starting to take up most of my time, yet I knew they didn't take up most of his, that he was doing other things, "many many of them." I acquired a sense of awe at the energy that had coincided so forcefully with my own. You really needed your chops for this, you'd feel like some poor traveler caught in a ground blizzard, three to thirty times a week and mostly after ten at night, when he usually started wailing. Sometimes, I'd duck his calls.

We talked this way, with occasional visits to the house, dinners and movies, until he found Gustav Hasford's *The Short-Timers,* bought the rights, wrote a long treatment of it, and asked me to work on the script with him. Then we really started talking. By then I knew I'd been working for Stanley from the minute I met him.

2001: A FILM

by Stanley Kubrick

The film critic of *The Village Voice* called it "a disaster." *The New York Times* and *New York* magazine panned it, too. And influential critic Pauline Kael dismissed it as a "monumentally unimaginative movie."

The weren't writing about *Battlefield Earth*. They were writing about *2001: A Space Odyssey*, a film that is revered today as one of the greatest ever made. How could the Big Apple's most powerful critics have gotten it so wrong?

That's exactly what Maurice Rapf set out to discover more than 30 years ago. In 1968, not long after *2001*'s disastrous first preview, the *Life* magazine critic sat down with director Stanley Kubrick to talk about the landmark science fiction epic. By that time, Kubrick had made several cuts to his film, and it had gone on to wide critical acclaim and boffo box office.

What follows is the result of that conversation: an in-depth monologue in which Kubrick talks about his visionary film, its meaning, its ground-breaking special effects and the less-than-visionary initial reviews. The article was originally printed in the January/February 1969 issue of *Action*, the now-defunct magazine of the Directors Guild of America. (It's showing up again in the book *Stanley Kubrick: Interviews*, which is being released by the University of Mississippi Press in January.)

Now that the year 2001 is finally upon us, we thought it was time to revisit Kubrick's masterpiece. And just in case you've never seen it (hang your head in shame if you haven't, science fiction fans!), Warner Bros. will give you the chance to atone for your sin: The studio plans to rerelease the film in theaters later this year.

From the day it opened, *2001: A Space Odyssey* got great reaction from the paying audience. All the theater managers say the only adjective they can use is "phenomenal," because of the numbers of people who buy tickets a second, third, and fourth time to see the film. The managers report that after each show people come up and want to know where they can buy tickets again. So this poor reaction on that first [preview] screening I attribute to the audience and to the originality of the film. The film departs about as much from the convention of the theater and the three-act play as is possible; not many films have departed further than that, certainly not big films. I don't know why there was this concentration of nonreceptive people, but there was.

First of all, the audience that is seeing the film now is reported as being 80 percent 35 or under, down to 5 years old. I would say the audience must have been 90 percent from 35 to 60 at that screening. So the preview audience and the paying audience have been two ends of the moviegoing scale.

Secondly, the lukewarm New York reaction has not been the case anywhere else, for some strange reason. I haven't had time to look through this, but in Chicago we got three rave reviews out of four. In Boston we got all rave reviews, including critics whom you wouldn't expect to like it, such as Marjorie Adams, who said the film is like adding a new dimension to life. It's gotten virtually unanimous rave reviews out of New York. I don't know the reason for the New York reaction. The audience, with the exception of a few mumblers that go out, has reacted more intensely, more favorably than to any other picture that the managers can remember.

I myself usually get 10 or 12 letters about a picture over a period of the whole life of the film. I've been getting about two letters a day since the film opened. Two or three have been cranky letters, asking for their money back; the rest are from people saying, "This film has changed my life" and "I've seen the film six times" and things like that. So all indices of the film would indicate that for some strange reason, chemistry that night was bad and also very unrepresentative of anything that's happened since then.

I tightened the picture all the way through. I had started thinking about doing it right from the first screening because even though the total reaction of that screening was not representative or good, I could still see places that, as I watched it with an audience, I thought were just going on a bit. It's probably the hardest thing to determine, as to how much weight to give. I just felt as I looked at it and looked at it that I could see places all the way through the film where I would tighten up, and I took out 19 minutes. The picture had been originally two hours and 41 minutes long.

A number of very perceptive people, and a lot of just ordinary people, saw the long version and flipped over that. I don't believe that the change made a crucial difference. I think it just tightened up, and some marginal people who might have gotten restless won't get restless. But the people that dug the film dug it in its original length, and the people that hated it hate it at the present length.

Special effects were the reason the film was late, the reason that it was so close to the wire. I spent a year and a half, June 1965 practically up to the beginning of March 1967, running through the 205 special-effects shots. The last ones were arriving in California as they were doing the negative printing. You can't finish this picture without the special effects; they're integrated in almost every sequence so the thing never really got put together except a sequence at a time to look at it, or a reel at a time.

All of the money spent on the film shows on the screen. In most films, you have a bunch of guys talking to each other and you make use of about three or four sets and that's about it. There really isn't a lot to look at, and everybody is waiting for the big action sequence. I remember as a child being frustrated by one war picture after another where John Payne and Randolph Scott would talk and talk and you'd be waiting for the big attack. It would finally come at the end of the film for two minutes with some process shots and a lot of cheated action. Forgetting all the other things that a film is, there is always—to me anyway—a disappointment in not really seeing anything up on the screen that is beautiful or interesting to look at. Largely it's just a matter of photographing a lot of people talking to each other on sets that are more or less interesting with actors that are better or worse.

Essentially films are confined to being elaborated three-act stage plays. They have had a great problem breaking out of that form.

In *Space Odyssey*, the mood hitting you is the visual imagery. The people who didn't respond, I now, for want of coming up with a better explanation, categorize as "verbally oriented people." Every child that sees the film—and I've spoken to 20 or 30 kids—knows that Doctor Floyd goes to the moon. You say, "Well, how do you know?" and they say, "Well, we saw the moon." Whereas a number of people, including critics, thought he went to the planet Clavius. Why they think there's a planet Clavius I'll never know. But they hear him asked, "Where are you going?" and he says, "I'm going to Clavius." Now, I knew at the time that most people wouldn't realize that Clavius was a crater on the moon, but it seemed to me a realistic way of talking about the moon. He wouldn't say, "I'm going to the moon to the crater Clavius." With many people—BOOM—that one word registers in their head and they don't look at 15 shots of the moon; they don't see that he's going to the moon.

Communication visually and through music gets past the verbal pigeonhole concepts that people are struck with. You know, words have a highly subjective and very limited meaning, and they immediately limit the possible emotional and subconscious designating effect of a work of art. Movies have tied themselves into that because the crucial things that generally come out of film are still word-delivered. There's emotion backing them up, you've got the actors generating feeling, etc. It's basically word communication.

"The Blue Danube" is a magnificent piece of music for the

beautiful, graceful motion of the space station. To me it just seemed like a perfect representation of what was going on. Also, it helped to get away from the idea that space would be eerie and strange. Space travel will become very ordinary very soon, and it will be particularly significant for its beauty. It seemed to me "The Blue Danube" was a magnificent piece of music to use, particularly since I had decided to use existing music and not original music.

The screenplay is the most uncommunicative form of writing ever devised. It's hard to convey mood and it's hard to convey imagery. You can convey dialogue, but if you stick to the conventions of a screenplay, the description has to be very brief and telegraphic. You can't create a mood or anything like that, so the screenplay that was written was about a 40,000-word prose piece by Arthur C. Clarke and me. That was the basis of the deal and the budget, etc. Then a screenplay was made from that by me and Arthur, and then Arthur afterwards wrote the novel based on the screenplay.

I've always said the two people who are worthy of film study are Charlie Chaplin and Orson Welles as representing the two most diverse approaches to filmmaking, Charlie Chaplin must have had the crudest, simplest lack of interest in cinematics. Just get the image on the screen; it's the content of the shot that matters. Welles is probably, at his best, the most baroque kind of stylist in the conventional film-telling style. I think perhaps [Russian director Sergei] Eisenstein might be a better example because where Chaplin had all content and no style, to me Eisenstein has all style and no content. *Alexander Nevsky* stylistically is possibly one of the most beautiful movies ever made; its content to me is a moronic story, moronically told, full of lies. It's the most dishonest kind of a film. And I would have thought that perhaps a study of Chaplin's greatest films and *Alexander Nevsky* would be worthwhile, because somewhere within that you'd see how two complete diverse approaches can make a fascinating film.

People now realize how easy it is to make a film. Everybody knows that you use a camera and everybody knows that you use a tape recorder, and it's now getting to the point where a filmmaker almost has the same freedom a novelist has when he buys himself some paper. I haven't seen all the underground films; I've been away for three years. If they haven't already, there's no doubt that at some point someone's going to do something on a level that's going to be shattering. First of all, they all need a little more experience. It's getting to the point now for a few thousand dollars you can make a film, and a hell of a lot of people can lay their hands on a few thousand dollars if they want it badly enough.

WHOA, TRIGGER! AUTEUR ALERT!

By Rick Lyman

The six-by-eight-foot flickering rectangle of light turns the white wall to amber above Quentin Tarantino's fireplace. Not far away, back through a Spanish archway, a 16-millimeter projector rattles with a persistent click that never quite disappears beneath the bleating of the soundtrack, like static on a shortwave radio.

"I love this scene," Mr. Tarantino says. "It's a really tough scene, a tough, tough scene. But it's not the kind of scene you expect, all right. The emotion is right out there. But if you buy it, and I totally buy it, then it can make you cry."

This is the guy who made ear-severing a dance routine, turned sadomasochistic basement torture into comic relief and created the scene where Uma Thurman takes a six-inch hypodermic in the chest. So when the director of *Reservoir Dogs* and

Pulp Fiction, the celebrity prototype for an entire generation of Sundance-bred, film-geek auteurs, tells you that you are about to see a scene that is tough, you listen to him, don't you?

Roy Rogers is standing off to one side, elegant and stoic, with that thin, shiny mouth and those exotic eyes. Dale Evans is a few steps behind him, plump and fretting. A few steps away, the sheriff's men have Trigger, Rogers's famous stallion, held tightly on a rope. Trigger bobs his head up and down, shifts from foot to foot, his preternaturally floppy mane slapping across his forehead. It doesn't look good for the good guys. Rogers and Trigger have been found standing next to the body of a villain whose head has been bashed. We know the horse is innocent, but circumstantial evidence points to Trigger.

"In this case, Roy, circumstantial evidence is enough," the sheriff sadly intones.

Yes, Trigger is about to get one between the eyes, right now. There is no court of appeals for killer horses. The screen is suddenly filled with the face of Rogers. Somehow, fear, regret and calculation all begin to wash out of his eyes even though his face doesn't move a muscle. He drops his head, a decision made. "Wait, Sheriff," Rogers says, and then confesses to the killing. "Roy, don't you know what you're doing?" Dale whimpers. He knows. He's saving his best friend from a bullet, even if it means several years on a chain gang for him.

Mr. Tarantino leans forward and rests his elbows on his lanky legs, his face riveted to the flickering image on his living room wall where *The Golden Stallion* is playing. He says the film is one of the three or four masterpieces of a now all-but-forgotten journeyman director named William Witney.

Mr. Witney, 85, an Oklahoma native now living in quiet retirement in rural California, is the sweetest fruit of what Mr. Tarantino says has been a year and a half of gorging on film history and B-grade filmmakers. Mr. Tarantino says he had a suspicion that there were "forgotten masters" out there, workaday moviemakers who had carefully chosen their assignments and then transformed them into art, but who had been overlooked in the post-auteur critical landscape.

"People think that the only good westerns made in the 40's and 50's were by John Ford or maybe Howard Hawks," Mr. Tarantino says. "Film guys might add, oh, Anthony Mann and Budd Boetticher and Andre De Toth. But I just had this suspicion that because they didn't make A-list movies or didn't work with A-list stars, a lot of really great masters were getting lost in the shuffle."

So while he was working on the two screenplays that he intends to begin shooting, one after the other, after the first of the year, Mr. Tarantino says he also indulged his film-scholar fantasies and dived into the world of the forgotten genre flicks.

BEST HORSE AND BEST FRIEND

"I've found directors of some of these movies who I'm really into, but William Witney is ahead of them all, the one whose movies I can show to anyone and they are just blown away," Mr. Tarantino says. "He makes you accept everything on his terms, and his terms are that Roy and Trigger are best friends. Trigger is not just his best horse; he's his best friend. You know, in some movies, a cowboy might go to jail to save his best friend from being shot down dead. Well, Trigger is Roy's best friend. It's the easiest leap to have him do that here, yet it's so powerful and so unexpected. What's great is that you buy it, you absolutely buy it, and I don't know that I really would buy it from anybody else but Roy and Trigger."

The idea behind this series is to sit down—with accomplished filmmakers or actors or screenwriters or cinematographers, people who have contributed something to the history of film—and simply watch a movie, not one of their own films, but someone else's, a film that has some special resonance for them. Perhaps it was a film they saw as a teenager, something that inspired them or has grown mysteriously in their estimation over the years, or maybe something like this, something they have stumbled across with shocked delight.

The goal is to get some sort of understanding of how film artists absorb the movies they love, and how those movies have informed their own work. Instead of just another profile about the last project or the most recent award or the next big deal, this is to be about the work.

That's the idea. And so Mr. Tarantino, champion of everything from B-grade 1950's genres to 70's black exploitation to life as a bitter and ironic cocktail, was asked what he wanted to watch and he said, *The Golden Stallion,* a 1949 minifeature from the days of the Saturday morning cowboy serials, neither bitter nor ironic. Tough? Quentin Tarantino thinks so. You think you know better?

JUNGLE GIRLS TO COWBOYS

"The thing about William Witney is that he was really a director of genre movies," Mr. Tarantino says. "He started making serials in the late 1930's, and he made some of the best of them, from the Dick Tracy ones to Spy Smasher to Jungle Girl. And when they stopped making serials, he moved over to Saturday morning cowboy pictures and did pretty much everything Roy Rogers shot between the late 40's and the early 50's"—when Rogers stopped making movies and shifted to television.

As the lanky Mr. Tarantino grows more effusive about his subject, he also becomes more mobile, pivoting on his hips as he chatters, then leaping up to pace the room, peppering his long, fast sentences with earnest expletives like "all right" and "cool." The faster he talks, the faster he walks. The more intricate his sentences, the more baroque his gestures.

"When they stopped making Saturday morning cowboy pictures in the 50's, when Republic Pictures closed down, he moved over and made juvenile delinquent films, and they are some of the best of those movies ever made;" Mr. Tarantino says. "And when they stopped making those, he moved over and did some rock 'n' roll movies in the 60's. He flitted with the A list a couple of times, but mostly he was a guy who moved from one B-list genre to another, all right, for something like 40 years. And all the while he is churning out TV shows. He did a ton of 'Bonanza' and episodes for almost every western of the period. And do you know what his last movie was? A black exploitation flick in the 70's. He ended with *Darktown Strutters* in 1975, about a female black motorcycle gang. I think it's so cool that he began as the king of the cowboy serials and he ended with a black exploitation film. That's a career, man."

A spokesman for McFarland and Company, which published Mr. Witney's 1995 memoirs about his years as a serial director—*In a Door, Into a Fight, Out a Door, Into a Chase*—said that Mr. Witney had suffered a stroke a few years ago and was not able to be interviewed, but that he had been informed about Mr. Tarantino's interest in his work.

COMMON DECENCY

The rap on Mr. Tarantino, 37, is that he doesn't make as many movies as he should; years and years come between his films. It's been three years since his most recent, *Jackie Brown,* and that one was a long time coming. This is all just about to change, he promises. One of his new projects is a tasty little noirish thriller starring Uma Thurman. "My fans are gonna love this one," he says. "They've been waiting a long time, and I think they're really going to be happy with it." The other is a big, epic World War II adventure; he is just now trimming and polishing the screenplay.

Yet what does this very deliberate filmmaker, who spent a lot of his time in the last decade trying to generate an acting career, find to love about a true Hollywood salaryman like

William Witney, who was making five movies a year when *The Golden Stallion* came out?

The flickering image shifts: Rogers is off in prison now. There was no last-minute reprieve. He had to do his time, and hard time it was. Not only that, but he also had to watch as Trigger became the property of the bad guys. And yet he never became bitter. Mr. Tarantino finds it odd that this is so moving to him.

"Normally, I would be drawn to movies where a good-guy Roy Rogers character becomes corrupted through life," Mr. Tarantino says, transfixed on the screen again. "In one of my movies, this guy would probably have come out of prison wanting to kill somebody. And he would kill somebody—while riding Trigger.

"Nowadays, Roy Rogers seems almost too good, but you buy it from him somehow. I find myself being moved by his common decency. Life's events and other people's actions have no effect on him and his heart. He didn't save Trigger to become a bitter man; he did it because it was what he had to do. His code is his code. The whole world can change, and it doesn't change his code."

Mr. Tarantino first came across Mr. Witney's work when he watched an old print of *The Bonnie Parker Story* (1958), a kind of juvenile delinquent movie set in the Depression, with Dorothy Provine playing the infamous gangster. "I was blown away," he says, "It was like, whoa, who made this? I have to see everything he ever did." And so began the hunt for the half-forgotten works of Mr. Witney. One after another, he found them, watched them and, with one or two exceptions, found them absolutely riveting, the work of a real lost master, just what he had been looking for.

He has whittled Mr. Witney's oeuvre— more than 100 films from 1937 to 1975—into what he considers to be his four greatest masterpieces. The earliest is *The Golden Stallion*. Then comes *Stranger at My Door* (1956), another western, this time with Macdonald Carey playing a frontier preacher whose homestead is invaded by a robber on the lam. ("I showed this to a group of friends, all film people, and it just blew them away," Mr. Tarantino says. "We talked about it for hours afterward.") Then *The Bonnie Parker Story* and, in 1959, *Paratroop Command,* a realistic World War II adventure about a platoon pariah who has to prove himself.

'DROPPING LIKE FLIES'

"I was showing *Paratroop Command* to Peter Bogdanovich one day, and there comes this moment in the film where he goes, like, hey, wait a minute, what the heck is happening?," Mr. Tarantino says. "These guys, who you've been getting to know throughout the movie, suddenly start dying. And I don't mean a big, glamorous cinema death. They're just dropping like flies, unceremoniously. It's so realistic. You know that it was a movie made by a guy who had been there. William Witney was in the Marines in World War II for something like five years."

The projector is still clicking away, and the wall above the fireplace is filled with motion. Trigger is running through a broad valley, the sun backlighting his mane and a team of wild horses following behind. Dale Evans, in voice-over, is reading a letter she is writing to Rogers, back on the chain gang. "I find this so poetic, so beautiful." Mr. Tarantino says. "The letter is beautifully written, her delivery is great, and these images of the wild horses are just stunning. Wait, I want to run it back."

He jumps up and runs back to the projector and rewinds to catch the last few minutes again.

Appreciating William Witney begins with understanding what he did with Roy Rogers, Mr. Tarantino says. "Roy's movies at this time had turned into these sort of western musicals, like frontier jamborees, where he's singing and walking around in outfits with fringes," Mr. Tarantino says. "After their first few movies together, Witney had gotten Roy out of his fringe-and-sparkle attire and was dressing him in normal attire, blue jeans and stuff. They stopped being these crazy musicals. He turned them into rough, tough violent adventures. Audiences loved it. Nobody had ever seen Roy fight like that, so it was kind of cool to everyone that he was such a good fistfighter. And a fistfight in a William Witney movie is a fistfight. They're tough. People get bloody noses."

Mr. Tarantino says he admires Mr. Witney for his rough and believable action scenes, but also for his taste, as shown in his choice of assignments over the years. He compares him to Howard Hawks, a director who spanned genres but managed to bring something of himself to each of them. "It shows you how important taste is," he says.

A VISUAL STYLIST

And there is something unpretentious about the way Mr. Witney worked that appeals to the young director.

"He's a visual stylist, but he's a visual stylist in the way that a lot of those guys were back then," Mr. Tarantino says. "It's always about moving the camera like 'Hey, Mom, look, I'm directing.' He was clever about camera movement. One of the things I got from looking at his films is that the camera movements are so elegant. You have to have made movies for 30 years to be able to move the camera so unpretentiously. His camera movements, when they happen, are so cool. They're either completely artful, in a cool, don't-call-attention-to-yourself kind of way, or they're visually about how to tell the story. These guys were storytellers. They knew how to move the camera to convey information so they didn't have to shoot another dialogue scene to explain something."

And something else has jumped out at Mr. Tarantino.

"Look at the way he uses Trigger in this film," he says. "William Witney is the greatest director when it comes to working with animals. In his films, if there's an animal, it's another character in the movie. If a homesteader has a dog, it's not just yapping in the background. You get to know this dog; you might even follow it on its own little adventure in the middle of the movie. And *Golden Stallion* is his masterpiece when it comes to working with animals, perhaps because he's working with Trigger, the greatest animal actor who ever was."

A NOBLE PURSUIT

In the long run, Mr. Tarantino says, he hopes Mr. Witney has influenced him in subtle ways, perhaps helping him build his instinct for when to move the camera and how. He did, while still in the first flush of admiration for Mr. Witney's work, write two animal scenes into his World War II epic, though he says that the script has grown too long and byzantine and must be trimmed back and that both of the animal scenes, sadly, will probably have to go. In one, a refugee girl hiding in a barn is attacked by rats and saved by a dog; in the other, a soldier separated from his platoon finds and befriends a runaway horse. Never to be filmed, he says with a shrug: "That's the way it goes."

Has this year in the film-scholar trenches been worth it? These are, after all, years in which Mr. Tarantino could have been making a lot of money and a lot of films.

"This is a very noble pursuit," he says. "I've turned quite a few friends on to William Witney, so he lives through us, at least."

It's easy, he knows, to "get hung up on somebody when you do something like this," and perhaps exaggerate a filmmaker's gifts or importance. But he has thought about it and really believes that Mr. Witney is the genuine article. So has it been worth it? Yes.

"You know, in this business right now, there are a whole lot of people making movies to pay for their incredibly extravagant lifestyle," he says. "There's just a whole lot of that going on. I'm not judging, but that's not why I came here, to make movies to pay for my pool. I never want to have to do that and I don't have to do that. But you know, if you come at this as though it's a religion, as opposed to a job, then sometimes you have to keep close to God a little. That's what this last year was. It was my way of renewing myself."

CHEESE WHIZ

by Rebecca Mead

Last month, something unusual happened on the *Billboard* video-sales charts. First and second place were taken, predictably enough, by the insuperable *Titanic,* and Disney's audiovisual pacifier *Lady and the Tramp.* But close behind them, climbing as high as third place one week, to outrank even video-store sure things like *Austin Powers* and *Playboy's Freshman Class,* was a movie called *The Evil Dead*—a cheese-and-ketchup horror flick from 1979 with an absurd plot, bad acting, and all the production values a mere three hundred and fifty thousand dollars can buy (not many).

Though less well known than other splatter movies of the same era, *The Evil Dead,* which is about a group of college students trapped in a cabin who are turned one by one into zombies by an unseen monster, is a genre cult classic. When I bought a copy at my local video store and asked the dyed-and-pierced youth behind the counter whether it was good, he gave me a withering look and replied, "It's the best movie ever made." The energetic sales of *The Evil Dead* and its sequel, *Evil Dead II—Dead by Dawn,* which was rereleased last summer, coincide with a horror renaissance. Wes Craven's 1996 movie *Scream* and last year's *Scream 2* both grossed more than a hundred million dollars, and this summer's *Halloween: H20,* in which Jamie Lee Curtis reprised her role from 1978's *Halloween,* was a critical and commercial success.

The *Evil Dead* movies appeal not only to teens who like to scare themselves witless; they are also celebrated by a certain kind of cineaste. Film buffs note the wildly unconventional camera moves, racing along almost at ground level to convey the viewpoint of an on-rushing monster. (Fellini is said to have been an admirer of *The Evil Dead.*) Comedy fans praise the two *Evil Dead* sequels (the third is called *Army of Darkness*) for their raw slapstick humor: in *Evil Dead II,* the star Bruce Campbell, chainsaws off his own hand because it has been colonized by an evil spirit, then straps the saw to his stump to become a kind of avenging proto-cyborg (Jay Douglas, of Anchor Bay Entertainment, which has rereleased the videos, compares Campbell to Harold Lloyd and Charlie Chaplin.) Moreover, connoisseurs of schlock find in the *Evil Dead* movies the kind of ham acting, crude special effects, and cartoonish poor taste that distinguish this American genre. The contemporary analogues of *The Evil Dead* are not just today's horror films but gross-outs like *South Park* and cheesy, so-bad-they're-good reruns on *Nick at Nite.*

Sam Raimi, who directed *The Evil Dead* when he was just twenty years old, is a master of cheese, which might be defined as an offness of taste and mood, akin to camp but without camp's knowing distance. Since making the *Evil Dead* series, Raimi has gone on to direct several studio movies with grown-up budgets. In 1990, he made *Darkman,* a comic-book superhero melodrama starring Liam Neeson, which spawned two straight-to-video sequels that Raimi produced but didn't direct. (The straight-to-video sequel is categorically cheesy.) In 1995, he made a Western, *The Quick and the Dead,* which was half homage, half spoof, and was noteworthy for being the first major motion picture in which Leonardo DiCaprio died tragically and Sharon Stone kept her clothes on. Then Raimi helped create the goofy Ancient Greece-meets-Santa Monica television series *Hercules* and its crypto-Sapphic spinoff, *Xena: Warrior Princess,* which for three seasons has been the most successful first-run syndicated drama on television, considerably enriching Raimi and his partner, Rob Tapert.

For almost two decades; Raimi has fulfilled a cultural role comparable to the bit part he played in Joel and Ethan Coen's 1994 movie *The Hudsucker Proxy,* where he was an adman trying to come up with a name for a new toy (the Hoopsucker? the Hudswinger?) that is eventually called the hula hoop. Raimi has dedicated his imaginative powers to the invention of simple, diverting pleasures, and has done so with engaged enthusiasm, rather than with the cool, aloof stylishness of his friends, the Coen brothers. The Coens, who have known Raimi since Joel was an assistant editor on *The Evil Dead,* are teasingly fond of him. In their office they have a framed still of him getting blown away in his role as the "snickering gunman" in *Miller's Crossing,* and when they talk about him they sound the way Beavis and Butt-head would if they had doctorates in cinema studies and watched the Independent Film Channel instead of MTV.

Joel: "Each successive *Evil Dead* becomes purer and purer, more like esoteric art films. Getting closer and closer to, like, Tarkovsky."

Ethan: "Sam was going to do an *Evil Dead* which just consisted of Bruce alone in a cabin. One actor; one set. Very arty. It would have been a really good movie: you know, the inner and the outer. Just Bruce, man. A contemplation of Bruce."

Joel: "Just Bruce."

Ethan: "And Sam wrote this really great script about the demolition derby, the romance of the demolition derby."

Joel: "He wrote it a long time ago, and we have been trying to convince him to do it ever since. I think he thinks it's silly."

Ethan: "He should do more art movies, like the *Evil Dead*'s and the demolition derby. Sam, you know, he's misunderstood. Even by himself."

I met Sam Raimi for lunch recently to talk about his new movie, a thriller called *A Simple Plan,* which opens next month. Lunch was at midnight, and we ate in a church, but the site and the hour were not due to the nocturnal demands of horror. Raimi had been shooting night scenes in the bar of the Waldorf-Astoria as part of *For Love of the Game,* a project that sounds entirely wholesome, starring Kevin Costner as a baseball hero.

Raimi seemed wholesome, too, with the combined mischievousness and earnestness of a twelve-year-old. He had a courtly, understated manner, addressing his bit-part actors respectfully as "sir," and thanking extras for their work. ("Sam's very polite," Joel Coen told me. "He has always helped little old ladies across the street. That has always been a part of Sam, along with the evisceration and dismemberment.") You would call him baby-faced if it were possible for a baby to have a day's growth of gray-flecked stubble. He wore a sports coat, as he usually does on set, as a sign of respect for his team; but he wore it over a rumpled pair of blue chinos and a pair of scuffed, clompy brown leather shoes.

In conversation, Raimi had a habit of smoothing his hair down on his forehead into choppy bangs, and he was attentive, and given to an occasional half-giggle when something amused him. Friends say he used to perform a party trick in which he would open a beer bottle with his eye socket. Scott Smith, the author and screenwriter of *A Simple Plan,* described some more recent practical jokery: "Sam would introduce me to a producer from Paramount by saying, 'This is Scott Smith's assistant,' to see if this person would treat me differently, not knowing who I was," Smith says. "He's like the kid in school who wouldn't get into trouble himself but would get *you* into trouble."

A Simple Plan is the story of two brothers who find millions of dollars inside the wreckage of a crashed airplane and scheme to keep the money; a decision that leads inexorably to brutality, betrayal, and death. The film marks Raimi's return to the movie business after a few years out. The hiatus was due, in part, to Raimi's decision to spend more time with his two small children—Lorne, a boy of four and a half, and Henry, who is almost two. (Raimi's wife, Gillian, the daughter of the television cowboy Lorne Greene, is expecting the couple's first girl in January.) "I stopped shooting pictures, and I started getting into television, where you can drive to work every day and be back for dinner," Raimi explained. His chief project was producing a horror series for CBS Television, called *American Gothic*, about a small South Carolina town where the sheriff is actually the Devil; it died during its first season.

But Raimi's absence from the movie industry was also a function of his reputation as a genre director: he had a hard time being seen as anything else. There was a moment in the late eighties when studio executives apparently regarded Sam Raimi as the next Tim Burton, but it failed to pan out. (Raimi was at one time attached to *Jack Frost,* a movie opening this Christmas about a child whose dead father comes back as Frosty the Snowman, but another director ended up making the film.) Even *A Simple Plan* is Raimi's by default. The novel was optioned by Mike Nichols, bounced to Ben Stiller, and finally landed with Scott Rudin, whom Raimi petitioned for the position of director. "Scott Rudin told me, 'You know, I want to work with you, but truthfully, there are a lot of other directors that I think are more right for this project, and you are, like, number fifteen down on the list,'" Raimi said. Finally, when John Boorman had to abandon the project after casting the two leads and scouting locations, Raimi was brought in.

Though Raimi has always had devotees, his movies have never been quite good enough. His longtime partner Rob Tapert says, "I think *A Simple Plan* is the first time Sam has shown his potential. I have always felt that he is a better director and filmmaker than the reception that the movies have received would suggest."

A Simple Plan is Raimi's first effort to make an altogether mainstream movie, albeit it an offbeat one. The influence of the Coens' *Fargo* flavors the film: like it, *A Simple Plan* is set in a snowy Midwestern town where unexpected violence lurks. But the film is less ironic than *Fargo,* more heartfelt. To an eye accustomed to Raimi's signature cartoon violence and oversized characters, *A Simple Plan* is the picture of restraint. Bruce Campbell says, "You watch *A Simple Plan* the way you watch a normal movie. Sam has a certain visual style, where the camera is always racing around and twisting up and down. But here he just shot it. He made that leap to storytelling, instead of 'Sam Raimi, star of the movie.' "

Raimi says that he was intent on making a character-driven drama this time. "I appreciate the artistry of the horror film," he told me, "but the movies I see are not those. They are stories of real people, or a mix of real people and adventure, like *The Treasure of the Sierra Madre,* which I love." *A Simple Plan* contains the first fully rounded characters that Raimi has ever had to deal with, particularly in Billy Bob Thornton's portrayal of the older of the two brothers, who is a bit simpleminded, yet psychologically complex. Still, there are moments in which Raimi's horror expertise is evident, as in a scene where the younger brother, played by Bill Paxton, first climbs into the cockpit of the crashed plane. For all Raimi's talk about the power of character, he knows exactly what to do with a pilot's decomposing corpse, a trapped, thrashing black crow, a lot of dark, cold metal, and a camera to leave his audience aghast with anxiety.

Raimi's defining memory of the power of film is watching his father's home movies. "I remember seeing footage of my seventh-birthday party," he says. "It was a Halloween party and he showed all the kids playing party games outside, and then he showed them leaving the party, and then, on the same reel, he showed them arriving at the party. I was so taken with the fact that he had shuffled the order of reality. I thought, This is unbelievable. Something about it made me giddy. It seemed like we were tampering with God's world, altering something that was far beyond our ken. That was what I was attracted to. I wasn't attracted to 'the movies.' I've often read about these filmmakers who were attracted to great movies, and that had nothing to do with it for me."

Raimi was the fourth of five children, and he grew up in Franklin, Michigan, where his mother had a retail intimate-apparel business, Lulu's Lingerie, and his father ran the furniture and appliance store that Raimi's grandfather had established. (The name Raimi is abbreviated from the German Reingewertz.) "Our house was littered with comic books, Three Stooges paraphernalia, and Fig Newton bars—that was our reality," says Ivan Raimi, Sam's older brother, who is now an emergency room doctor and a sometime collaborator on Raimi screenplays. Another brother, Ted, is a star of *Xena*.

An early influence was the eldest Raimi brother, Sander, who was six years Sam's senior. "He used to perform magic at my parties when I was younger," Raimi told me. "Incredible magic, with electricity and chemicals and fire." By all accounts, Sander was the brilliant boy in the family. At the age of fifteen, he was selected to go on a scholarship trip to Israel. There he drowned in a swimming-pool accident.

"My parents pulled their strength together to make sure we survived it," Raimi said. "But it colors everything you do for the rest of your life." After Sander's death, Sam learned how to do the tricks himself. (He recently brushed up on his skills to perform at his son's preschool.)

Raimi's first movies were made on a Super-8 camera his father gave him when he was thirteen years old. He collaborated with a crowd of neighborhood boys, including Bruce

Campbell, whom he had met in junior high school. "I remember seeing Sam dressed as Sherlock Holmes and sitting on the floor at school playing with little dolls, and I knew immediately the guy was different," Campbell says. Other members of the team were John Cameron, who has gone on to produce for the Coen brothers, and Scott Spiegel, now a screenwriter and director in Los Angeles.

"We would meet every Saturday and Sunday, and make Civil War movies," Raimi said. "We made *The Civil War,* Part 1, Part 2, and Part 3. Me and those boys made *The Jimmy Hoffa Story,* Part 1, Part 2, and Part 3. We read in the paper about him being kidnapped, and the next Sunday we went to the place where it happened and shot it. We made *James Bombed,* starring Bruce Campbell. We made *Six Months to Live,* the story of a guy who finds out he's got an incurable disease and decides he is going to spend as much money as possible, and then, of course, he learns that he is not going to die, and he has to kill himself.

"Up until eighth grade, we would play the women's roles in drag. Our backward social skills prevented us from knowing women, but finally we overcame that. We'd say to girls, 'O.K., come and be in *Pies and Guys* next Sunday—you're the baker.' Or we'd say, 'Bruce Campbell comes home and he catches you with the six-months-to-live guy in the sequel we're making, called *Six More Months.*' "

After high school, Raimi went to Michigan State, where he and his roommate, Rob Tapert, made movies to show on campus. *The Happy Valley Kid,* a Super-8 movie that cost seven hundred dollars and grossed thirty-five hundred dollars, was the story of an M.S.U. student who goes on a rampage the week before finals. "It was a big hit on campus, because the kids really liked watching the professors get blown away, Raimi said. "I learned, 'Oh, it is the exploitation aspect that sells.' "

After a year and a half of college, Raimi dropped out, as did Tapers, and they started to work with Bruce Campbell on *The*

Evil Dead, raising money by working as busboys and cabdrivers and janitors. (The working title was *The Book of the Dead,* but a foreign-sales agent vetoed it. "He said, 'Book? That won't sell anything,'" Raimi said.) They chose horror because, Raimi said, it could appeal to the drive-in market, and it offered the best chance of recouping investors' money. "I didn't really like horror films—they frightened me," he recalled. "But, as I studied them, I began to see that there is an art to them, and there is a craft to making suspense, and I realized how interesting that process was. I would watch the suspense build in a picture, and it would be released and the audience would jump and scream, and I thought, This is kind of fantastic: they are being brought to a level here, and how long can we sustain that level? And should we break it with a scare, or should we bring it down gradually, or should we end the scene on a high note? I began to understand that making a horror was like writing a piece of music: it's like watching the work of a composer."

Raimi and team shot *The Evil Dead* in a freezing cabin in Tennessee over the course of twelve weeks, burning props for firewood as they went, and improvising camera techniques to compensate for their lack of high-tech equipment. The unsteady, racing shots were done with the use of a "shaky cam," otherwise known as a "Sam-Ram-a-cam"—a camera screwed onto a two-by-four, which could be carried along at ground level. "It was like a punk horror film," Rob Tapert says. "Sam was the one who kept saying, 'We are going to make the audience hurt.'"

"Back then, it was a much more infantile goal," Raimi said. "Get a response, get a visceral, audible response. Will they jump, and how high? And can we measure their movement in inches?" Joel Coen, who worked on *The Evil Dead* with a veteran editor named Edna Paul, recalls, "It was clear when we were cutting it how great it was. There was a moment when Edna and I were cutting, and Sam wanted some trims made, and I remember Edna getting very mad at him, and saying,

'Sam, you are cutting all the humanity out of the picture.' And Sam and I looked at each other, like '*What* is she talking about?' "

I went to visit Raimi in his apartment, and it was littered with toys and kids' videos. Raimi has moved his family into a sublet in the East Seventies while he's shooting *For Love of the Game* in New York, but the family home is in Brentwood, and there he is an avid gardener. "He has a big green thumb," Bruce Campbell told me. "He kills things during the day and grows them back at night."

I asked Raimi how old his children would have to be before he would let them watch *The Evil Dead,* and he shot back, "When they are thirty." Then he reconsidered. "I think they might enjoy *Evil Dead II* when they are older, because it has a sense of humor. It is not really as vile." Raimi seemed slightly embarrassed about his work, as if he's yet to deliver something that has really satisfied him artistically.

Raimi says, with unguarded earnestness, that what he wants to do now is make some good movies for his kids. He sounds like any other anxious parent who doesn't want his child to watch rubbish—a situation that is bound to be complicated when that rubbish happens to be your life's work, and isn't actually rubbish at all. Although it's understandable that Raimi wants to make movies, like *A Simple Plan,* that are straightforwardly good, as opposed to movies that are so bad they're good—or even movies that are simply bad—he can't repudiate his pedigree.

"When I was eleven or twelve, I had a friend whose father was really wealthy, and he had one of the first video cameras," he told me. "So we were making skits over there every day after school. We would put toy soldiers down on the ground outside, and we would pretend the camera was a helicopter coming toward them—a battle scene. And then we would cut to the soldiers themselves, and that would be us, being participants in the fight.

"But no one watching it had any idea what we were trying to communicate. People didn't understand why we were showing toy soldiers, and then why we were suddenly bigger than they were. So we thought, O.K., how can we make this clearer? At that stage, it wasn't even about making *bad* movies—we were making movies that no one could understand. The movies had to improve, just so that people could understand what we were trying to tell them. They had to improve for people even to realize that it was a bad movie. We didn't even have that."

CEREMONY AND REVOLT: BURN! AND THE LAST SUPPER

by Natalie Zemon Davis

Gillo Pontecorvo was born in Pisa in 1919 into an Italian-Jewish family. During World War II he was a Communist partisan and leader of the Resistance in Milan. He said later that his experience of fascism, "the cancer of humanity," and of the war had "shaped [his] idea of the world. . . . I am passionate about people and their suffering. . . . I felt that I would be able to . . . really communicate these ideas."

His first attempt to communicate after the war was as a journalist in Paris, where he also studied music composition. Then he saw Roberto Rossellini's *Paisan,* the great World War II film made in 1946, which became a founding inspiration for Italian neorealism. He later compared the experience with being struck by lightning. Film became Pontecorvo's medium. After a series of documentaries and films around brief episodes in Italy, he turned to historical films on grand themes: *Kapò* (1959), set in a Nazi concentration camp, The *Battle of Algiers* (1966), and *Burn!* (1969).

To each of these films Pontecorvo brought attitudes and sentiments at creative variance with each other. He had left the Communist party in 1956 in the wake of the Russian invasion of Hungary, but his passion to show "the difficulty of the human condition" grew:

> I have made political films with the idea of creating something powerful that can help to change something else. And I do so because I feel very near to the tragic conditions of people. My compassion is with them, so I have felt a spontaneous urge . . . to tell their stories.

But those stories had to be carefully and thoroughly researched. With Franco Solinas, his regular collaborator on his film scripts, he read and reread books and conducted interviews, all "under the dictatorship of truth." Even then he was not satisfied: described by one of his biographers as having a perfectionist streak, Pontecorvo knew how far he was from grasping the complexity of these historical situations. In his *Battle of Algiers*, for instance, he made a tremendous effort to achieve balance. Pontecorvo's compassion for human suffering would not lead him "to paint black all the action on one side and white on the other." Instead, he would "enter into [different] logics, and see everything that was possible to see." Once he had hoped to be a composer, so it is not surprising that musical themes are very important in his films: they mark and add to the moments of resistance and hope. But for those who listen carefully, there is another tone as well.

In *Burn!*, Pontecorvo said, there were several stories entwined in the same narrative. One was a romance of adventure, in the style of, the nineteenth-century English novel (Joseph Conrad's *Nostromo* from 1904 is surely one of the books he had in mind). Another was a confrontation between two sets of ideas: those of the "liberal bourgeoisie" of enterprising England, represented in the person of Sir William Walker; and those of the oppressed of the colonial world, as represented by José Dolores, leader of the black revolts. In all, the film was a fictional parable of linked historical transitions: from slave regime to free labor; from old imperial colony to independent nation dominated by foreign capital. Pontecorvo, together with scriptwriters Solinas and Franco Giorgio Arloria, put together events from Brazil, Saint-Domingue, Jamaica, Cuba, and elsewhere and set them on the imaginary island of Queimada.

The film opens in the early 1840s as Sir William Walker's boat nears Queimada and the ship's captain explains that *queimada* means "burned" in English. The Portuguese had once set fire to the entire island to put down initial Amerindian opposition to their conquest. Walker is on a clandestine mission from the British Admiralty, with approval from the Royal Antilles Sugar Company, to foment a slave uprising along with a Creole declaration of independence from Portuguese rule. Just as he arrives, Santiago, the current leader of the slaves, is discovered by the authorities and executed. Walker looks about for a new leader and finds him in the young José Dolores, who had carried his valises when he got off the boat. First he taunts Dolores into defiance against himself, then inspires and trains him for resistance against slavery and the Portuguese. The initial step is a bank robbery, followed, as Walker foresees, by an attack on the white soldiers who track down the money, and then by a general slave uprising led by Dolores.

Meanwhile, Walker persuades the Creole elite and plantation owners of the economic advantages of free workers over slaves. He plots with them the assassination of the Portuguese governor. These events come together on a night of slave carnival, at the end of which the new president, Teddy Sanchez, declares the independence of Queimada and, shortly afterward, the abolition of slavery.

Dolores, who is now called General Dolores by the people, comes to town with his armed entourage, wanting to claim a leadership role in the new republic. After a month, with no agreement on a constitution between him and President Sanchez, and with the sugar rotting in the harbor, Dolores returns to his encampment, where the blacks are still in arms and refusing to work on the sugar plantations. Walker has already tried to persuade Dolores that "civilization is not a simple matter. You cannot learn it overnight." Dolores, now very troubled, finally instructs his followers to lay down their arms and go back to the plantations. He warns Walker to tell his white friends that "they may know how to sell sugar, but we are the ones who cut the cane."

Ten years pass. Sir William Walker has been to Indo-China, among other places, and has returned to London "another man," quarrelsome, dissolute, and living in a poor neighborhood. The Royal Antilles Sugar Company has made immense profits from its plantations all over the Caribbean, except in Queimada, where the sugar-cane cutters have been in revolt under General Dolores and have won several victories, despite being outnumbered by the Queimada soldiers. The film resumes the tale as Walker is employed by the Royal Antilles Sugar Company, with support from Her Majesty's government, to put down the revolt. Efforts at negotiation fail when Dolores refuses to see Walker. Walker learns from one of Dolores's followers of the general's revolutionary critique of the white man's civilization: "It is better to know where to go than how to go."

Walker coldly plans military actions, which are carried out by Queimada troops, including many black soldiers, and additional British troops. As black families are herded out of their huts, the mountain villages that give support to the rebels are burned. Before long, most of the other villages and the plantations also go up in flames. Altogether, there is much loss of life. President Sanchez wants to stop the attack, but Walker engineers his arrest by the commander of the Queimada troops, and Sanchez is executed for treason.

When Dolores is finally captured, he refuses to say a word to

Walker, but tells the black soldiers who are willing to listen: "One of us will remain. We will be born later." Walker tries to get Dolores to escape, so he will not be executed and become a martyr and a myth. Dolores looks at Walker in silent triumph and shouts as he is led off to be hanged: "Inglese, but what civilization? Till when?" While workers load the cargo of sugar, Walker walks to the boat to return to England. A voice like Dolores's asks if he can carry Walker's bags, and, as Sir William smiles and turns, he is killed with a knife.

Pontecorvo cast Marlon Brando for the role of Sir William Walker, and followed his preferred practice of casting José Dolores and the other black figures from the rural population of Colombia, his initial site for shooting. He saw Evaristo Marquez riding horseback in the countryside one day and decided he was perfect for the leader of the blacks. Marquez's only language was a Spanish-African Creole, and he had to be coached into speaking English, just as José Dolores was coached into making revolution.

Unlike *Spartacus*, *Burn!* gives some background to slave revolts. Santiago's rebel movement, centered in a mountain village of free blacks, or maroons, has been crushed, but it provides a tradition of resistance on the island. Dolores seems not to know of it, however, or at least not to build on that tradition when he meets Walker, even though Santiago's head has been paraded around the villages as a warning. Walker chooses Dolores when he sees him sneak food to a newly arrived slave mother in chains with her infant, and then throws a stone at a soldier trying to prevent Dolores from doing so.

The path to armed revolt is a double one. Most evidently, the white gentleman, acting for the interests of Britain, the sugar trade, and "progress and civilization," manipulates the black slave porter until he is prepared to kill Portuguese soldiers to be free. This transfer of energy and intention is expressed at critical junctures through the faces of the two men: Sir William looking at Dolores with eyes narrowed in intense expectation; Dolores changing his expression from doubt to certainty, then breaking into a smile.

"If I had told you, José, to start a revolution," Walker says to Dolores after the first victories, "you wouldn't have understood. To rob a bank, yes, that was possible. First you learn to kill to defend yourself. Then . . . to defend others. And the rest came by itself." Dolores goes on to ask Walker, "And you, what do you get?" We film spectators wonder whether the former slave agrees with Walker's patronizing account of how he came to rebel. Enlightenment ideas played a role in the formation of the real Toussaint L'Ouverture's revolutionary sensibility in Saint-Domingue, but they were not bestowed on him by a Frenchman. Rather, Toussaint acquired them from within his own circle on the island. Pontecorvo and Solinas could have learned that from C.L.R. James's *Black Jacobins,* which was available in both French and English when they wrote their film script.

Burn! also shows another path to revolt—that of religion and ceremonial festivity. This route was omitted in *Spartacus,* and it comes into its own in historical scholarship on popular uprising only in the late 1960s. Vodou spirits and Vodou songs of liberty and uprising played their part in preparing, sustaining, and remembering the Haitian revolution. The leaders of the slave revolts of 1835 and earlier in Bahia were Afro-Brazilian Muslims, and the rebels brandished phrases from the Koran along with their machetes. In *Burn!*, versions of African song and ceremony burst on the screen at important moments, sometimes mixed with Christian motifs as well. There is a cross near Santiago's coffin, but his wake is marked by drumming, African chanting, and dancing. Men, women, and children dance after Dolores's first victory over the Portuguese, some of them brandishing rifles and wearing soldiers' hats. The carnival that culminates in the assassination of the Portuguese governor lasts all day. It is infused with African motifs, the slaves are brilliantly costumed, their children are covered with white fluid to make them look like ghosts, and their cries and dances transfix the soldiers until it is time for the attack. Ennio Morricone's music underscores the same message, and the theme associated with revolt is heard in counterpoint with an African song.

Sir William Walker is performed with intensity and absorption by Marlon Brando. He fought ferociously with Pontecorvo during the film, but has said recently: "I think I did the best acting I've ever done in that picture." Walker is in many ways the central figure in *Burn!*, yet his story is always placed against that of Dolores. Whereas in Kubrick's film, Spartacus and Crassus are opponents throughout, in Pontecorvo's film Walker and Dolores are collaborators. They are cheerful collaborators in their first encounters—exchanging Dolores's rum for Walker's whisky and toasting each other's projects—and enemies in their last.

Their life trajectories move in opposite directions. Walker begins with belief in "civilization and progress," in freedom of sorts along with managing and profit making. He ends in doubt, commenting with icy accuracy, as he watches the capture of Dolores, on the irony of the English treatment of the black leader. He says he no longer knows *why* he is in Queimada, but affirms that he still likes to do things well. Dolores begins in uncertainty, without a clear plan or a moral and social philosophy. He ends in belief, challenging the goals of the "white man's civilization," which cares only for technical progress, and asserting, "if a man works for another . . . he remains a slave."

The final conflict between the two men is not just political or ideological, but personal. Sir William wants to win as a man over General Dolores. He holds out his hand in vain to the captured leader. He insults the silent Dolores, who then spits in his face. Dolores's victory is in their final moments together, when he refuses to escape. Pontecorvo intended this scene to show the cost of Dolores's martyrdom to Walker himself: "If

José is killed . . . without even speaking one word to him, José would become greater than Walker, who would then feel as if he had lost everything." In his last words to the silent Dolores, Walker bursts forth with the question he has abandoned for his own life and which the rebel leader thinks all important: "Why?" Why does José want to die? Why?

Burn! is a tough movie, with more balance to it than *Spartacus*. The violence of the Queimada and British forces is horrendous—the burning, the uprooting of population, and the setting of dogs on the rebels (as was done in Saint-Domingue by Napoleon's army in 1802)—but Dolores also teaches, "We must cut heads instead of cane," and refuses negotiation by sending back a wagon of dead men. The ex-slaves are not all brothers: the troops of independent Queimada who hunt down the rebels are mostly black, and some of these black soldiers cruelly mock the captured Dolores. The rulers do not all become as ruthless as Walker, the commanders of the Queimada and British troops, and the agent of the Royal Antilles Sugar Company: the mestizo President Sanchez is a moderate who believes that independence should have brought something better than domination by foreign capital and massive violence, and he pays for it with his life.

Apart from the power of its celebratory and festive scenes and the terror of its scenes of destruction, the historical achievement of *Burn!* is in its successful experiment in telling specific and general stories at the same time. *Burn!* not only suggests how events of the past are experienced by village groups or lived out in the personal rivalry of two men (the microhistorical potential of film) but also tries to give a general account of shifts in power and class and the rhythm of historical change (the iconic potential of film). Pontecorvo once said that his ideal director would be three-quarters Rossellini, the focused storyteller, and one-quarter Eisenstein, the teller of grand sweep.

In *Burn!* this general picture is offered in part by having individual persons stand for a large social process: the British consul to Queimada in the Portuguese period becomes the representative of the Royal Antilles Sugar Company in the period of independence. It is also offered by commentary, as Sir William Walker both performs his strategic and manipulative tasks and, like a chorus, comments on them. At Walker's first meeting with President Sanchez and his colleagues on his return to Queimada, Sir William suddenly pauses and reflects on the interval in which he has been away:

> Very often between one historical period and another ten years might certainly be long enough to reveal the contradictions of a whole century. And so often we have to realize that our judgments and our interpretation and even our hopes may have been wrong—wrong, that's all.

By skillful acting, Marlon Brando is both out of character and in character as he makes this uncolloquial observation; the film audience catches the convention of commentary being displayed and then the slippage of Walker back to his own life, as he lowers his eyes and his voice on the phrase, "even our hopes may have been wrong." Many historians would find Pontecorvo's historical schema oversimplified and would substitute other terms for his Marxist "contradictions," but they would agree that there are time intervals that seem to participants to have a distinctive character and a sense of shift (our own *fin de siècle* seems to be one).

Pontecorvo adds complexity to his narrative not by words, but by images and sounds that close and open the history. There is Dolores's face, caught twice in a still in Walker's telescope: early in the film in anger as he picks up a stone to throw at the Portuguese soldier; at the end as he climbs a mountainside and reaches back to help a fellow rebel. There is the color white: at the opening the white of a big rock off the coast of Queimada, which, the ship's captain recounts, is said to come from the bones of the Africans who had died while crossing the ocean and were cast off there; the white covering of the children at carnival; the whiteness of the ash overlying the mountains of Queimada at the end. Then there are the parallel futures imagined after the burning: in Walker's words to the sugar company man, the destroyed island will be green again after ten years and producing sugar, restored as it had been after the Portuguese burning; in Dolores's words to a sympathetic black soldier: "It is natural that fire destroys everything. A little life always remains. One of us will remain. We will be born later."

In *Spartacus*, the child that survives can be a form of resistance as well as the hope for the future. In *Burn!*, the child—here the boy child—plays both the role of hope and the role of sorrow. During the heady days of early rebel success, when slavery is being destroyed and the island has declared its independence, José Dolores is a charismatic figure: the women and men of the villages and city streets dance around him with joy. The women in particular hold their little boys up to him, to be touched and held. During the days of burning and the eviction of villagers, the little boys are at the center again, but now alone, baffled, terrified as they run crying in the smoke and gunfire. They are a reproach both to Sir William Walker and to General José Dolores. In Ennio Morricone's music for these scenes, the crying of a little boy cuts through the grand motifs, reminding us of the costs of both rebellion and oppression.

PEOPLE WHO NEED PEOPLE

by David Geffner

There's a telling moment halfway through Kirby Dick's sad yet riveting documentary *Sick: The Life and Death of Bob Flanagan, Supermasochist.* As the artist struggles through another breathless attack from his cystic fibrosis, Dick asks if biographers are "vampires," pillaging the lives of their subjects to satiate their own artistic thirsts. The thoughtful and intelligent Flanagan pauses briefly and smiles: "No, I think they're more like vultures. Circling around with their cameras until I cough again."

Whether fowl or foul, the relationships directors have with their real-life subject matters are about as complex as filmmaking gets. After all, biographical or portrait documentaries are only as compelling as the people portrayed in them. And a slew of recent indie docs—*Sick, Crumb, The Cruise, On the Ropes, American Movie, Sex: The Annabel Chong Story*—proves that in spades. Each film charts the life of a flamboyant character existing on the margins of society. And each film's subject fully consented to the process of being captured on celluloid. They became actors in their own life stories.

Indie doc-makers' burgeoning interest in biographical portraits mirrors, in fact, a parallel interest by the mainstream media. VH-1's Behind the Music, A&E's Biography, and E!'s True Hollywood Story are some of television's most successful shows. Of course, the independent film model is usually predicated on more marginal characters, personalized approaches, and, sometimes, the presence of the filmmaker in the biographical narrative.

And, of course, the feature-format of indie docs demands real storytelling. Accordingly, indie docs, more than anything, have come to resemble fiction films. But, in a narrative feature, of course, actors get paid, careers are born, and bank accounts are fattened. What, then, do documentary subjects receive for having their lives invaded for months, sometimes years at a time, by ambitious camera crews bent on sculpting their worlds into art? Some obviously bask in the "15 minutes" an indie release provides. But, the long-term payoffs are slim next to what the filmmaker receives. If these films are more partnerships than documents, as many directors polled for this article admit, who really benefits? Should filmmakers give their doc subjects "final cut" over their own life stories in the interest of making the deal? Or, should all bets be off once the cameras start to roll?

REAL IS AS REAL DOES

Boston-based Frederick Wiseman, who has been making documentaries for over 30 years, calls his own films biased, prejudiced, subjective, condensed, but also a fair representation of how he saw a situation at a particular time. "The idea that documentaries are objective reality is comic," Wiseman insists. "It's simply one person's version of events, that's all."

N.Y.-based doc producer, cinematographer, and docfest programmer, David Leitner, builds upon Wiseman's observations, adding that every time a filmmaker aims a camera at a subject, he or she is editing reality for his or her own purposes. "Introducing microphones, a crew, and lighting equipment clearly alters the flow of natural events," Leitner observes. "There might have been a time, back in the '60s, when the pretense of reality was pushed on us. But, I don't think anyone today would dare to call documentaries the complete truth."

Snatches of several truths, perhaps. But, many of today's successful indie "portrait" docs do have more in common with narrative features—a linear storyline, a larger-than-life protagonist, added-on music and/or narration to enhance presentation—than the "fly-on-the-wall reality" of '50s and '60s cinema verité. If the current slate of indie docs are intended more as "entertainment" than as instruments of social change, should the thornier issues of documentary ethics intrude into the filmmaking process?

"I'm not sure I would do it this way again," observes Bennett Miller, director of *The Cruise*, a portrait of New York tour guide Timothy "Speed" Levitch, "but we had no arrangement whatsoever when we began making our film." Tim was homeless when we shot and had been for six years. He was making just enough money to scrape by, and his job on the bus was frustrating because he desperately wanted to connect with people through his work and art. I think, for all those reasons, he was eager to be the subject of a film when I approached him."

First-timer Miller had considered making documentaries on two other "passionate outsiders" before Levitch. However, both died before he got around to filming. Introduced to Levitch through Miller's younger brother, with whom Levitch had gone through high school and college, the director built up a close rapport with his subject. He filmed over 100 hours of digital video, occasionally buying meals, even offering up his apartment as a crash-pad.

"Documentaries are built on trust," Miller observes. "We didn't ask Tim to sign anything until he had seen a fine cut of the film. And, in return, he gave us complete access for many months and was never involved in the editing process of what was, ultimately, an intimate portrait of his life alone."

Miller's approach, a common one for many of the films mentioned above, was sincere, yet risky. Without written consent, the subject can, in the worst case, reject the film and attempt to stop its exhibition. Many attorneys familiar with documentary filmmaking urge filmmakers to obtain written consent upfront with either a simple written declaration or an involved legal form. This is often more to satisfy a film's distributor or a TV network, rather than as ammunition for some far-off legal showdown.

"Regardless of how sensitive it may to be to obtain consents before shooting begins," remarks Wilder Knight, a N.Y.-based entertainment attorney at Pryor, Cashman, Sherman, and Flynn whose documentary credits include *The Brandon Teena Story* and the soon-to-be-completed HBO documentary *Gordon Parks*, by Saint Clair Bourne, "it's just a smart thing to do. The business bottom line is that distributors and errors-and-omissions insurance carriers generally require them. You don't want to have your project be unsellable because you lack a few key releases."

"There is also a very practical reason to obtain releases," Knight continues. "In many of my clients' documentaries I have been unconvinced that releases were absolutely necessary from a legal perspective. To the extent you are portraying real-life events there is a strong public policy in favor of allowing journalists to operate without constraints. But a significant problem arises when a suit is brought. Even though it may be clear you will 'win on the merits,' it is equally clear that you will 'lose on the legal fees.' Obviously, trying to obtain a release up front may color the relationship you have with your subject. It may be difficult to run around getting everyone to sign releases during a riot. The final decision is a call the filmmaker must make. There are filmmakers who have successfully filmed without obtaining releases. But from a strict business standpoint, you should try to get a release whenever possible."

"As a general rule, I believe if you're making a documentary about an individual who is still alive," adds Knight, "you shouldn't offer payment. That's just a personal opinion and relates to the idea that a journalist should not be influencing the person being interviewed. The payment of funds may create an artificial situation. *The National Enquirer* pays its subjects for their stories, and *The New York Times* doesn't. I tend to believe more of what I read in the *Times*, although *The National Enquirer* wins hands down as far as entertainment is concerned!"

HE LOVES ME, HE LOVES ME NOT

While Timothy "Speed" Levitch did receive minor compensation at the conclusion of *The Cruise*'s editing, "pizza money" as Levitch has said, few can argue the former tour-bus guide has not benefited from the film's release. According to Miller, Levitch has "gotten off the bus." He has signed a book deal, had a play produced, appeared on *Leno*, was featured in a *New York Times* Metro section article, travelled with Miller to various European film festivals, and essentially became the toast of the indie-film party circuit. For the first time in more than half a decade, Levitch was able to afford his own sublet in Manhattan; the most tangible proof of *The Cruise*'s effect on this formerly homeless man.

Not all indie docs have such happy endings. Kirby Dick's sharp, harrowing portrait of sado-masochist and cystic fibrosis sufferer, Bob Flanagan, culminates in Flanagan's death. Dick brings the viewer terrifyingly close to the actual moment of the artist's passing. In any other context, a still-photo montage of a disease-ridden corpse could easily qualify as exploitation. But, *Sick* is about its subject's desire to control a disease that is destined to take his life. Dick's respect and affection is obvious—the ending is done much the way Flanagan attacked his life and illness: raw, truthful, and unadorned.

"When I approached Bob about this film," Dick observes, "I told him it would be very intimate, that I would shoot just about everything he did. We both anticipated it would probably include his death and that was something he supported. Most of Bob's work focused on his illness and his impending death, so he was very open to my approach. I'd say there was a real sync between us from the moment we began."

As in *The Cruise*, Dick and Flanagan never focused on financial compensation, opting instead for a creative give-and-take during the making and editing of the film. "We never thought it would make any money," Dick relates. "So, the main concern was always to respect Bob's wishes about how his work was portrayed. Bob knew himself, and his disease, better than anyone. I would've been a fool to ignore his suggestions. I think he let me into his life because he felt I understood his work, perhaps, on theoretical level, better than anyone, and would not screw things up."

If the aftermath of *The Cruise* and *Sick* represent opposite yet compatible prisms of the same spectrum, *Sex: The Annabel Chong Story* falls hopelessly in-between. This frustrating, muddled indie doc was a cause célèbre at the '99 Sundance Festival, mostly because of its salacious subject matter. Pitched somewhere between a rousing feminist manifesto and a stomach-churning look at the L.A. porn industry, *Sex* is a prime example of what happens when the director/subject partnership breaks down.

As the film's executive producer and co-distributor, David Whitten, tells it: "it was clear in our preliminary meetings with Gough Lewis [the film's director] and Grace [Grace Quek, aka porn star Annabel Chong], that they were having a romantic relationship. We knew that could mean a very bumpy road, particularly if the romance fell apart. On the other hand, because Gough was so involved in Grace's life, he had an unusual level of access and trust. About three quarters of the way into shooting, they had a falling out, and Gough went off on his own to edit the film. He basically just went up to Canada and didn't talk to anybody."

In fact, as the film nears its February release, director and subject are no longer speaking. But, Whitten's company continues to work with Quek, using her to publicize the film on the festival circuit, having her speak at seminars about her experiences in the porn industry (where she is still active), even documenting each festival visit in DV for a potential "documentary sequel"

"From a publicity standpoint," Whitten baldly states, "It has been an easy call whom to maintain the relationship with: an articulate porn star who slept with 251 guys and is the subject of the film, or a first-time filmmaker who feels he deserves more fame than the movie's subject matter."

Ultimately, then, whose film is it—the director's or the documentary subject's? In the case of all those involved in *Sex: The Annabel Chong Story*, that's a fairly fuzzy question. Director Lewis describes his current state of mind regarding his debut feature as being "completely burned out and beyond caring."

As Lewis describes: "it was very awkward, at times, being involved with the person I was filming. Seventy percent of this film was made entirely by myself. That's 120 hours of footage over two-and-a-half years. Of course, I won't deny the chemistry facilitated a level of trust which made the film stronger. I was able to get a complete picture of a woman who was seductive, intelligent, and filled with contradictions. Those qualities, which I believe I captured quite accurately on film, were what made me fall in love with Grace once we started shooting. Needless to say, I would never, ever do it that way again!"

Lewis compares his experience to another noisy Sundance entry, *Crumb*. "Terry Zwigoff had a long-time friendship with Robert Crumb," Lewis says. "Because of that relationship it allowed for a deeper level of character study. Yes, it's Terry Zwigoff's film. But, it's about Robert Crumb. Likewise for me: it may be my film, but at the end of the day, it's about Grace Quek. I believe that's why she's being used as David Whitten's mascot for the film's promotion. Quite frankly, I was relieved that Grace and I broke up before I began editing. It gave me some distance and helped me to make a better portrait. The woman asked me to marry her, for goodness sake! I wasn't about to do a character slam on her once editing began."

And, what's Annabel Chong, aka Grace Quek's, take on this?

"The first time I saw this film," Quek begins, "was a few weeks before Sundance, when it was a finished cut. I was disappointed because it was apparent that so much of the film had Gough's personality woven through. Many moments—like the cutting scene and the rape scene—are not contextualized and that bothers me."

Quek is nothing if not candid as to how the partnership began: "I was in my early twenties and didn't consider the consequences of getting sexually involved with someone making a movie about my life. Gough was so inexperienced as a filmmaker, that I wasn't even convinced he would get it off the ground. But, once we began shooting, I felt like I had a stake in it. I think both of us wanted to advance our careers, and we saw this film as a means to achieve that."

According to Quek, Lewis was close to abandoning the project after the relationship dissolved, although Quek never considered bailing out. "After we broke up," Quek continues, "I was concerned that Gough's feelings for me would color the way he cut the movie. Yet, on the other hand, I had to respect the sanctity of the artist. Once you agree to have your life filmed, it does, in a sense, become the property of the director. I think he has the right to his interpretation, even if I disagree with it."

BACK-END MY ASS

According to David Whitten, Grace Quek was promised 15% of the back-end profits of *Sex: The Annabel Chong Story* by the film's director before production began. Gough Lewis retained 85%, of which he parceled out roughly 30% to private investors. The deal has since gone through various adjustments, due to budget overruns, but Quek still retains her original 15% of the back-end. The film is being co-distributed by Strand Releasing and will roll out in ten cities with as many as 50 playdates on tap if it takes off, a huge release by indie doc standards. Yet, controversy continues to dog it. When *Sex: The Annabel Chong Story* played the Mecca of American indie festivals, Sundance, the documentary community reeled over Lewis' approach.

"People were literally screaming at me because they believed we had compromised what Sundance was all about," Whitten recalls. "The idea that Grace had a financial stake in the film and that some scenes were obviously staged freaked people out. The attacks may have been valid. Was it a contrived effort by two people to enhance their fame? At the very least, it has forced festivals like Sundance to question what a documentary is in today's world."

Sex: The Annabel Chong Story may not score with critics, but its underlying business model might represent the future of small-scale indie portrait docs. Speed Levitch was given "points" in *The Cruise* after he'd approved the fine cut and before Artisan had picked up the film. Sheree Rose, who was an integral part of *Sick* and indeed, Bob Flanagan's life, will share profits from the film with Kirby Dick once the film goes into the black, which Dick projects happening this year.

As Dick notes: "Personally, I don't think there's anything wrong with subjects benefiting from their own films. I also think there are many advantages to having the subject give creative input. The idea of this pure journalistic position that's somehow tainted by the subjects being paid is absurd. I just don't buy it."

Some indie veterans, like Frederick Wiseman, are wary of creating a false intimacy with their subjects, opting, instead, for a very clear dividing line. "I tell all the participants in my films that I retain complete editorial control, and that they may not get a chance to see the film before it airs on public television. If they object to having their picture taken I simply don't include them. Nobody has asked for profit-sharing in my experience. I don't want to mislead people to think that an enduring relationship will result from this film. I'm very straightforward about that."

Examining a profit-sharing arrangement, it's easy to ask what all the fuss is about. Given the current market for indie docs, neither the director nor subject is ever likely to see much money. With few exceptions (*Hoop Dreams, Roger and Me*), the genre never yields hefty back-end profits. So, why bother? Most directors polled for this article felt that a profit-sharing arrangement, particularly one put in place after the film's editing, would help to solidify trust between filmmaker and subject, a bond more fragile than dollars and cents could ever approach.

"I believe if you're making a documentary about an individual who is still alive," relates attorney Knight, "you shouldn't offer payment at all. The subject's behavior can, and often will, change if they think they have a commercial stake. That being said, however, I know my documentary clients are driven by an intense passion, not by the sense of profit. Giving points can be viewed as a show of good faith, even if they have little, or any, real value."

Adds *The Cruise*'s Bennett Miller: "Hardly anyone starts a documentary because they want to make money. In fact, it's usually the filmmaker who is putting out his or her own funds just to get it finished. If someone were to ask me what I would recommend, I'd say do whatever is comfortable for both parties. Whether it's one point or 100 points on the back-end doesn't ultimately matter. It's more about keeping the relationship you have with this person open and fair. That's what will determine the value of your film."

IT TAKES A VILLAGE

In these self-reflective times, when movies about making movies are sprouting up like Satan's young'uns, no recent venture better illustrates the implicit faith at the core of indie docs than the upcoming Sony Pictures Classics release *American Movie*. A big favorite at this year's Sundance Film Festival, *American Movie* is a hilarious, low-key chronicle of Mark Borchardt, a Wisconsin-based filmmaker desperate to make an independent feature. One memorable scene has the young director mercilessly driving his aging uncle (the sole investor in the-film-within-a-film) to finish multiple ADR takes. Borchardt is fearless in showing his own obsessions on camera, and anyone who's ever been foolish, or arrogant enough, to make an indie film, will cringe and laugh in the same instant.

"I think what's fairly unique about *American Movie*," notes director Chris Smith, "is that you see our [Smith co-made the film with his partner, Sarah Price] relationship with Mark, and his family and friends, evolve on-screen. Mark and I met as casual acquaintances while editing our respective movies in a basement at the University of Wisconsin. I started with very little knowledge of his life, and four years later, what ends up on-screen is, I believe, the product of a real friendship."

In fact, Smith wasn't even sure he had a movie worth making until Borchardt was forced to put his own project, *Northwestern*, on hold. Once all the frenetic production meetings stopped, the filmmakers had no choice but to go deeper into Borchardt's personal life. The tonal shift is apparent. What starts out as a funny, if familiar, story of a driven young indie filmmaker slowly turns into a heartfelt examination of the emotional cords that bind an American community.

"Not all documentaries require such an intimacy with the subjects—some are documents of single events or whatever," observes cofilmmaker Sarah Price. "But, for us, Mark's personal relationships with his family and friends were what made this movie worthwhile—it became so much more than just following an indie filmmaker around. Not only did Mark trust us to come into his life on a daily basis for several years, but his family and friends showed a lot of faith that we'd be able to edit a movie which would depict them in an accurate way."

Following in the footsteps of another indie doc about Midwesterners and the communities they live in, *Hoop Dreams*, Smith and Price worked out profit percentages for the film's major participants before their successful Sundance screening. As for Borchardt, Smith and Price made him an equal third partner in all *American Movie*'s profits.

"There was never any question between Sarah or myself as to Mark's deal—it had to be what it was."

Borchardt, at the time this article went to print, had just completed a summer-long stint working 50-hour weeks in a Wisconsin shutter factory. He was preparing to move out of his parents' house and back into his apartment to once again fine-tune the script for *Northwestern.* Despite the critical hype *American Movie* has had prior to its release, including all the attendant publicity Borchardt has had to shoehorn into his life, the 33-year-old director still struggles and yearns to get his dream project made.

"If there are benefits to be had from its release," Borchardt explains, "then of course I'm going to try and take advantage. For example, the trailer for *American Movie* shows the website for *Coven.* Hopefully that will help increase my sales. But, ultimately, I'm still going to make *Northwestern* the way I want to. I won't shoot in color, or put somebody's girlfriend in it just to get finishing money! I believe I am accountable only to myself, and I can't count on other people to make my film, no matter how much exposure Chris' movie brings."

Borchardt holds Smith in great regard as a filmmaker, and he does not run from the more negative aspects revealed in the film. "The Super Bowl scene, when I'm drinking, is a dark, ugly scene," Borchardt notes. "But, it shows I needed to change. It's my responsibility to take action when stuff I don't like is revealed in a film. That's the give-and-take between the director and the subject. If you insist they show everything all pretty and shy away from the problems, you may be protecting yourself from the public but you're not moving ahead as a person."

As Borchardt's comments emphasize, trust is the currency in which director and documentary subject inevitably must deal. Sometimes that trust can result in a film so shockingly intimate, like Terry Zwigoff's *Crumb,* that the viewer is stunned by what the camera has revealed. Other times the portrait is more gentle and forgiving, like Bennett Miller's *The*

Cruise, and the subject is plucked from obscurity, to the delight of the audience. Either way, the results are determined by the filmmaker's subjectivity. It is a tremendous leap of faith for anyone to be followed intimately for an extended length of time by a filmmaker with a camera. Indie docs typically take on a life of their own once released, and all the public has to judge is what the director has elected to put on-screen, rather than the hundreds of complex, daily events the subject encounters.

As Kirby Dick, who was as intimate and friendly with his subject as any filmmaker could be, concludes: "One of the reasons I do documentaries is for that relationship. You simply have no idea where it's going to go. It's unpredictable, and it's not always in service of the film. I see the relationship as a kind of reversal which can throw everything up in the air and allow things to come down in unexpected ways. Because of things like DV, which allows you to shoot, basically alone and without a crew, I'd say that relationship is more open than it has ever been. So, it's a very exciting time to be shooting documentaries."

> "Film is too vast a medium for self-indulgence. It's a dangerous tool and you must be responsible when you use it."
>
> —FRITZ LANG

NAZIS

FASCISTS HAVE ALWAYS understood the power of movies. Mussolini built Cinecitta Studios in Rome and Franco encouraged foreign movie production in Spain. The Shah of Iran threw a fabulous film festival in Teheran, as did Marcos in the Philippines. The Nazi Minister of Propaganda Josef Goebbels avidly pursued the production of motion pictures.

Stewart Klawans has written a book entitled *Film Follies, the Cinema Out of Order.* In the chapter excerpted here, *An Interlude,* he tells the history of the Nazi film *Kolberg*. As you will read, this movie had enormous resources poured into its production at a time when Germany was losing the war.

Just what exactly is it about the Nazis that continue to fascinate us so much? Besides having very stylish uniforms, I think the overwhelming purity of their villainy is what remains so outstanding.

J. Hoberman's article *When the Nazis Became Nudniks* ponders the true symbolism of Mel Brooks's *The Producers* in relation to the history of the Third Reich.

John Landis

AN INTERLUDE

by Stuart Klawans

As part of its contribution to the 1937 Paris World's Fair, Germany exhibited the architectural model for a work in progress: the Nazi Party's Nuremberg rally site, designed by Albert Speer.

The project was a culmination of work Speer had done at Nuremberg since 1934. Within the public yet private space of the rally site—public because thousands gathered, private because they did so only at the Party's pleasure—Speer created settings for events that were spectacular: made to be seen, by on-site viewers and by the camera's eye. Of these events, the one that had served the party best was staged in large measure so that an antimodern, antifeminist New Woman, Leni Riefenstahl, could create *Triumph of the Will*. With the exhibit at the Paris World's Fair, the Nazis promised their viewers an even greater work of total cinema.

Budgeted at 700–800 million marks, the rally site was to cover 65 square miles. At its south end was a parade ground, the Marchfield, encompassed by grandstands with seating for 160,000 spectators. Guests of honor would sit on a platform dominated by an allegorical sculpture that was to be 197 feet tall. As Speer noted in his memoirs, such a figure would have been 46 feet higher than the Statue of Liberty. The Marchfield itself, he pointed out, would have covered twice as much ground as the palace of Kings Darius I and Xerxes in Persepolis.

Leading north from the Marchfield was a processional avenue. It was to be a mile and a quaver long and 264 feet wide, with a reviewing stand on the right and a colonnade for the display of flags on the left. At the end of this avenue stood the Great Stadium, which was to seat 400,000 spectators. (The Circus Maximus in Rome, Speer wrote, had held at the most 200,000.) Beyond the stadium was a reflecting pool, or more properly lake; and beyond that stood two more buildings: a Kongresshalle and a Kulturhalle, the latter designed especially for Adolf Hitler's speeches on cultural affairs.

The judges in Paris awarded Speer's design a Grand Prize. Despite this success, Germany declined to contribute a pavilion to the World's Fair held in New York in 1939. When that exposition opened, on April 30, its most popular attraction proved to be the Futurama, a ride-through exhibit in the General Motor's pavilion, designed by the scenic artist Norman Bel Geddes. Visitors moved past the model of a clean and happy Metropolis of 1960; upon exiting, each received a pin that read 'I have seen the future.' As for Hitler's work of art of the future: he invaded Poland on September 1.

The war, too, was staged for the cameras; it was a continuation of the Nuremberg rallies by other means. The German nation got to see itself in a starring role, with a great many tributary peoples, prisoners, and stiffs cast as extras. Produced for Hitler by a group that prominently included his Minister of Propaganda, Josef Goebbels, the war played successfully on screens in Germany and its occupied lands for month after month, augmented by radio broadcasts, concerts, newspaper and magazine articles, and still more rallies.

Of course, this all-encompassing production also had its commercial aspects. Goebbels noted one of these in a diary entry for October 21, 1939: 'The financial success of our films is altogether amazing. We are becoming real war profiteers.'

The movies to which he referred seldom forced an explicit political message upon the audience. As writers such as Eric Rentschler have shown, Goebbels wanted the regime's films to serve as come-ons; most of them were musicals, melodramas, light comedies, adventure yarns, biographical dramas about great men of the past. So long as they accorded with the tone the Nazis wanted to set, these genre pictures were allowed to leave the preaching to other films: the newsreels, documentaries, and short subjects that were shown on the same bill. Only a handful of each year's features were propaganda vehicles. Their messages varied with the needs of the moment.

In 1940, for example, the Nazis wanted to step up their promotion of anti-Semitism. The Jewish population of Germany had shrunk from 503,000 in 1933 to 234,000 at the onset of the war. Then, through conquest, the regime quickly added some 8 million Jews to its European subjects. Goebbels, having planned ahead, was ready with two films to meet the challenge: Fritz Hippler's pseudo-documentary *Der ewige Jude* (*The Eternal Jew*) and Veit Harlan's costume drama *Jud Süss,* about the wiles of a Jewish moneylender who perverts and debauches the court of Württemberg. As Erwin Leiser notes, *Jud Süss* 'was shown to the non-Jewish population when the Jews were about to be deported. Concentration camp guards saw it. And at the Auschwitz trial in Frankfurt former SS Rottenführer Stefan Baretzki admitted that the effect of showing the film was to instigate maltreatment of prisoners' (pp. 84–5). *Jud Süss* was Germany's biggest box-office hit of 1940, attracting more than 20 million admissions.

Beginning in summer 1941, Hitler withdrew from public view. Perhaps to compensate for his absence, Goebbels increased production of the genre known as genius films. Although the Führer had become invisible, figures who exemplified his most celebrated qualities showed up in many productions released in 1942–43: *Mozart, Andreas Schlüter, Diesel, Rembrandt, Paracelsus.*

On January 31,1943, Goebbels began to face the need for yet another phase of the propaganda war: Field Marshal Friedrich von Paulus surrendered his 90,000 troops to the Soviets at Stalingrad. Two weeks later, in a speech made at the Sportpalast, Goebbels called for austerity measures and the mobilization of all citizens. For the first time, many Germans began to face the possibility of defeat—a notion that was driven home on May 12, when a quarter of a million Axis troops surrendered to the Allies in North Africa.

On June 1,1943, Goebbels wrote a memorandum to Veit Harlan, the director who had served him on *Jud Süss*:

> I hereby commission you to make the epic film *Kolberg*. The film is to demonstrate, through the example of the town which gives it its title, that a people united at home and at the front will overcome any enemy. I authorize you to request whatever help and support you deem necessary from all Army, Government, and Party agencies, and you may refer to this film which I have hereby commissioned as being made in the service of our intellectual war effort (Leiser p. 122)

According to Harlan's memoirs, Goebbels had spoken of making a film about the town of Kolberg as early as 1940. Now, wanting to ready the home front for a period of sacrifice and suffering, Goebbels committed unlimited resources to a film about a citizens' army of the early nineteenth century, defying the forces of Napoleon despite impossible odds. In his diary, he wrote that *Kolberg* "fits exactly the political and military landscape we shall probably have to reckon with by the time the film can be shown."

Within one month after Goebbels commissioned the film, a four-night air raid on Hamburg destroyed 80 percent of the city and killed 30,000. The Allies invaded Sicily, Mussolini was deposed, and the German army failed in its all-out attack against the Russians at Kursk. Meanwhile, at the Ufa studio, Veit Harlan worked on completing *Opfergang* (*The Great Sacrifice*), an Agfacolor melodrama with a sub-Nietzschean theme. Its hero was torn between his duty toward one woman (representing a wan, indoor realm of books and music) and his passion for another (representing a vibrant, outdoor world of horseback riding and skinny-dipping). Girl number two (played by Harlan's wife, Kristina Söderbaum) was clearly to be preferred, though a lingering death was somehow the consequence of her living as a blonde beast who thinks with the blood.

Around this time, Auschwitz II (Birkenau) went into full operation, its four new gas chambers/crematoria having been inaugurated between March and June 1943. Farther east, forces under the command of SS Colonel Paul Blobel were destroying evidence of an earlier, less efficient phase of genocide. In June, one of the Blobel units was in Lvov, digging up mass graves and burning the corpses; in August, another such unit began work near Kiev, at Babi Yar. During these months, the Nazis also devoted significant resources to rounding up the few Jews who remained alive in the ghettoes. As Goebbels's ally in the home front mobilization, Albert Speer, began to centralize military production in September 1943, Germany was deporting some 2000 Jews from Minsk to Sobibor. By September 25, the Nazis had wiped out the Vilna ghetto.

In early October 1943, Veit Harlan and Alfred Braun finished the screenplay for *Kolberg*. (Klaus Kreimeier writes that Thea von Harbou was said to have been an uncredited collaborator.) Filming began on October 28, with interiors shot in Neubabelsberg and exteriors in Königsberg and on the Baltic coast near Kolberg itself. In order to have a town he could blow apart and burn, Harlan also began constructing a Kolberg-folly in Gross-Glienicke, a suburb of Berlin near Potsdam and Wannsee. In November, as production started to move forward, the Allies began their bombing campaign against Berlin. That same month, some thirty Jews in the Janowska camp staged a revolt; off the set, too, there were acts of defiance, despite impossible odds.

The filming of *Kolberg* continued through August 1944. According to Harlan's account, the production cost 8.5 million marks—more than twice the usual budget for a first-class feature—and eventually employed 187,000 people, including entire army units. For one sequence, in which Napoleon's soldiers attempt to advance across flooded fields, Harlan drafted 4000 sailors to serve as extras. (Soldiers could not be trusted to fall into the water properly.) When the Admiralty refused the request, Goebbels overruled the Admiralty. Harlan also managed to requisition a hundred boxcars of salt (to sprinkle over the fields as fake snow) and 6000 horses. Factories were put on overtime to manufacture blank bullets for the production. Some 10,000 period uniforms were sewn; when those ran out, the soldier-extras who were to march in the rear ranks were told to dye their own uniforms and decorate them with sashes made of toilet paper. The Western Allies landed at Normandy, the Soviets began their offensive against Army Group Center, Colonel Claus von Stauffenberg attempted to kill Hitler, Goebbels was named Reich Plenipotentiary for Total War, and still the shooting continued on *Kolberg*.

Harlan wrapped the production in August, around the time the Allies entered Paris and the Nazis began the final deportations from the Lodz ghetto: another 67,000 Jews sent to Birkenau. The following month, Goebbels began organizing a Volkssturm, or People's Army, made up for the most part of very young and very old men. Children aged 10 to 15 were conscripted to work on farms and at antiaircraft installations. Women, too, were conscripted in large numbers for the first time; exemptions were discontinued, and the age limit for women for compulsory labor was raised from 40 to 50.

In November 1944, Harlan attempted to hand over *Kolberg,* but Goebbels declared the picture a complete disappointment. He demanded extensive cuts, especially in sequences that showed too vividly the sufferings of war. Harlan later estimated that the excised footage had cost 2 million marks to shoot. Around this same time, the Nazis began to dismantle the gas chambers and crematoria at Birkenau and to destroy the camp's documents. On Christmas Day 1944, Goebbels held his final discussion with Harlan about the editing of *Kolberg*. The following day, an Allied air strike all but finished Germany's counter-offensive in the Ardennes.

The film was ready for its scheduled premiere on January 30, 1945, the twelfth anniversary of Hitler's appointment as Chancellor of Germany. Goebbels was determined to hold the premiere on the Atlantic coast of the Reich. By this time, Germany held only one position on the Atlantic, La Rochelle. Since it was behind Allied lines, Goebbels had the print of *Kolberg* dropped in by parachute. The commander of La Rochelle sent back his thanks:

> Profoundly moved by the heroic stand of the fortress at Kolberg and by this artistically unsurpassable rendering of it, I convey to you . . . a renewed vow to emulate the heroic struggle of those on the home front and not to lag behind them in endurance and commitment.

On January 31, *Kolberg* was given its premiere in Berlin, at the UfaTheater on Alexanderplatz and at the Tauentzien-Palast. (Ufa's greatest theater, the Palast am Zoo, had by this time been destroyed by Allied bombing.) According to Kreimeier, the guests at the Tauentzien-Palast were given only a cold buffet, "consumed in haste by a worried public eager to get home before the next air raid."

On March 19,1945, in the face of the Red Army's advance, German forces evacuated Kolberg (today known as Kolobrzeg). That had pretty much been the result in 1807, too, despite what Harlan and Goebbels showed in the film.

Kolberg is narrated in flashback. The frame story, set in 1813, begins with thousands of citizens marching through the streets of Breslau. Although they sing most stirringly of their desire to fight Napoleon, King Friedrich Wilhelm III holes up in his palace, refusing to hear. Into his inner chamber strides General Wilhelm von Gneisenau (Horst Caspar), who reminds the out-of-touch leader of the events of seven years earlier, in Kolberg:

With Napoleon victorious at Jena and Austerlitz, the military commander of Kolberg, Colonel Loucadou (Paul Wegener), seemed prepared only for token resistance. So the burgermeister, old Nettelbeck (Heinrich George), took matters into his own hands: organizing a militia, bringing in his own artillery, and otherwise showing up the furious Loucadou. Nettelbeck was assisted by a dashing cavalry officer, Ferdinand von Schill (Gustav Diessl) and later by Gneisenau himself, once he took over the military command of Kolberg.

Put in a love story, Goebbels had said. Harlan, never slow to give his wife a job, cast Kristina Söderbaum as Maria, a farmer's daughter, who falls in love with von Schill. She also crosses enemy lines to convey a message to Queen Luise, consents to have her home burned to the ground to prevent its use by the French, and provides a useful contrast to her brother Klaus (Kurt Meisel). The latter is one of Harlan's whipping-boy characters: a culture-besotted weakling who swoons over the *Moonlight* sonata when real men should be fighting and making love, who toasts the French on demand, who dies (as he should) trying to rescue his violin from a flood.

For those interested in establishing auteurist credentials for Harlan—an initiative taken up in recent years by a number of writers—this figure of the degenerate art-lover should be of some consequence. It is unquestionably one of Harlan's thematic signatures; his most notable stylistic tic is a tendency in dialogue scenes to push the actors toward either somnambulism or apoplexy. (In *Kolberg,* the exchanges between Heinrich George and Paul Wegener look so much like spitting contests, they might have been directed by an oral surgeon.) Those who feel that Nazi cinema was redeemed by such traits may seek more of them in Harlan's work. I will note only that his authorial credit for *Kolberg* must be shared with Goebbels, who closely supervised not only the editing but also the screenplay (sections of which borrow from his speeches) and who seems to have thought of the film as his answer to *Gone With the Wind*.

Goebbels also seems to have conceived of *Kolberg* as a personal testament. According to Harlan, Goebbels spoke of Nettelbeck as the hero of the film and identified with the character. But I think Goebbels was much closer to Gneisenau, both in physical type (he somewhat resembled the thin, sleek-haired Horst Caspar) and in the role he played: making speeches and providing an interpretive frame for events. If we imagine Gneisenau to be a self-portrait of Goebbels, then we may find in *Kolberg* some instruction on how to be a Minister of Propaganda. When the French send an envoy to request surrender, Gneisenau steps out onto a balcony and addresses the citizens gathered below, informing them that he chooses to fight on. Anyone who disagrees, say so now, Gneisenau orders; and everyone remains silent. Anyone who agrees, go back to what you were doing; and the crowd disperses in all directions. A striking picture of the mechanism of consent: those who would object must find the courage to speak up as individuals, while those who accept their leaders' policies need only go about business as usual.

Not that anything was still usual by 1943. If we ask why Goebbels, as advocate for total war, should have allocated military resources to a mere film, precisely when Germany's situation in the field was crumbling, we also must ask why the Nazi regime simultaneously allocated its shrinking resources toward the completion of genocide. The mystery becomes intelligible only if we realize that the Nazis were carrying out not one war but three; a war of geopolitical conquest, an intellectual war (to use Goebbels's phrase), and a war against the Jews. These three were related, of course; Himmler, for example, made it plain to his chain of command that the presence of a Jew—any Jew at all, anywhere in Europe—should be considered a danger to German forces. Similarly, certain productions of the intellectual war clearly were expected to influence for the better the war in the field. But the hierarchy among these three projects was never stable. Sometimes the Nazis produced films to help their troops make war; but they also made war for the sake of producing films, or killing Jews and other undesirables.

To speak in this way, linking, the production of *Kolberg* with the systematic murder of millions, is to compare small things to great, and in the most tasteless way possible. I am tempted to write "grotesque." Yet in its original sense, as applied to the wall paintings of Nero's Golden House, that word described something far removed from the Nazis' enormities. "Grotesque" described a style in which incommensurate things were mixed to create a decorative pattern, for the amusement, of sophisticated people at their leisure. (Strictly speaking, this book is grotesque.) As a domestic refinement, the grotesque had no deep connection to its presumed Dionysian origin in the archaic, disorienting rites practiced in caves and caverns. Far from inspiring awe or ecstasy, the grotesque in Nero's time probably functioned as an ironic contrast to the Empire's aboveground, Apollonian system of temples—which (for the upper classes) were themselves sites of disbelief.

It was the conviction of the young Nietzsche that a full-blooded engagement ought to be restored between Dionysus and Apollo, the grotto and the temple. This engagement, he felt, should be sought not in religion but in art, specifically in the music-dramas of Richard Wagner. Nietzsche's later, horrified recantation of this notion does not concern us here; nor is this the place to do justice to Wagner by considering the actual texts of the music-dramas as distinguished from their aura. For our purpose, it is enough to understand that what Nietzsche analyzed and articulated a century ago, many other people were sensing and acting upon. The "progressive" culture of which Wagnerism was the highest expression brought together people with many different agendas, and so it generated many results. In one of them, the temple became a rally site in Nuremberg; the grotto, a crematorium.

And the connection between the two? Conventionally, we speak of a dialectic, as if one were succeeded by the other in an endless cycle. Perhaps the folly of *Kolberg* may remind us that there is a third term that temporarily resolves the dialectic, a type of building that exists between the extremes. The midpoint between a grotto and a temple is a ruin.

WHEN THE NAZIS BECAME NUDNIKS

by J. Hoberman

"It's springtime for Hitler and Germany, winter for Poland and France," the uniformed tenor warbles. "Come on, Germans—go into your dance!" His command is the cue for a stage full of goose-stepping chorines in storm trooper caps and lederhosen hot pants to take their places in a rotating swastika formation, filmed from an overhead angle like the climax of a Busby Berkeley musical number.

Was "Springtime for Hitler," the "gay romp with Adolf and Eva at Berchtesgarden" that is the subject and centerpiece of Mel Brooks's first feature film, *The Producers,* the big shock of 1968? Or was the spectacle of hoofing Nazis just business as usual? Roger Ebert, then starting out as a film reviewer in Chicago, recalls his first encounter with *The Producers* as something "so liberating that not even *There's Something About Mary* rivals it." But Mr. Brooks's chutzpah was not to every taste.

When *The Producers* opened several months later at a midtown Manhattan art house, it was greeted with severely mixed notices—including pans from New York's leading critics, Renata Adler, Stanley Kauffmann, Pauline Kael, and Andrew Sarris. This week, Mr. Brooks's adaption of *The Producers* opens as a Broadway musical.

Even in 1968, "Springtime for Hitler," the movie's title until the distributor Joseph H. Levine prevailed upon Mr. Brooks to change it, was a gag that its author had nurtured for years —an ultimate "Show of Shows" skit, complete with a dialect role perfect for Sid Caesar, the television star for whom Mr. Brooks had created countless comic German characters.

As befit a movie directed by one of the most manic writers in show business, *The Producers* piled shtick upon shtick. A seedy impresario, Max Bialystock (Zero Mostel), who finances his shows by romancing and bilking elderly women, and a timorous, if ultimately crooked, accountant named Leo Bloom (Gene Wilder) hatch a scheme to defraud their investors by overselling shares in a Broadway show so terrible that it is certain to close after one performance. (Among other things, *The Producers* is credited with introducing the phrase "creative accounting.")

The partners select a musical by an unreconstructed Nazi, Franz Liebkind, who, once they have tracked him down at his Greenwich Village bunker, enthuses that his play gives "not the popular conception of the Führer but the young, beautiful inner Hitler who danced his way to glory." (Mr. Brooks considered taking the part of Liebkind himself, before giving it to Kenneth Mars.) Bialystock and Bloom further guarantee their show's failure by hiring a self-confident, if dimwitted, cross-dressing director, Roger De Bris (Christopher Hewitt), and bestowing the role of Hitler on a mind-blown method-acting hippie known as L. S. D. (Dick Shawn). As ultimate insurance, Bialystock proffers an opening-night bribe to *The New York Times* drama critic. The reviewer angrily throws the hundred-dollar bill to the ground; the show, however, is a hit.

Critics pointed out that a similar premise had been employed in two George Kauffman plays, an episode of the television show *Racket Squad* and even, according to one review, a theatrical producer who was then active. (Possibly, it was first used in one of the lost plays of Aristophanes.) But *The Producers* was made with an improvisatory quality that had largely been absent from Hollywood since the wacky Paramount comedies of the early 30's and that, unstinting in its comic aggression, gave the sense—not altogether uncommon in the 1960's—of putting something on the screen for the first time.

The credit sequence presents Max Bialystock, sporting the world's most flagrant comb-over, playing "dirty young man" to a succession of amorous crones. Bialystock is a sort of frenzied Groucho Marx (complete with asides to the audience) inflated to Falstaffian dimensions. A fount of libidinal energy and rampant orality, Mostel not only chews the scenery and devours the lens but kisses everything in range, not least the manuscript of *Springtime for Hitler.* (In another turn of phrase credited to the movie, Bialystock gazes out of his dirt-encrusted office window and, spying a white limo below, longingly screams, "Flaunt it, baby, flaunt it!")

Mr. Brooks has said that this outrageous character was inspired by a theatrical producer for whom he once worked, "a guy well into his 60's who made love to a different little old lady every afternoon on a leather couch in his office." *Time* magazine suggested that Bialystock was a parody of David Merrick—and others have proposed Merrick's mentor Arthur Beckhard as the model. In any case, the part was written for Mostel, a monstre sacré, who first had to be persuaded to take the role and then proceeded to embody it with an almost terrifying gusto. (Reports of on-set tension between Mr. Brooks and the sometimes difficult Mostel hardly seem unreasonable.)

Mr. Wilder, appearing in only his second movie, plays Stan Laurel to Mostel's manic Oliver Hardy. The extended one-on-

ones between the bellowing Bialystock and his accountant, a flaming neurotic complete with security blanket, are classic, although Mostel also demonstrates a touching rapport in his "romantic" scenes with a kittenish Estelle Winwood, then 84.

"I want—I want—everything I've ever seen in the movies," the repressed Bloom explodes at one point. Mr. Brooks wanted that and more. *The Producers* is nothing if not self-conscious filmmaking and, although far less flashy in its technique than several of its contemporaries like *The Graduate* and *Bonnie and Clyde* (which also quoted Busby Berkeley), the movie was, in its way, one more example of a Hollywood new wave. Mr. Brooks flaunted his own historical references by evoking the movies of the 1930's, predicating gags on knowledge of such Partisan Review heroes as Joyce, Kafka, and Dostoyevsky—as well as incorporating the sort of Yiddishisms that were a leit-motif of Mr. Caesar's skits. (Roger De Bris is named for the Yiddish term for circumcision.)

The words "Jew" and "Jewish" are never used. One of the movie's best gags is the Nazi playwright's obliviousness to the evident Jewishness of his producers. Not only are their names, professions, and demeanors meant to be stereotypically Jewish, their interpreters were as well. Having created the role of Tevye in *Fiddler on the Roof* four seasons earlier, Mostel was a Jewish icon; in 1969, after Mr. Wilder was nominated for an Oscar for best supporting actor, The *Hollywood Reporter* noted that he was now in "dueling contention" with Dustin Hoffman for the title role in a movie version of Philip Roth's just published *Portnoy's Complaint*.

Some found *The Producers* not only coarse but overly ethnic. Pauline Kael wrote in *The New Yorker* that it "revels in the kind of show-business Jewish humor that used to be considered too specialized for movies." In its confrontational, bad boy attitude, *The Producers* was a late manifestation of the "sick comedy" associated since the late 50's with those, mainly Jewish, stand-up comedians—Mort Sahl, Shelly Berman, Mike Nichols and

Elaine May, Tom Lehrer, and especially Lenny Bruce—who treated such apparently unfunny subjects as mental illness, racial prejudice, religion, and nuclear fall-out. (The most celebrated antecedent was the Bruce routine known as "Hitler and the M.C.A.," in which two German talent agents in 1930, desperate to find a dictator, discover and recruit a handy house painter.) That the film's financing was arranged by Sidney Glazier, the Oscar-winning producer of a movie as dignified as *The Eleanor Roosevelt Story,* seems like one of Mr. Brooks's bad-taste jokes.

Was *The Producers* seen as an expression of Jewish anti-Semitism? Neither the New York nor Los Angeles offices of the Anti-Defamation League have records of any complaints. *The Producers* is far less redolent of self-hatred than of self-love, even narcissism. Far from self-deprecating in its Jewish humor, the movie conveys cultural confidence: it is a rebellion against invisibility, the equivalent of dancing on Hitler's grave. Indeed, *The Producers* opened in New York with a full-page endorsement from Peter Sellers, himself a Jew, who called it the "ultimate film" and "essence of all great comedy." (Four years later, Sellers announced his own never-realized equivalent to *The Producers,* a movie in which the comic-strip hero the Phantom pursues the 90-year-old Hitler, to be played by Sellers, from the South American jungle to the stage of the Royal Albert Hall.)

"Those of us who have seen this film and understand it have experienced a phenomenon which occurs only once in a lifetime," Sellers wrote. Anarchic as it is, *The Producers* has an undercurrent of seriousness and even catharsis. No movie has more economically evoked the Third Reich as a regime of failed artists and crank aesthetes embarked upon a demented project to "beautify" the world—through war and mass murder. (Magnet for a mad abundance of dancing, singing, sieg-heiling would-be Führers, *Springtime*'s casting call anticipates the multiple Hitlers who appear throughout Hans-Jürgen Syberberg's 1976 epic *Hitler, a Film From Germany.*) And no movie has ever succeeded so well in reducing that totalitarian project to travesty, to one more tawdry show biz episode. Although *The Producers* anticipates the flood of Nazi kitsch that would soon appear, the musical *Cabaret* was already on Broadway and the prisoner-of-war sitcom *Hogan's Heroes* was among the most popular shows on television by the time the movie opened.

In contrast to a less vulgar Holocaust comedy like *Life Is Beautiful,* Mr. Brooks succeeds in implicating the audience in his joke. Our culture's continuing fascination with the Nazis is a factor not only of their absolute evil but also of their status as pioneers of spectacular politics—ecstatic mass rallies, orchestrated media campaigns, eroticized violence, pseudo-documentaries created to glorify a pop star-political leader. There is nothing more prescient than the telegram sent to Mr. Brooks's shell-shocked, and ultimately naive, producers: "Congratulations. 'Hitler' will run forever."

"It's the biggest train set a boy ever had."

—ORSON WELLES

TECHNOLOGY

THE TOOLS WITH which films are made are constantly evolving. Color and sound were two seismic changes in the way we watch and make movies. As computers and digital technology advance, it is becoming apparent that soon film itself will be obsolete. Not the movies as an experience, but the means by which that experience is delivered to us.

I cut my first film (appropriately called *Schlock*), on a Movieola. When my editor George Folsey Jr. began using a flatbed system called a Kem, we were literally on the cutting edge. Starting with my television series *Dream On*, I was editing on a computer software system called Montage, which has morphed into Lightworks, the Avid and countless others. Although these methods are definitely faster and more versatile, I do miss the tactile smell and actual feel of handling film.

Cinematographer John Bailey talks about his own experience with the future.

With the steady improvement in computer software and digital compositing, the field of animation has been revolutionized. Very few have the patience or skill required for traditional stop-motion photography. Computer generated animation has grown so sophisticated that now no matter how stupid the movie, the monsters look great! What these films often lack is a real sense of magic and personality.

Michael Atkinson's appreciation of Ray Harryhausen, *Stop-Motion JimJams*, pays tribute to the man whose work has inspired so many. As a "special effects man" Ray's place in cinema is unique. He is perhaps the only "technician" who can be considered the auteur of his movies, almost always written and directed by others. Yet, conceptually, and in the exquisite execution of his visionary FX work, the movies are in a very real sense his.

Harryhausen is a remarkable and unassuming guy who has recently celebrated his 80th birthday. Ray and his wife Diana travel the world accepting accolades wherever they go. Nice work if you can get it.

John Landis

FILM OR DIGITAL? DON'T FIGHT. COEXIST.

by John Bailey

The ninth-floor screening room of DuArt Lab, on West 55th Street in Manhattan, is a home away from home for many exhausted filmmakers. They collapse into its chairs late at night to munch pizza while watching the "dailies" of their current production. I know it well. I have photographed a dozen feature films in New York in the last 15 years. So what was I doing a few weeks ago arriving in broad daylight carrying a roll of 35-millimeter film that had just arrived from a lab in Los Angeles?

I just had to see 15 minutes of *The Anniversary Party,* the feature-length drama starring Jennifer Jason Leigh and Alan Cumming, which I had photographed this past summer, as soon as the film was ready. In the strictest sense, *Anniversary Party* is not a "film" at all. It is a movie shot—"captured" is the term of choice—on digital videotape. And this reel, which I pass to the whimsical projectionist Norberto Valle Jr., is the first segment processed for theatrical release: color corrected and transferred to 35-millimeter film by two Los Angeles companies in the forefront of digital imaging.

As Norberto threads the projector, he proudly tells me of his daughter's studies at Princeton. And the moment seems to crystallize the meeting point of several different journeys: her future, my past and the possibilities for a technology that could become the launch vehicle for Hollywood movies as they soar somewhat uncertainly into the digital skies—trailing behind them the last vestiges of many jobs like Norberto's.

The American cinema's past has for the last 30 years been intertwined with the rise of American film schools. Many of the producers, directors, writers, cinematographers, and editors making mainstream movies today are graduates of those schools, and, like me, most have made their movies on 35-millimeter motion picture film. But a friend who teaches cinematography at a major film school recently lamented that his students were refusing to shoot their projects on film. This generation of filmmakers-to-be grew up with camcorders, and they find it bothersome to learn what they call the "technical stuff," like focus and exposure. They relish the immediacy of video and consider its hands-on ease of operation a birthright.

But in 1969, a few years out of film school at the University of Southern California, I happily joined the major film union, The International Alliance of Theatrical Stage Employees, as an assistant cameraman—to do the "technical stuff." The first studio film I worked on was Monte Hellman's cult classic *Two-Lane Blacktop*. Seven years later, I was the camera operator on *Days of Heaven,* a film by Terrence Malick. The Academy Award-winning cinematography of the late Néstor Almendros on this movie remains a touchstone for the ravishing beauty and luminous detail that celluloid film can capture. Since 1978, I have used this medium to photograph more than 40 feature films, from *American Gigolo* and *Ordinary People* to *As Good as It Gets*—all of them photographed, printed, and exhibited on motion picture film. When *The Anniversary Party* is released later this year, it too, will be printed and exhibited on film. But its capture, on digital video, was my first foray into the world my friend's students take for granted.

I used the European PAL 25-frame system, which promises a clearer, more resolved image than the current American standard, NTSC. But all the video systems being embraced by a new generation of "digerati" are poor stepchildren to the one developed by Sony and Panavision. Called HD 24P because of its higher definition, this is the camera George Lucas recently used to photograph the forthcoming *Star Wars: Episode II,* the one for which he expressed such unqualified enthusiasm, the one whose result he called "indistinguishable from film."

His claim has ignited a firestorm of rebuttal from dissenting filmmakers, some of whom have seen and used the HD 24P video camera in tests and actual production. Many filmmakers are convinced that celluloid film is still far superior to digital videotape in tone, texture, color, and the capacity to resolve detail and complex patterns. They further claim that film cameras have more flexibility and reliability in actual work conditions, and that motion picture film and cameras are capable of significant refinement beyond current levels. No less a filmmaker than Steven Spielberg has said that so long as film labs remain open, he will make his movies on film.

When I began photographing *Anniversary Party* in Los Angeles for its costars, who also wrote and directed it, I had no intention of being sucked into this maelstrom. For me, the worst part of the hysteria is that it is the manufacturers and studio marketers who seem most invested in getting rid of film and who stand to rake in the most profits. For them, it is not an issue of creative expression aesthetics, or improved picture quality. It is an issue of bottom-line economics. In their hoped-for environment of total control of the means of distribution and exhibition, millions of dollars would be saved on each film by eliminating bulky film negatives and prints. Elaborate encoding formulas would also act as a curb on piracy and unlicensed exhibition.

But what is at stake is too important to be left to the number crunchers. If cinema is the defining art form of our time, the artists who make the movies, who create the drama, and execute the images that so move us, should also be its custodians. If image capture is now the major battlefield in this film-versus-video war, the cinematographer is on the front line. His skilled eyes see to it that the work of writers, directors, editors, and designers is conveyed properly to the audience; the cinematographer must be heard, not just enlisted for an ex-post-facto rubber stamping (as happened in the development of the 16-by-9 format for high-definition TV). For if the video-equipment manufacturers and the accountants looking for ever larger profit margins have their way, movies on celluloid film will soon exist only in temperature- and humidity-controlled vaults, nothing more than revered icons of a lost, lamented "Silver Age."

On the other hand, times do change, and no one wants to be left behind. Which brings me back to *The Anniversary Party.* Jennifer Jason Leigh and Alan Cumming wanted to tell the story of an intimate gathering of friends that goes terribly wrong. They asked some of their friends—Kevin Kline, Phoebe Cates, John C. Reilly, Gwyneth Paltrow, Jane Adams, John Hickey, Parker Posey, Mina Badie, and Jennifer Beals—to act in it with them. Because of its very low budget (despite the cast), its superfast 19-day shooting schedule and its informal video techniques, Jennifer and Alan call it their "home movie."

In agreeing to photograph it for them on video, I was responding to their desire to give the movie a sense of immediacy and spontaneity while reflecting the lush, upscale lifestyle of its characters. I was also hoping to answer for myself questions that had arisen during my participation in a panel discussion on new technology at last year's Sundance Festival. The audience of predominantly young filmmakers seemed, along with most of the panel, convinced that film (celluloid) was dead. This was news to me, even though dozens of articles have been consistently making the point for a year. But it did seem that the days when student filmmakers complained bitterly of having to use video cameras on their first-year projects were gone. Film had become, in these circles, decidedly unhip.

I have sympathy with these young film artists seeking to redefine the medium. My own generation of film students—Martin Scorsese, Paul Schrader, Francis Ford Coppola, William Friedkin, Brian De Palma—fell under the spell of the French New Wave of the 60's, which had taken film and sociopolitical issues onto the streets and into the cafes of Paris. Within a few years, my peers were adapting the New Wave's revolutionary techniques to American cinema creating a radical and fresh style that is now established movie grammar. How different are these young people, dazzled by the possibilities opened by Dogma 95, the Danish movement?

Begun by the directors Thomas Vinterberg and Lars Von Trier, Dogma 95 rejects the use of lighting, camera dollies, scored music, and a host of other tools of mainstream cinema. Its reductionist aesthetic is a perfect framework for the spontaneity and improvisatory tendencies of many digital video movies. It argues for a democratization of the medium. Thousands of these movies are now being churned out by young people working without any studio oversight, hopeful that their cinema will capture the ever-elusive zeitgeist of a culture hell-bent on moving on to the Next New Thing.

So when Jennifer and Alan asked me to photograph *Anniversary Party* on digital video rather than film, I embraced the concept in a spirit of discovery and reinvention. My wife, Carol Littleton, who is editing the movie, speculated that if our friend Larry Kasdan were to make *The Big Chill* with us today, we might encourage him to use digital video (even though we know that posterity might not have access to it, just as we can no longer view some of the more than 70 video formats that have come and gone since videotape was introduced).

So here I am at the DuArt screening room to review this first reel of film rendered from the original video. These final scenes of *Anniversary Party* contain both day and night sequences and shots made in very high-contrast sunlight. What I see is a surprise: after watching it a few times, I decide that the video-to-film footage looks much better than I had expected.

Of course, this isn't an accident. Throughout the shooting and postproduction, state-of-the-art techniques were used to optimize picture quality. First, a master digital videotape was assembled from a clone of the original camera tapes. Then, using a DaVinci 2K digital color-correction system, Mike Sowa at Laser-Pacific Media Corporation made a final master on the D1 format. From this, David Hays at the video facility E-Film made a 35-millimeter film negative on an Arri laser recorder, the best of all the current tape-to-film machines. The negative was further corrected for color and density at Deluxe Lab by the film timer Mike Milliken. This is the elaborate, costly and time-consuming journey any digital movie makes to reach the projectors of a local multiplex; a movie captured on 35-millimeter film is simply printed at the lab.

Is this final result in the tape-to-film process as good as film, as good as film printed from an original film negative? Well, I can only say it is different, fundamentally different. To understand why, we have to look at the differences in the capture surfaces, where the image is created. The silver halide crystals embedded in the film emulsion, the surface that contains the pictorial record, are random and continuous. There is no definite pattern to the crystal array, called grain, and it is assuredly an analog process. Shadow and highlight detail, color definition and image sharpness can have an enormous range and subtlety, limited only by the size of the negative frame itself. Whether Super-8 or Imax, it is the same film. Video capture, however, happens on a chip called a CCD. The limiting factor is not just the size of the chip but the number of pixels on it. These pixels are not random or shifting. Their position is fixed. A good analogy for the pixel array is an image made of mosaic tiles.

Imagine that the position and defining borders of the tiles remain static as the images on the tiles continually change. The question arises: is this pattern apparent even subliminally? Does the static pixel array of digital video render images whose quality is fundamentally different from those created by the ever shifting, random movement of film grain? Is the dreamlike state of suspension that we associate with film inherent in its photochemical architecture?

Joerg Agin, president of the Entertainment Imaging division of Eastman Kodak, compared the current state of film and digital video capture in a report in a recent issue of the International Cinematographers Guild magazine. In Mr. Agin's view, if you were to scan a single frame of 35-millimeter color negative film, you could convert it to a digital file of 9 million to 12 million pixels. The CCD recording chip of the Sony HD 24P camera records effectively about two million pixels for each of the three primary colors, significantly less than the number of a high-quality film frame. This is a theoretical comparison, and some video engineers dismiss such numbers, as the technologies are totally different. But I find it a helpful way to explain the difference to nontechno-geek filmgoers. Many other technical and aesthetic considerations—contrast, exposure latitude, color definition, frame rates, and exposure sensitivity—also enter the equation; and none of these seems to tip the balance toward any existing video system. In addition, in an era of "run and gun" production, working cinematographers and directors must assess the equipment's portability, speed of setup, and reliability under extremes of weather.

While serving on the foreign film committee of the Academy of Motion Picture Arts and Sciences over the last six weeks, I watched feature films from more than 35 countries. Several used elaborate digital techniques, like the Taiwanese *Crouching Tiger, Hidden Dragon.* But some, like Portugal's *Too Late* (shot in the mud and tidal waters of the Tagus River) or Iran's *Time for Drunken Horses* (shot in the extreme cold and snow of the mountains bordering Iraq), favor the proven durability of film cameras.

After finishing the film rendering of *The Anniversary Party,* I had the opportunity to participate with two fellow cinematographers, Aaron Schneider and James Chressanthis, in a test sponsored by Eastman Kodak. Kodak, deeply involved in digital imaging as well as its traditional film business, wanted a fair comparison of film and video for presentations. So we shot with film and video cameras side by side under exactly the same conditions.

BOTH systems were used in challenging photographic situations—all the tests I had seen previously were made under very controlled conditions favorable to video. I attempted to use both the film and video cameras in more stressful and revealing settings. The results are being finished on both tape and film, and will be shown in both media. On the basis of my initial viewings, I don't expect to abandon film any time soon. And that is the medium I will employ with the director Callie Khouri for *Divine Secrets of the Ya-Ya Sisterhood,* which we will start shooting in early April.

For the most part, *Anniversary Party* was shot with the technical polish that is the hallmark of mainstream Hollywood films. We adopted a Dogma 95 aesthetic only for an early scene of a game of charades, and then in the climactic scenes in which the characters' close-knit relationships begin to unravel under the influence of the drug Ecstasy. So *Anniversary Party* is a kind of hybrid, a movie made by traditional filmmakers using tools and techniques of the newer medium. And here, it seems to me, lies the lesson at the core of the whole film-or-digital debate.

In the mid-19th century, within a decade of the invention of photography, writers announced the imminent death of painting. But in fact the rise of photography freed painting from its more onerous task of simply recording reality. Beginning with Impressionism and onward through Abstract Expressionism, painting re-created itself. Photography and painting cross-fertilized each other in an ongoing dialogue throughout the 20th century. Film and video can do this in the 21st. They should coexist, not compete, each pursuing and further developing its unique qualities. It is unfortunate that much of the current dialogue consists of partisans of one medium attacking partisans of the other from behind ever more entrenched battle lines. Perhaps it will be a new generation of viewers now in their infancy, with eyes not yet trained to the look and texture of film, who will calmly assess and accept the limits and merits of each.

STOP-MOTION JIMJAMS: RAY HARRYHAUSEN

by Michael Atkinson

For me it was the harpies. At 10 already my medulla throbbed with images of appalling, haywire lunacy—dinosaurs stalking the streets of Tribeca, 30-foot fiddler crabs, two-headed Roc hatchlings, alien saucers crash landing into the Capitol dome, gargantuan octopi ripping down the Golden Gate Bridge, hydras and cyclopes and platoons of sword-brandishing skeletons. At least I could sleep. for the most part, through the lurching, proportion-screwing dreams it all spawned. But the harpies, bluish, leathery, and creepy as a cold spot in a strange cellar, kept fluttering over me, *picking* at me, and I couldn't sleep peaceably for weeks.

Revisiting the berserk stop-motion world of Ray Harryhausen, after a childhood spent retrieving my eyeballs from under the TV and slapping them back in my head in time for the next centaur to gallop across the screen is like picking through old toys you'd thought the Salvation Army had carted away long ago. Ridiculous, sublime, and sadly antiquated by industry standards ever since the body-snatching infestation of digital animation (which places us somewhere in the mid-80s; even the *Star Wars* films, in their original versions, relied on Harryhausenish frame-by-frame figure movement), Harryhausen's is the most literal mythopoeic cinema ever constructed. He reigned supreme for three decades as the single most accomplished F/X wizard in the world, running from his apprenticeship to Willis O'Brien on *Mighty Joe Young* (1946) to *Clash of the Titans* (1981), his official swansong. Nearly anyone whose home harbored a TV in the 60s and 70s has the familiar Harryhausen topos imbedded on his or her alpha waves: the lizard-hipped postures, roiling reptilian tails and many-armed sabre-fights, the disturbing flexibility of stone and bronze colossi, the skeletons come to life in the ancient-Greek noonlight, the warping of scale perspectives, the in-our-face manifestations of nightmarish mythic archetypes, the weird, jittery sharpness of impossible entities, etc. There could have been no casual dalliance with fable, Biblical or otherwise, in the Indy Jones movies, nor the theropodian thrills of *Jurassic Park*, without Harryhausen's precedent. If there is a Jungian collective unconscious that can indeed be glimpsed through the looking-glass of primitive myth, then

Harryhausen alone gave its archetypes cinematic life. If movies are indeed universal, then Harryhausen's images are their bete noires, the shuddery daydreams of ancient man terrorized on the plain by the new idea of half-man/half-anything monsters and godly whim.

Though they do literally belong to an exclusively preadolescent universe—these are the best *toys*, after all; who didn't want an 18-inch-high, fully posable latex cyclops to play with?—Harryhausen's movies opt less for Joseph Campbell's heroic brand of mythmania than for the mythic image's hellzapoppin expression of disquiet and horror. Only rarely did a Harryhausen critter's breach of the reality web not tap into a primal fear—the tiny Eohippus in *The Valley of Gwangi*, the R2D2-ish owl in *Clash of the Titans*, for two. Otherwise, welcome to the jungle: the pterodactyl lifting a cowboy off his horse and flying away in *Gwangi*, humans trapped in a giant honeycomb by a 20-foot honeybee in *Mysterious Island*, the seven skeletons ("the children of Hydra's teeth") rising swords-first from the dirt and falling en masse into battle stances (squa tront! as the old E.C. Comics used to say) in Harryhausen's premier achievement, *Jason and the Argonauts*. The dynamic of human-meets-leviathan is perpetual, hopeless combat. *Jason* also features the unsettling vision of the bronze giant Talos, tottering across a Greek beach before Jason unplugs his heel and lets the water out, as well as those harpies, which still plague me. Maybe they embody, like much of Harryhausen's work, a deathless instinct for superstitious loathing within that collective unconscious; maybe they're just fucking scary.

Archetypal anxiety had always been Harryhausen's basic text, whether he knew it or not; his first full-length films were classic Cold War expressions of atomic unease, Otherliness and cosmocentric hate. *The Beast from 20,000 Fathoms* is a seminally American take on primeval chaos visiting death upon the modern metropolis (and, eventually, Coney Island), and the freeway-decimating octopus in *It Came From Beneath the Sea* abstracted that idea further, into pure aquarium jimjams. *Earth vs. the Flying Saucers* remains one of the era's most rabid UFO movies, whose aliens display unbridled, even unreasonable, hostility toward the old U.S. of A.; though the film remains a template for any reading you'd care to give, the emphasis on military confrontation and federal icons is targeted directly at Moscow. After Hiroshima, America imagined anything could happen, and in a Harryhausen movie it certainly, dependably would, preferably in or around a familiar and disposable landmark. (And the films were his; the credited directors were as negligible as the actors.)

His move to ancient myth, Raquel Welch dinosaur sagas and Jules Verne seemed prescient, as the tense and placid Cold War segued into the more complicated 60s, but his shuddery world-gone-mad scenarios just got buggier. All the same, the primitive allure of their frame-by-laborious-frame F/X was just as fascinating—we all knew how the effects were managed, and the subtechnological beauty of the tarnished Talos or the manacled dragon in *The 7th Voyage of Sinbad* seemed, well, myth-like in its own right. Whether it be Méliès, the German Expressionists, the cheaply contrived monster insects of the 50s, or the contemporary junky retro-designs of Gilliam, Caro/Jeunet, and Guy Maddin, the *artificiallia* of fantastic imagery—the zipper on the monster suit, as it were—has a distinctive, instantly antiquated lustre that seamless visual effects cannot match. The fantastic tangibility of Harryhausen's creations is what made them memorable—unlike computer animated figures, which move with an unnatural yet unthreatening fluidity, Harryhausen's homely behemoths obey the same laws of movement that constrain the actors, and inhabit the same space, turf, and sunlight. Their three-dimensionality is not illusory, and their hesitant, unblurred motions are strangely poignant.

Sinbad's cyclops or Jason's Talos aren't real, after all, and yet their liberation from the rush-hour time tunnel at the back of each kid's skull made reality a dubious quantity. More literal than Bosch or Giotto, Méliès or De Mille, Harryhausen's images take the possibility of phantasmata seriously, without once succumbing to showbiz tricksterism or even expressionistic rifts. At all times, the dinosaurs and griffins obey physical laws, mythic prescriptions, and the logic of magic. (Who knew that you could raze a 100-foot bronze titan by unplugging his heel? It seemed to make perfect sense.) Indeed, Harryhausen's world became truly timeless once his Cold War sci-fi days were over; his submersion into myth and Mesozoic tarpits was complete, never acknowledging current fashions or cultural obsessions, never referencing anything outside the hermetic demands of his ancient sources. When his filmmaking methods approached obsolescence, he retired rather than pollute his deranged, pantheistic biosphere with slicker technology. He'd already shown us a cyclops and dragon fighting to the death—even if it's filmed again with the liquidiest computer visuals megabucks can buy, we've already seen it, for *real*. As F/X capabilities accelerate, I can easily imagine Harryhausen's rough-hewn images taking on the raw, gritty integrity of news footage. Perhaps that's what Ray had in mind all along.

Studies in an alternate physical truth of a kind only cinema can muster, movies like *Jason, Mysterious Island, It Came from Beneath the Sea* and the Sinbad epics could be read as an audiovisual library of mythic experience—the jolt of seeing those harpies for the first time can't help but approximate the funky disquiet of a B.C. plebe hearing about them around the pre-European cave fire. At the very least, the films should be required viewing for anyone under

12, the soil of whose brainpans have dampened and grown moldy in recent times with the vigorous polishing playing Sega provides. One three-fingered, many-headed Harryhausen monster chasing real people through a torchlit cavern could set the mud on fire.

"When the major studios began to do a similar type of film, they couldn't really call them exploitation pictures. I like the words 'high concept' very much.

—Roger Corman

GENRE

GENRE IS A fancy word for type, as in, "what type of movie is it?" Musical? Western? Film noir? War? Action? Horror?

Maria Di Battista discusses one of my favorite films, *His Girl Friday.* While some would say this qualifies as a Screwball Comedy, Ms. Di Battista calls it a *Female Rampant.*

I made a movie in 1991 called *Innocent Blood* from a clever screenplay by Michael Wolk. I mention it because David Remnick's article *Is This the End of Rico?* is about HBO's smash hit *The Sopranos.* In Remnick's discussion of the Gangster Genre is the key as to why my approach to my gangster/vampire movie has similarities to David Chase's approach in *The Sopranos.* We even share much of the same cast!

John Landis

IS THIS THE END OF RICO?

by David Remnick

Ever since the early thirties, when Charles (Lucky) Luciano tamed the more anarchic impulses of the Mob, it has been an article of local faith that the greater metropolitan area is controlled by the Five Families. There are, as it happens, five and a half—the half being the DeCavalcantes of Union County, the only freestanding Mob family in New Jersey. Like their more powerful cousins across the river, the DeCavalcantes have in recent years suffered the indignities of federal investigation and the decimation of their numbers, so much so that they are experiencing the *agita* of existential dread. National franchisers now haul most of the trash; the pharaonic earners of Florham Park and Belleville are sweating over subpoenas; and, in the city, Little Italy dissolves into Chinatown while tourists stand on Mulberry Street summoning the memory of Crazy Joe Gallo's last supper. It's all on the fade. As the late columnist Murray Kempton once asked, "Where are the scungilli of yesteryear?"

The first blow to the DeCavalcantes came in the early sixties, when the F.B.I. planted a bug in the Kenilworth offices of the don, Simone Rizzo DeCavalcante, known as Sam the Plumber—plumbing supplies being one of his favored businesses. Already, in those wiretaps, one could sense that the Mob's influence was not quite what we believed it to be. "We got thirty-one or thirty-two soldiers," DeCavalcante is overheard saying. "Most of them are old people who ain't making much." In another tape, he sounds like a salaried municipal worker computing his pension: "If I can continue for two or three years, I will be able to show forty thousand or fifty thousand dollars legitimately and can walk out. Then my family situation will be resolved." Sam the Plumber's plans for his golden years were derailed only slightly—he spent 1971 through 1973 in prison. A few years after his release, he abandoned north Jersey for a condo in Fort Lauderdale. He died, at liberty, in 1997.

The DeCavalcante family is centered in Elizabeth, with branch offices at the Jersey shore, in Toms River, and in southern Brooklyn. In January of 1998, investigators started to undermine the DeCavalcantes as thoroughly as they had the Five Families. Federal agents wired an informer, who proved so cunning a rat that he almost won his stripes as a made man. Finally, the F.B.I. took the snitch out of action, spirited him away to the witness-protection program, and arrested fifty-eight men, among them one of the family's acting bosses, Vincent (Vinny Ocean) Palermo. Dozens of members will come to trial soon on charges of murder, extortion, loan-sharking, bookmaking, robbery, mail fraud, and trafficking in stolen property.

The wiretaps were both useful and sad. According to the *News,* the F.B.I. learned of the family's grandest designs, their plans to sell everything from stolen Viagra tablets on the Internet to an ersatz "original" screenplay for *The Wizard of Oz*. One can hardly imagine the omnipotent Corleones planning, as the DeCavalcantes did, to forge "vintage" Superman comic books and sell them. "That would kill the comic industry," an associate named Sal Calciano says with evident satisfaction. "Nobody ever did it. Nobody ever [expletive] thought of it before."

Perhaps all that will be left of the DeCavalcante legacy is the plaintive tone of their wiretaps. Joseph (Joey O) Masella, Palermo's driver, seems typically forlorn, an emblematic mobster at the fin de siècle. The F.B.I. has served his grandmother with a subpoena. His wife has thrown his clothes onto the lawn. His kid needs a therapist; his girlfriend wants breast implants. He can afford neither. Masella is in debt all around town. Fatherhood drives him mad. He calls his ex-wife and begs her to take the kids off his hands. "Come and get your daughters. I can't take it no more," he says. "You left me this responsibility. I'm fifty years old. I can't [expletive] breathe. I'm dyin' over here." His humiliation is complete. "I don't want it," Masella says. "The whole [expletive] life. Who the [expletive] wants it, I don't want it." But Masella can't get out. He owes a hundred thousand dollars to various gangsters, who are not likely to forgive him or his debt. In June, 1998, Palermo, by way of warning, kicks Masella in the groin and tells him he'd better get square. "You know, by rights, I gotta kill you," Palermo says. Not good. On October 10, 1998, Masella was found dead in a parking lot in Marine Park with bullet holes in his pancreas, stomach, spleen, and intestine. Palermo was charged with the hit.

A couple of months later, Home Box Office began broadcasting a new series about a New Jersey crime family, *The Sopranos.* Their domain is Essex County, not Union—a critical difference. The show, a creation of a television writer and producer from north Jersey named David Chase, has none of the operatic moralism and ambition of *The Godfather* pictures but, rather, combines the *gavone* camaraderie of *GoodFellas,* the free-associative comedy of *Portnoy's Complaint,* and the kitchen-table agonies of *The Honeymooners.* Tony Soprano, played sublimely by the Gleasonesque James Gandolfini, is paterfamilias to both his crew (Big Pussy, Silvio, Paulie Walnuts, et al.) and his extended suburban family. Like the late Joey O Masella, Tony Soprano is everywhere persecuted by circumstance and the dramatis personae of his life: his demonic mother, Livia, despises him; his uncle Junior betrays him; his sister, Janice, exploits him; his wife, Carmela, lectures him; his sullen children, Meadow and Anthony, Jr., ignore him; and the F.B.I. surveils him. And, like Joey O, Tony is depressed. It's all too much. He has nightmares and panic attacks; he sees a therapist; he takes Prozac and Xanax.

The critics have swooned. Even the most expert commentators admire the show. On March 3,1999, some DeCavalcante members, an enforcer named Joseph (Tin Ear) Sclafani and a capo named Anthony Rotondo, are overheard on the wiretaps remarking on the uncanny resemblance between this thing of ours and this thing of theirs. "Hey, what's this fucking thing, *Sopranos*?" Tin Ear asks. "What the fuck are they? . . . Is that supposed to be us?"

Rotondo knows all. "What characters. Great acting." He adds, "Every show you watch, more and more you pick up somebody. One week it was Corky, one week it was, well, from the beginning it was Albert G."

Sclafani, however, feels ignored, a Jersey guy's anxiety: "I'm not even existing over there," he says.

The producers of *The Sopranos* shoot the exteriors in Lodi, North Caldwell, Verona, Newark. The interiors—the Soprano house, the office in the Bada Bing strip club, and the office of Dr. Melfi, Tony's therapist—are shot in Queens, at the old Silvercup bakery, which has been a television studio since 1983. I visited the set a few weeks ago, as Chase was filming the thirteenth and final episode of the season. Chase is fifty-five, a trim, wary, almost expressionless man with hooded eyes and the sardonic wit of one who seems utterly distrustful of his current success. He has spent his adult life working in television, all the while dreaming of making feature films. There is a vestigial core of self-loathing in him. "Television is crap, and I don't watch it," he told me. "I only watched it as a kid." At Stanford film school, Chase made a gangster movie, for twelve hundred dollars, called *The Rise and Fall of Bug Manousous,* about a man who is fed up with life, escapes into a fantasy of being a twenties mobster, and then dies in his own fantasy.

"I thought that maybe one day I would get to smoke Gauloises and make little dark enigmatic pictures," Chase said. In the beginning, he worked on the crew of a few soft-core features, "pussycat-theatre stuff." Chase said he had a job on one film "with two legitimate actors, about a senator's daughter who meets a handsome guy at a ski lodge. They wanted to distribute it as a legitimate picture, but if it failed they would do some 'insertion footage.' "

Over the years, Chase has written nine feature scripts, none of which have been produced. There were some close calls with the likes of Ridley Scott and Michael Mann, but, he said, "I could never get anything going." Soon he was making money, quite a lot of money, working in television, including some decent shows like *The Rockford Files* and *Northern Exposure*, and yet he complained all the while, to his wife, to his daughter, to his therapist. "I felt cowardly," he said. "The most important piece of career advice my wife gave me was, if it's fulfilling for you, do it. And I mostly have not followed that." Then he revamped a lingering idea: to portray a suburban American family and cloak the story in the details of an ancient genre—the gangster film. Fox, CBS, NBC, and ABC all turned down Chase's pilot for *The Sopranos*. And a good thing, too: with commercial breaks and network censors, *The Sopranos* undoubtedly would have become castrati.

At HBO, Chase has nearly unlimited creative control and *The Sopranos* wins, by cable standards, unprecedented ratings. For all that, Chase is still dubious about television—"I always wanted to get out of the television business and would still like to"—but on the set he seemed to work in a warm zone of engagement and satisfaction. He sat behind the director, John Patterson, as Gandolfini and Lorraine Bracco, who plays Dr. Melfi, started working on a therapist's-office scene in which Tony despairs of his son and of his failures in school. Gandolfini appears in practically every scene and, as a result, often works shooting days that run fourteen, sixteen hours. Like certain athletes, he psychs himself into concentration through a weird verbal violence: a shout, a snort, a nasty, self-directed epithet. When he blows a scene, his reaction can be volcanic.

Bracco was as lighthearted as Gandolfini was fierce. This was her last scene of the season. It began with Tony expressing his concern for a friend of the family, Jackie Aprile, Jr.

"Twenty-two years old, living in a housing project. Can you imagine the shame for the family?" All the while, Gandolfini is twitching, scratching his earlobe, working out a crick in his neck, wincing, every gesture another betrayal of anxiety and dread.

"In the end," Tony says, "I failed him." He shrugs, shrugs magnificently. "What the fuck you gonna do?" This is Tony's customary reaction to death, to disaster: his defense mechanism. "What the fuck you gonna do in this world today?"

And then Lorraine Bracco lets rip with a whoopee cushion that she sneaked onto the set. Gandolfini, it can be fairly said, loses his concentration.

"Next line!" he barks.

Again with the whoopee cushion.

"Jesus!"

Now Bracco and Gandolfini are laughing.

Chase leans over and whispers, "It's the last week of school."

Bracco has pulled such stunts before. Not long ago, in another therapy scene, she stuck hair extensions under her skirt, and, just as Gandolfini was delivering a line, she crossed her legs, a parody of Sharon Stone in *Basic Instinct*.

"I don't think we've got anything here yet," John Patterson said.

Bracco could not stop laughing: "I can't help it. At least they're not the silent, stinky ones."

They settle down. Action!

"Twenty-two years old. Living in a housing project. Can you. . . . Fuck!"

Gandolfini gets out of his chair and walks to the office's antechamber. He takes a long sip of Coke and makes a call on his cell phone. He hangs up and sighs hugely. "It's like pulling fucking teeth!" he barks. Gandolfini's Jersey accent (he's from middle-class Park Ridge, in Bergen County) is softer than Tony's, but it is not entirely clear from the sound of his voice who is talking. "Fuckin' teeth!" Then he goes back inside and tries again. And screws it up again. "It's fucking unbelievable. I can't say anything!" He goes out, and says, "I don't know what I'm fucking talking about."

Finally, Gandolfini returns to the analyst's chair and nails the scene. Time for lunch. It is five o'clock in the afternoon.

David Chase grew up on Mob movies, and even with a considerable awareness of Mob reality. He watched *The Untouchables* on Thursday nights and *The Public Enemy* on *Million Dollar Movie*. His family, which changed its name from DeCesare to Chase, was middle class. His father had a hardware store, and his mother worked for the telephone company. In school, he knew the son of a mobster, and he read transporting crime stories in the now defunct Newark *Evening News* about the Boiardo family, a Genovese crew working in Essex County. And yet the most powerful autobiographical presence in *The Sopranos* derives not from the Mob but from family. Tony's mother, Livia (the name of Tiberius's harridan mother in *I, Claudius*), is modelled on Chase's own, he told me, "though I should point out that she never tried to have me killed." Nancy Marchand, who died last year, played the role so chillingly that, with the mere wave of her hand, sons across the nation, Italian or otherwise, could feel the zing of guilt along their spines. "My mother was so downbeat, so relentlessly pessimistic—and that, in Livia, all comes from her," Chase said. "That way of waving her hand in disgust, that comes from her, too. And all those lines: 'I wish the Lord would take me now'; 'I won't talk to anyone on the phone after dark.'

"I used to tell people stories about talking to my mother, and I got endless laughs with the shocking things she said—how she made a mandate of 'I have to speak my mind' and 'Do you think you're going to change me now?' and 'I'm no phony,' all under the banner of honesty. I remember she told me, in front of my wife, 'You'll get bored with her.' We're married thirty-three years. . . . I felt sometimes that she was like a performance artist, and her act was her level of pessimism about everything."

In *The Sopranos,* the Mafia life is not so much the central subject as it is the intensifying agent. The conventions of the Mob heighten the conventions and contradictions of a modern family. The violence, which is horrific but rare, undermines everyone's ambition to be normal. Livia does not merely disapprove of her son. She tries to get him whacked. Tony tries to help his friend Artie Bucco, so he burns down his restaurant. Carmela is full of churchly moral posturing ("What's different between you and me is you're going to Hell when you die!"), but she happily spends Tony's blood money, and, with his skill for threat, she shakes down a woman to write a college recommendation for her daughter, Meadow. ("I want you to write that letter," she says evenly.) And at Meadow's school, Verbum Dei, the soccer coach turns out to be a child molester. The great surprise is that Tony, blissed out on Vicodin and booze, doesn't have Coach Hauser killed. From therapy, he has learned proportion.

An episode of *The Sopranos* typically has a primary and a secondary plot, with thirteen or so scenes, or "beats," each; there is a tertiary plot, with five or six beats; and there are, possibly, one or two additional miniplots, with just a couple of beats. In one of the shapeliest of Chase's episodes, "College," from the first season, Tony takes Meadow on a trip to look at schools in Maine. This is a signal event for a parent and child of the upper-middle classes, a period of enforced intimacy, just as the child is about to leave home forever. It is a time for truthtelling. For the Sopranos, everything is somehow more so. In the car, Meadow asks her father, "Are you in the Mafia?" Tony confesses, up to a point, but protests that if he wasn't doing what he was doing he'd be selling patio furniture on Route 22. In Maine, Tony encounters a former rival who was in the witness-protection program, and, while Meadow is interviewing at Colby, he garrotes the rat with an electrical cord.

Afterward, Meadow seems to know what's happened. ("Your hand is bleeding!") Meanwhile, at home in Jersey, Carmela, played with deadpan brilliance by Edie Falco, feeds baked ziti and red wine to the parish priest, Father Phil—and they *almost* have a one-night stand as they watch the repressed lovers in *The Remains of the Day* on DVD. This season, the parental theme has got even more pronounced as Anthony, Jr., descends into the murk of adolescence and Meadow, now a freshman at Columbia, dates a half Jewish, half African American young man, whom Tony refers to, alternately, as "Sambo" and "Buckwheat." The Soprano kids are not, as kids are elsewhere on television, funny, triumphant, or powerful; they are grotesquely, realistically confused.

A few days after shooting ended, I met Chase for coffee. We talked about a particularly good scene in the season opener in which Anthony, Jr., is trying to figure out *Stopping by Woods on a Snowy Evening*. Meadow, with a few weeks of Columbia behind her, helps out with all the critical self-possession of Northrop Frye. She tries to get him to see that the whiteness, the snow, in Robert Frost's scheme is symbolic of death. Anthony, Jr., cries out, "But I thought *black* meant death!" In *The Sopranos,* even homework is ominous.

"Instead of doing *Eight Is Enough* or something, we set it in a situation of life and death," Chase said. "The Mob provides an essential set of contradictions in Tony Soprano's character. It also gives you the possibility of danger and then hours of nondanger. And it gives you a world that is something allegedly private and secret.

"I thought the Mob was expired as a movie form before we ever started," Chase went on. "I wouldn't care if this were the last Mob movie. I have nothing invested in Mob movies."

Does *The Sopranos,* with all its postmodern self-awareness, with all its evidence of decline, signal the end of the Mafia movie? Will the Mob movie go the way of the Western, revived rarely and only then as something nostalgic (*Unforgiven*), sensational (*The Wild Bunch*), or comic (*Blazing Saddles*)? It is remarkable to think now how such a rich movie genre came out of such a small, violent, and hermetic world. There were a few silent Mob pictures of distinction—D. W. Griffith's 1912 short *The Musketeers of Pig Alley,* Raoul Walsh's *The Regeneration* (1915), and Josef von Sternberg's *Underworld* (1927)—but the first golden age was ushered in by two events: the advent of sound, in 1927, which gave us the jolt of gunfire and the bite of the gangsters' slang and wit, and the St. Valentine's Day Massacre, in 1929, which made Al Capone a national media figure. Three films released between 1931 and 1932—Mervyn LeRoy's *Little Caesar,* William Wellman's *Public Enemy,* and Howard Hawks's *Scarface*—set the standard. Both David Chase and Tony Soprano adore them and the theme they established. As Robert Warshow pointed out in his 1948 essay "The Gangster as Tragic Hero," the appeal of these pictures, beyond their visceral excitement and their opportunity for escapism, resides in "that part of the American psyche which rejects the qualities and the demands of modern life, which rejects 'Americanism' itself," the comfort and conformity, the sunny optimism and unbounded opportunity. The gangster in these movies is a man whose response to harsh circumstance is brutal and ultimately doomed. He is possessed of perverse ambition and perverse nobility. With our ids, we enjoy his murderous ascent, we delight in his malapropisms and limitless appetites, and with our superegos we are satisfied by his inevitable fall, we feel a sense of superiority and relief.

The enjoyment of gangster pictures is a guilty pleasure, and, in the early thirties, Hollywood could not distribute these movies without at least making a show of contrition. Both *The Public Enemy* and *Little Caesar* begin with warning labels in the guise of sermons. After seeing the name James Cagney and the rest of the cast list for Wellman 's picture, we read the message "It is the ambition of the authors of *The Public Enemy* to honestly depict an environment that exists today in a certain strata of American life, rather than glorify the hoodlum or the criminal." *Little Caesar* begins with a quotation from the Book of Matthew printed on faux parchment: " . . . for all they that take the sword shall perish with the sword."

In both pictures, the hero (or antihero, as he would be called later on) rises from small-time criminal to singular status in the big city and is then pursued and killed. This is, more or less, the arc of all Mob pictures: the brutal man who believes himself invulnerable and then ends up dead in the gutter. And that is the moment when Edward G. Robinson, as Enrico Bandello—clearly a Capone figure—is dying and breathes the immortal line "Mother of Mercy! Is this the end of Rico?"

Howard Hawks, in trying to make *Scarface,* suffered worse than Wellman and LeRoy. Hawks and his main screenwriter, Ben Hecht, wanted to make a picture that somehow combined Al Capone and the Borgias, But the Hays Office, headed by the former Republican Party chairman Will Hays and his deputy, Colonel Jason Joy, would not give a movie the production seal of the Motion Picture Producers and Distributors of America without a thorough review. Hays and Joy scoured scripts for any traces of amorality. Joy's reading of the script of *Scarface* was particularly damning and left Hawks despondent. For weeks, it seemed that there would be no movie at all, according to Todd McCarthy's biography of Hawks. Hays, for example, complained that Scarface's mother was a "grasping virago, distinctly an Italian criminal type mother"; he insisted that the mother "present to the son a dialogue telling him what the Italian race has done for posterity and that he, Scarface, is bringing odium and shame upon his entire race." Most galling of all to Hawks, the Hays Office threatened to withhold the production seal unless he added a finale scene with a judge condemning Scarface on the gallows. "You've commercialized murder to satisfy your personal greed for power," the judge intones. "You've killed innocent women and children with brutal indifference. You are ruthless, immoral, and vicious. There is no place in this country for your type." Hawks and his producer, Howard Hughes, battled with Hays and Joy for nearly a year, but there was no getting around most of these compromises.

In 1933, with the end of Prohibition, the image of the mobster as a misbegotten freedom fighter became obsolete; in 1934, with the formalization of the Hays Code, it became untenable. In *Dead End* and *Angels with Dirty Faces,* the gangster became an object of sociological study and audience pity; in comedies like *The Amazing Dr. Clitterhouse* and *Ball of Fire,* he became the butt of the joke; and in Raoul Welsh's *The Roaring Twenties,* made in 1939, the mobster became a figure of nostalgia.

Crime films headed off in two main directions: treating the psychopathic lone criminal (Walsh's *White Heat,* Henry Hathaway's *Kiss of Death*) or highlighting the private detective. From John Huston's *The Maltese Falcon* to Howard Hawks's *The Big Sleep* and Edward Dmytryk's *Murder My Sweet,* Sam Spade and Philip Marlowe and their like were freelance survivalists in the crepuscular urban jungle. They were quick-witted and not averse to violence, and their instinct for survival was inhibited by an internal code of ethics that pushed them, if only grudgingly, to the side of order.

The first important Mafia film after *Scarface* was *On the Waterfront* (1954), in which the Mob appears in its new, post-war guise as a monkey wrench in the machinery of liberal capitalism. As the has-been fighter, Marlon Brando sacrifices himself in a last (and seemingly futile) stand against Lee J. Cobb and the men who control New York Harbor.

The big-time Mafia, the Mafia of great American Romans running New York, is the subject of Francis Ford Coppola's *The Godfather* (1972). Nearly thirty years later, *The Godfather* is still terrifying and remains, in many ways, the best of all gangster films—we are not likely to forget the solemn oneliners, the oaths, the assassinations of Luca Brasi and Sonny Corleone, or the Don's sunlit death in his tomato garden—but, like the many operas it recalls, the film is generously dressed with the tinsel of camp. To watch *The Godfather* now is not unlike going to hear Puccini; soap opera coexists with high art. Time has changed the nature of our pleasure. Similarly, when you see Brando in the opening scene of *The Godfather,* dispensing favors in his gloomy study, you can't help thinking of all the parodies that followed, including Brando himself as a bulked-up version of Don Corleone in the Matthew Broderick vehicle *The Freshman.*

The characters in *The Sopranos* are obsessed with *The Godfather,* but their maker is obsessed with Martin Scorsese and his street-level view of things. David Chase thought the Mafia movie had finally exhausted itself in 1990 with *GoodFellas.* Scorsese's gangster films, beginning with *Mean Streets,* in 1973, are about guys who sit around all day eating, gabbing, and collecting money in bags, guys who intimidate truck drivers and mailmen, guys for whom no petty scam is an indignity. Chase pays homage to *GoodFellas* by having the actor Michael Imperioli, who was shot in the foot in Scorsese's film, do the same thing to a bakery clerk in the series. Most of the criticism of Coppola's *Godfather III* focussed on the script, which was inferior to the first two. But, by the nineties, the problem was a proper suspension of disbelief. Somehow, the sight of Al Pacino, as the aging Don, trying to lean on the Vatican in *Godfather III* is no less funny than Pacino, as a nudnik gangster in *Donnie Brasco* (1997), trying to bust open parking meters with a sledgehammer. Chase's creative leap was to grasp the transformation of the Mob genre, its passage from tragedy to farce, and, against all odds, make something new.

There are still mobsters today in racketeering, labor unions, and gambling, but no one questions that Cosa Nostra, the real one, is fast expiring. As Tony laments in the pilot episode, "I came in at the end. The best is over." Prosecutors and gangsters agree on the reasons: federal initiatives like the Racketeer Influenced and Corrupt Organizations (RICO) Act and the effectiveness of investigators, who mastered the art of wiretapping and flipping witnesses, have nearly wiped out the Five Families. David Kelley, the chief of organized crime and terrorism in the United States Attorney's Office for the Southern District of New York, told me, "All the old rituals and codes have eroded over time, and the reasons are simple: greed and convenience. There's a sense now of every man for himself, a turn from 'this thing of ours' to 'this thing of mine.' " Gangsters used to talk righteously about avoiding the drug trade, but they couldn't resist the profit margins; and when a gangster is facing ten to life for narcotics trafficking—as opposed to a few years for hijacking a truck—he is more likely to testify for the government. Also, as Tony Soprano demonstrates, the Mafia life is highly stressful, what with all the beatings and the search warrants. Many elders would get out if they could ("I don't want it. The whole [expletive] life") and many of them do what they can to make sure their kids go straight. More and more, the Mafia has gone small-time. Pump-and-dump brokerage scams and truck hijackings are nice but they are hardly the stuff of *The Godfather.*

In the movies, gangsters are appealing because they embody not only a rude dominance but also a code and a sentiment, a fantasy of brotherhood. In the postindustrial world of no loyalties, of no commitments, gangsters trade blood oaths. "He's a friend of ours"—that's the way a Mob guy introduces a second guy to a third. But if that was ever true it was long ago. Real mobsters, especially our degraded contemporaries, are not as satanically charming as Bob Hoskins in *The Long Good Friday* or as hypnotically intelligent as Christopher Walken in *King of New York.* A few years ago, a friend, a prosecutor, asked if I wanted to write about a Mob assassin who was in the witness-protection program. He was living in what the prosecutor called "a warm state." Johnny Johnson (a bogus name, but why get him shot?) was small and middle-aged; he had, for a living, killed people on behalf of the Gordon Chandler Mob, one of Harlem's biggest heroin-and-numbers outfits. He had killed at least ten men, spent more than half his life in jail, fuzzed his mind with dope and angel dust, turned state's evidence, and, thanks to "the program," avoided a rat's assassination. Now he was selling aluminum siding and coaching Little League. He lived in a dim house on a busy street. Sometimes he slipped back to the city to see a woman, and sometimes the woman slipped down to see him, a practice that is not, strictly speaking, a bright idea.

For a couple of days, he talked about his life, about his horrible childhood and the squalid city institutions that made a pass at raising him, about his attraction to the glittering crooks in the neighborhood. ("My real father," he said, "was Bumpy Johnson," the infamous Harlem gangster, who died in 1968.) He talked about his first murder ("When it happened, I didn't give a fuck, no remorse"), and then he talked about his second and his third and his fourth. He talked about meeting John Gotti and "Jerry the Jew" and an entire rainbow coalition of thugs and how someone got his head bashed in with a baseball bat. On and on the pornography of his life unspooled, and sometimes he'd deliver it flat, like a machine, and other times he'd catch himself, and he'd cry awhile. He cried all through lunch at the International House of Pancakes. At times, he was terrifying to listen to, at others excruciatingly boring. Finally, as I was getting ready to leave, Johnny asked me, "So, how much?" He wanted to get paid for his interview. It was no simple thing explaining to a retired professional assassin why I couldn't do that. Johnny saw the interview as merely a first step. He wanted a book deal and then a movie. The aluminum-siding business wasn't coming through with the cash, and it certainly wasn't giving him what he thought was his due. He had only one commodity to his name: his story. But hadn't we heard it before? There are more black-Mob pictures than we know what to do with: *Black Caesar, Hoodlum, New Jack City.* What's left? A kreplach-Mob picture? Done: Sergio Leone's *Once Upon a Time in America.* A Russian Mob picture? Try *Little Odessa.* Even David Chase thinks the genre, like the cowboy movie, like the Busby Berkeley musical, has reached the vanishing point. And I don't care if I never see another one, he said. In one episode of *The Sopranos,* midway through the first season, the young, impetuous mobster Christopher Moltisanti, played by Michael Imperioli, tries to write a screenplay in the hours when he is not robbing trucks or picking up cannolis for Tony. He seems almost to speak for Chase.

"I love movies, you know that," Christopher tells his girlfriend. "That smell in Blockbuster! That candy-and-carpet smell? I get high off of it. Am I gonna let all this love and knowledge go to waste? My cousin Gregory's girlfriend, Amy, the one who works for Tarantino, said, Mob stories are always hot. I can make my mark!" But Tony would sooner see Christopher dead than let him spill the family secrets. And, besides, Christopher can barely spell, much less give new life to an old genre. That work is left to an outsider, to David Chase. And, as Chase told me, there's probably only one more season left in him before *The Sopranos* gets stale. He wants out. His next planned project is a feature, backed by HBO and distributed by Warner Brothers. And it is not about the Mafia. It's about the Christian-rock scene.

Mother of Mercy, is this the end of Rico?

FROM *FAST-TALKING DAMES* FEMALE RAMPANT HIS GIRL FRIDAY

by Maria DiBattista

The film's title blares out at us from a blur of newsprint. Its bold headline gives undisputed prominence to an ascendant female type with a jazzy moniker—His Girl Friday. The subject of this fanfare is Hildy Johnson, surely the fastest of the fast-talking dames of American screen comedy and perhaps the best newspaperman ever portrayed on film. She makes us aware of how "talking pictures" gave women the chance to speak up, speak out, and speak to their own desires, dreams, and ambitions. Presented with this opportunity, they made the most of it. They spoke fast and furiously, as if their survival depended on their doing so.

As, indeed, it did. The main business of comedy, unlike that of tragedy or melodrama, is to show us what makes a successful human being, happy in both work and play, sexually and professionally fulfilled. The comedies of the thirties and early forties teach us nothing if they don't impress upon us that slow-witted, reticent, or inarticulate women had little chance for sexual happiness, still less for professional success. In comedy, quickness is all. Why timing *should* be all is a good question, and this film does not hesitate to ask it. It puts this question to us in a particularly charged way: by showing us the relation between Hildy's work as a reporter, which she wants to abandon; her dream of a home, which she wants to pursue; and the impending execution of a convicted murderer, whose life it is in her power to save.

Yet my initial description of Hildy as regnant, by virtue of her quick wit, over the comic action, is somewhat belied by her apparent status as a girl Friday, a term that may strike us as dated, if not downright retrograde. Consider, for instance, the masculine presumption of that possessive pronoun "his," which intimates some claim to exclusive rights, a claim that editor Walter Burns (Cary Grant) converts into playful threat when he reminds Hildy (Rosalind Russell), his ace reporter and ex-wife, that he would kill her if she went to work for anyone else. Hildy treats this warning as a backhanded compliment: "Did you hear that, Bruce" she says to her fiancé, Bruce Baldwin (Ralph Bellamy). "That's my diploma!" She is amused at the notion that she can be "his" and rightly feels that she has graduated to a higher and more self-dependent status. Indeed, she announces at the beginning of the film that she will henceforth belong to herself. More accurately, she proclaims her intention of "going into business for myself."

The business, presumably, of getting married and leading, as Hildy declares, a "halfway normal life." Hildy is disgusted with the work of a newspaperman, a sordid scramble to gather all the news unfit to print. When Walter accuses her of being a traitor to journalism, Hildy retorts: "A journalist? Hell, what does that mean? Peeping through keyholes? Chasing after fire engines? Waking people up in the middle of the night to ask if Hitler is going to start another war? Stealing pictures off old ladies? I know all about reporters, Walter. A lot of daffy buttinskis running around without a nickel in their pockets. And for what? So a million hired girls and motormen's wives'll know what's going on." The class animus and misogyny of this diatribe, lifted from the film's source, Ben Hecht and Charles MacArthur's play *The Front Page*, where it is delivered by a man, is given an added sexual twist when spoken by a woman. In the play, the lament about the decline of manly journalism into sensationalist fare is part of the masculinist satire against the coarseness as well as imperiousness of female appetites. When a woman speaks derisively of the tastes of hired girls and motormen's wives, we get a different sense of the routine indignities, inflicted and suffered, of the newspaper trade.

The film will confirm Hildy's sense that the life of a newspaperman is the dramatic equivalent of farce, in which sexual and professional decorum, as well as "dignified" notions of truth, are the primary casualties. But Howard Hawks's comedy will also convince us, as it will Hildy, not to fret unduly about the mutual demise of both dignity and truth. This would be an odd moral, even an unacceptable one, if Hawks did not affirm something new—and newsworthy—in their place: an altered relation between the sexes that is breezily indifferent to, when it is not downright contemptuous of, the decorum that regulates a "halfway normal life."

Hildy has yet to learn that for her marriage will entail more than a move to Albany, where she hopes to spend her time in the company of a different class of women: it will entail a change of nature. In pursuing a halfway normal life, Hildy is working not only against her instincts as a newspaperman but against her destiny as a fast-talking dame. In Lubitsch's *That Uncertain Feeling* (1941), Jill Baker (Merle Oberon) tries to fend off her friends' suggestion that she see a psychiatrist to "cure" her recurrent and apparently psychosomatic hiccoughs by insisting that she's a "perfectly normal woman." "Don't say that about yourself, even in fun," is the friendly but firm rejoinder. Being normal is no laughing matter.

Hildy, of course, is not a perfectly normal woman, although for reasons she takes pains to explain to Walter, and other reasons that she is perhaps concealing, she aspires to become one. To begin with, Hildy was conceived as a man. She was born Hildebrand "Hildy" Johnson in the 1928 play; moved from stage to film in 1931 in the person of Pat O'Brien; and was reconceived and reborn in 1940, thanks to the majestic skill of Howard Hawks, as Hildegarde Johnson. Although she retains the surname and some of the lines of her namesake, she avoids the fate of imitated being, sexual mimicry, and masquerade. Hildegarde Johnson is a more original, endearing, and modern being than her male prototype, already identified by Hecht and MacArthur as a "vanishing type—the lusty, hoodlumesque, half-drunken caballero that was the newspaperman of our youth." So the playwrights at once tag and eulogize him, lamenting that "schools of journalism and the advertising business have nearly extirpated the species." Hildegarde Johnson is neither endangered species nor rowdy anachronism: she represents, rather, a new female mutation.

Hawks casts a knowing eye on his own predilection for such outlandish human developments when he concludes the film's prologue with the deliberate whimsy of "Once upon a time. . . . " I take Hawks at his word in presenting *His Girl Friday* as a modern fairy tale, but am not willing to concede that his reassurance that "you will see in this picture no resemblance to the men and women of the press today" is transparently ironic. Hildy and Walter, in fact, do *not* resemble the men and women of their day. They resemble only themselves, fantastical creatures whose nature is at once primordial and futuristic. By this curious description I hope to suggest how Hildy and Walter cannot be understood, much less appreciated, unless we see them as occupying and making their own kind of time. It was Manny Farber who first called attention to the way Hawks's romanticism—which "wraps the fliers-reporters-workhands in a patina of period mannerism and attitude"—makes his films appear not so much "dated as removed from reality, like the land of Tolkien's Hobbits." Hildy is a new female type very much of this company, a "once and future" woman, as it were.

Hawks's fascination with fantasies of regression is less indulged here than in his atavistic comedies, *Bringing Up Baby* and *Monkey Business* (1952), both also featuring Cary Grant. Indeed, it was Hawks's comic genius to see Cary Grant, surely the most debonair of romantic screen presences, as an evolutionary marvel who could revert, in the right comic circumstances, to the postures and devices of neolithic man and still retain, even enhance, his appeal as desirable mate. Hawks's complex manipulation of comic *time* as both regressive and visionary contributes to the illusion that what we are witnessing in his screwball courtship plots is, in fact, an exciting and perhaps dangerous sexual adaptation.

In transforming Hildy into a woman, Hawks was making obvious what the play presented as latent: a love affair between two men. He also seemed to have observed that their love affair lacked romance. I invoke romance here not just in its common amorous sense, but romance as an idealized depiction of charismatic individuals whose vitality explodes all the rules of right or even good behavior. No such romance is possible in the play because its sense of sexual difference is at once too complacent and too naive to admit of erotic enthrallment. Here, for example, is Hecht and MacArthur's description of Peggy, Hildy's fiancée:

> Peggy, despite her youth and simplicity, seems overwhelmingly mature in comparison to Hildy. As a matter of fact, Peggy belongs to that division of womanhood which dedicates itself to suppressing in its lovers or husbands the spirit of D'Artagnan, Roland, Captain Kidd, Cyrano, Don Quixote, King Arthur or any other type of the male innocent and rampant. In her unconscious and highly noble efforts to make what the female world calls "a man" out of Hildy, Peggy has neither the sympathy nor acclaim of the authors, yet—regarded superficially, she is a very sweet and satisfying heroine.

Peggy is regarded superficially as a sweet and satisfying heroine because she is conceived superficially. The iconoclasm of the play never targets the thoroughly conventional notion that the "female world" dedicates itself to one fundamental activity: domesticating the primal, renegade male. The playwrights, while grudgingly accepting the possible social necessity of this reformation work, clearly prefer the rowdy camaraderie of the pressroom, the last Hemingwayesque preserve of "Men without Women," that is, men at once "innocent and rampant." In affixing the heraldic as well as characterological term "rampant" to that generic American type, the male innocent, they endow him with a noble genealogy: Roland, D'Artagnan, Cyrano. Only an American male could fantasize such an ancestry in order to ennoble his arrested emotional development. For all the pungency of its idiomatic dialogue and keen satire on contemporary urban life, *The Front Page* remains oddly quaint, a curious amalgam of social cynicism and sexual sentimentalism that we might call urban pastoral. The play is a nostalgia piece that celebrates the pressroom as a "sort of journalistic Yellowstone Park offering haven to a last herd of fantastic bravos that once formed the newspaper offices of the country."

The modernity of *His Girl Friday*, then, cannot be attributed to a mechanical updating of an esteemed original. The film is determinedly of its own time and place, at once outlandishly contemporary and knowingly retrograde (as opposed to furtively elegiac) in delightedly reversing traditional sexual roles. The male reversals, by no means as visually spectacular as Hildy's sex-change (which we will consider in a moment), are equally inspired and, indeed, help fuel the comic competition for verbal as well as sexual mastery. Hawks, so expert in exploiting the Hollywood language of "types," enriches his film adaptation by splitting the Hecht-MacArthur "male innocent and rampant" into two competing characters: Hildy's rampant boss and ex-husband, Walter; and her innocent beau, Bruce. Comically speaking, Hawks doubles our sexual fun. Take the casting of Ralph Bellamy as Hildy's suitor. His very presence announces that Hecht and MacArthur's male innocent is no longer rampant but undeniably tamed. Bellamy has made this type so familiar that even within the film he is seen to be *sui generis*. Walter, faltering for a way to describe Bruce to Evangeline, the moll he dispatches to entrap him, resorts to the shorthand of a casting call: "He looks like, uh, that fellow in the movies, you know, uh, Ralph Bellamy." The in-joke carries a comic bonus in reminding us how types in the movies are embodied by actors or actresses with morally readable features that are translated from film to film and part to part. Ralph Bellamy is Ralph Bellamy, a human tautology who can be relied upon to be nothing other than what he appears.

Hawks's other famous in-joke works the opposite charm; it locates the charisma of the chameleon and rampant male, Walter Burns. Near the end of the film Walter Burns darkly warns that the last person to cross him was "Archie Leach a week before he cut his throat." Archie Leach is, of course, Grant's given name. Cary Grant is *never* redundant, although he is always and recognizably the star Cary Grant. The in-joke is in insidious keeping with the feeling, subtly but irresistibly growing in a film that would not seem to permit reflection, that death shadows the action and impels the more creative personalities to outwit death by *acting,* continually trying on new lives, inventing ruses that possess the shimmering radiance, if not the consistency, of truth. Walter fascinates, as truth often does not, because he is never redundant.

The man who esteems himself the lord of the universe (Hildy's phrase but one not disputed by her co-workers) first appears on screen primping before his mirror. Apparently one of the prerogatives of his lordship is enjoying the perks, courtesies, and pleasures traditionally accorded to women without jeopardizing his masculinity, losing his wits, or forfeiting his command. Walter's pleasure in usurping the courtesy normally extended to the fairer sex is hilariously evident in his wacky version of how Hildy "trapped" him into marriage. He claims he was tight on the night he proposed and Hildy acted dishonorably in taking him at his word: "If you'd been a gentleman, you'd have forgotten all about it." It's not important whether the story is true, only that it establishes that Walter is not male innocent and rampant. He is something more imposing: male rampant, reckless with the truth.

We can detect in his feminine preening and ironic vulnerability to Hildy's "ungentlemanly" advances more than a whiff of dandyish effeminacy: there is also a dash of mayhem in his scrambling of gender codes. So much is evident in his reliance on Diamond Louie, an underworld factotum who seems to have a whole repertory company of Runyonesque characters at his disposal to abet Walter's schemes. We may take Walter to be a man who flirts with crime as he flirts with femininity. Passing counterfeit bills and arranging for a kidnaping are two of the criminal offenses that this male rampant passes off as "innocent" maneuvers to keep Hildy from leaving him for Bruce—and Albany, too! Such maneuvers become less innocent when Walter, who mocks Bruce's innocence by warning him that he will depart on his honeymoon with blood on his hands should he prevent Hildy from writing the story that could save a convicted murderer, finds his own potentially stained with the blood of Hildy's future mother-in-law.

That Walter seems to be associated with dead bodies is no small obstacle to his romantic appeal. Take the most disturbing cut in the film, which links Walter to Mollie Malloy (Helen Mack), the Clark Street tart who befriended Earl Williams (John Qualen), the man slated to die at dawn for having shot a policeman. When Earl escapes during a state-mandated psychiatric exam, Mollie acts to distract the police and the press in their pursuit of him by jumping out the pressroom window. She is willing to commit her life to Williams because, it seems, he's the only man who wanted to talk to her, not buy her. As she takes her plunge, the camera cuts from reporters' shocked but professional interest in whether she survives to Walter's arrival on the scene.

Visually and dramatically connecting Mollie's suicidal exit and Burns's entrance is not Hawks's idea; it belongs to the play, with its more obvious moralism. In fact, in the play this is the first we see of Walter. In their stage directions, Hecht and MacArthur make clear that this dramatic entrance is calculated to impress us with the fact that Walter is at once a boss and a figure of nemesis: "Beneath a dapper and very citizen-like exterior lurks a hobgoblin, perhaps the Devil himself. But if Mr. Burns is the Devil he is a very naive one. He is a Devil with neither point nor purpose to him—an undignified Devil hatched for a bourgeois Halloween. In less hyperbolic language, Mr. Burns is the product of thoughtless, pointless, nerve-drumming unmorality that is the Boss Journalist—the licensed eavesdropper, trouble maker, bombinator, and Town Snitch, misnamed The Press."

To reduce grandiloquent Mephistopheles to a scandal-mongering town snitch is one way to contain the menace of Walter's unmorality. You needn't exorcize the devil, only familiarize yourself with the local demon and his typical mischief: "At this moment Mr. Burns, in the discharge of his high calling, stands in the door, nerveless and meditative as a child, his mind open to such troubles as he can find or create." Hawks adapts this characterization, and though he doesn't dispute Walter's devilish mischievousness, he does endow him with thought, point, and purpose beyond the childish motive of finding or creating trouble. To appreciate this complication in his character we need only remember that Hildy earlier had said that she, too, had metaphorically jumped out a window to escape her life with Walter.

Hawks doesn't dwell on Hildy's motives nor on Mollie's impulsiveness, but by connecting Mollie's literal jump and Hildy's metaphorical one he does alert us to the possibility that Walter may pose a real danger for Hildy. Hitchcock, in films like *Suspicion* and *Notorious*, openly elicited the demonic impulses lurking beneath Grant's worldly charm, but Hawks had in this film already begun excavating that dark side. Hawks's undercover work discovers a more comically heartless and potentially more dangerous Walter Burns than Hecht and MacArthur's dapper Mephistopheles.

Yet nowhere is Hawks's comic wizardry in animating and transforming the stock company of sexual types more in evidence than in the ingenuity with which he transforms a girl Friday, a generic figure from the classified ads, into a comic heroine who not only occupies the front page but gets top billing. Presuming that Hildy's "job" and her happiness depend on her remaining Walter's girl Friday, it is odd that, to my knowledge, no one has determined which component is more important to the formula—being a girl or being a manservant. What we can say is that Hildy, as girl Friday, is definitely not a woman, as she herself recognizes, nor do her mannerisms suggest a conventional femininity. This being the case, let us confer upon her a more heraldic identity: female rampant.

The conventions of screwball comedy permit, when they do not outright ordain, the most outlandish postures and unrefined gestures. In her enjoyment of this physical freedom, the screwball heroine is clearly the daughter of the slapstick comediennes, those "hoydens," as the appreciative Gilbert Seldes called them, who abjured the languorous poses favored by those females who sought to make their sexual fortune in the sedate world of parlor romance. Yet there is a qualitative difference between Claudette Colbert, in *It Happened One Night*, displaying her comely legs to illustrate that the limb is mightier than the thumb, and Hildy tackling a man in flight or, in the film's most stunning visual gag, bending over to display her backside, revealing the full breadth of her classified ads. Rosalind Russell carries herself in this role with a peculiar insouciance. Her self-indifferent carriage forms a fascinating contrast to Walter's narcissistic posing. She may be said to possess stature without being statuesque (the demeanor of Katherine Hepburn throughout most of *The Philadelphia Story*). Russell brilliantly conveys how Hildy's bodily reactions are keyed to her habits of attention. She can become instantly mobilized when a story—or a fleeing jailkeeper—crosses her line of vision.

There is as much fatality, then, as casualness in the use of the word girl to refer to Hildy in her role of newspaperman. Girl is a word that enjoys peculiar license in American slang. It entails, in the first and most common instance, an endearment that suggests both the dream of easy companionableness—a girl is a pal—and a reticence in admitting adult sexual feeling. Much of this camaraderie persists in the working relationship of Hildy and her fellow bravos in the pressroom, and it infuses the rhythms of her fast, knowing, and uninhibited exchanges with Walter. But "girl" is also a slang term used in uneasy proximity to the more explicit "tart," someone whose loose morals area function of her employment. In the play, Hildy jocoseriously holds no illusions about the genealogy of his trade: a newspaperman, he says, is a "cross between a bootlegger and a whore." His being a man limits the sting of the whore analogy and leaves his sexual dignity fairly secure—secure enough that he can even afford to mimic, as he does in a particularly loony moment, the whine of an androgyne. A woman could not say this line or claim such disreputable parentage, even in a comedy, without permanently sullying her moral integrity and, probably more to the point, undermining her physical appeal. In the film, it is through Mollie that journalism and prostitution are provocatively linked. That Mollie is the only other woman with a significant part in this comedy is not without point and pathos. In going into business for herself, Hildy finds a dispirited double in the working girl whose "business," like Hildy's, routinely, requires her to subordinate her rights and feelings to those of the man paying for her services.

To this the name Friday may attest. In the popular imagination, Defoe's complex creation is reduced to a "native" who assists Robinson Crusoe in the task of survival. His "nature" and his serviceability are conceived as inextricable, much as Hildy's "instincts" as a newspaperman are deemed indispensable but subordinate to Walter's captainship of the *Morning Post*. Yet how can Hildy be seen as a native of the pressroom? We are shown in those engrossing tracking shots that open the film and disclose its working spaces. The camera retreats before an advancing female figure who, because she is not the

Rosalind Russell of the title credits, we know not to be his girl Friday, but a girl Friday nonetheless. A more conventional director might have opened with an impersonal pan of the newsroom in which human figures would pass in and out of the frame, no single figure directing or arresting the camera's vision. But Hawks isn't interested so much in mise-en-scène for its own sake as in the motivated movement within it, the movement that attracts attention and imparts life. His camera tracks the advancing female figure until she is replaced by another worker, and the camera then follows him until he scurries beyond the preserve of the working staff to catch a departing elevator. It is then that Hildy emerges from the elevator at the right of the frame, and the camera reorients itself, drawn perhaps by the bold lines of Hildy's pinstriped suit, coordinated with a neo-stovepipe hat, or by the confiding way she reassures her companion, Bruce, that she will be back in ten minutes (the first of many such promises, none of them precisely kept).

The camera halts before resuming its tracking assignment, arrested by this tender exchange, just on the threshold of the swinging gate. Later the gate will be stilled to reveal a sign of "No Admittance." Its ostensible function is to keep visitors out, but given all the diabolic imagery surrounding Walter, we might be encouraged to read it as a moral advisory: "Abandon all sentiment you who enter here." Bruce cannot cross this barrier and enter Hildy's world of work but must remain outside it, "on the job," as Hildy says, waiting for her to complete one last reportorial errand, dispatching her "news" to Walter. Later, Bruce will tire of waiting for Hildy and enter the proscribed domain, the pressroom of the Criminal Courts Building. It proves to be a mistake. After pleading his case to a preoccupied Hildy, he will leave the room—and the film—as he entered it, unremarked. Now, too, the camera leaves him to follow Hildy back into the busy space it has just left. Only this time, with Hildy as the focus of the shot, we see the newsroom staff happily welcoming her back, and Hildy, returning their greeting, confers on them a fleeting but memorable individuality. "How's the advice to the lovelorn?" she asks one columnist. "Fine. My cat just had kittens again," she replies. "Your own fault," Hildy briskly but not unkindly tells her. In this brief exchange we understand at once the mark and the pathology of a professional: taking one's work home—advising, perhaps not wisely, but too well—confusing, as Bruce never would, business and home front.

The next time the camera traverses this space it will be to track Hildy and Walter as they leave the office to rejoin Bruce, stranded in the antechamber. On their way they enact a blithe parody of the male gallantry that yields the lead to the lady. Walter strides confidently forward, then defers to Hildy, but resumes his pride of place when Hildy opens the gate ("Allow me," she obligingly coos), permitting him to stride into the antechamber and perform his superb burlesque of male bonhomie, mistaking a senior citizen for Bruce, her Rotarian suitor: "You led me to expect you were marrying a much older man," he chides Hildy after learning of his "mistake" and, in mock courtesy, pumping Bruce's umbrella instead of his hand. The newsroom, at first animated background, then, briefly, personalized arena of working relationships, finally becomes properly scenic, the space where the sexual vaudeville of courtship is faultlessly performed. With exhilarating economy Hawks works the comic transformation, converting workplace into comedic theater.

These opening shots suggest the full powers of film to expose and shape reality according to its own lights and conventions. There is no attempt to compose within the frame, adjust the focus, or edit, invisibly or self-consciously, the life unfolding, at times unraveling, before us. That graduation from staged to filmed effects will be accomplished later, in the Criminal Courts pressroom and, most impressively, in the jail where Hildy interviews the condemned man, Earl Williams.

For now, what we observe is how the camera becomes absorbed in recording the scenic wonder of Hildy and Walter's reunion. The rapport between the two is a function of pure momentum; the pace of their repartee accelerates but keeps veering into dead ends. Hildy is exasperated here, as she is not in the more relaxed and expertly timed restaurant scene that follows. There she allows herself to share Walter's version of their mutual past, is entertained by his hastily devised, cockamamie stories, and receptive to his proposal to buy a life insurance policy from Bruce if she will do an exclusive interview with Williams. She seems to relax into the old rhythms and verbal intimacies of their former life together. In the newsroom, her timing, like her aim, is slightly off: while she misses few of Walter's cues, she throws back her lines as she hurls her pocketbook, just missing her target. Even her words seem to fly by and around him, searching to reach their mark. They finally do hit home when, showing him her ring, she blurts out the news of her engagement.

The news produces a stunningly quiet moment, another example that in talking comedies, silence is something not overcome but achieved. We will return to the moral import of such silences later. Here we remark that Hildy and Walter's reunion has played out the old motifs of their partnership without transforming them. She's amused, at times, by his bluster but resolute about her mission and, most important, deaf to his reminiscences: "Walter, I want to show you something. It's here. It's a ring. Take a good look at it. Do you know what it is? It's an engagement ring." He stops short. "I tried to tell you right away, but you would start reminiscing. I'm getting married, Walter, and I'm also getting as far away from this newspaper business as I can get." These reminiscences will resurface to bring them together, but for now they must be returned to silence before they can yield their inner, untheatrical essence.

Although the scene appears to develop improvisationally, it retains, as even a brief survey of its multiple if "invisible" cuts will show, a neat, even crisp, narrative line. Dramatically, the scene seems to hurtle forward toward a startling announcement, but its vector is initially controlled by Walter, who insists on taking us back, as he generously says he will take Hildy back. Back to the old complacency of his assurance that he will know her any time, any place, anywhere, back to the dreams of him he suspects Hildy has had as recently as last night, back to that prehistoric era in Hildy's life when she was only a doll-faced hick and he the Pygmalion who turned her into a first-class newspaperman. His comic rant about her ingratitude fails not only because it lacks real cause, but because it no longer captivates her as male performance. Hildy complains that she can barely get a word in edgewise, but when she does it stabs Walter cold. She brings him to a momentary but definitive halt when she caps his tirade with its commercial clincher: "Sold American!"

It is after this line that Hildy makes her show-stopping announcement, cutting Walter off from his memories and, of course, confuting *his* waking dream that he would know her any time, any place, anywhere. It is this line, delivered with an auctioneer's decisiveness, that alerts us to the dark logic of their relationship. It is the truthfulness of this comedy that this darkness will never be dispersed, although it will be lightened by Walter's more tender avowals, brought on by Hildy's tears, at the end of the film. For Stanley Cavell, it is a logic played and replayed throughout the "comedies of remarriage," a logic activated in this film by "the early, summary declaration that this woman has recently been created, and created by this man." Cavell's view of the genre and ritual of remarriage is partly based on a compelling reading of Milton's divorce tracts, but *His Girl Friday,* which mocks city politicians for alarums of the Red Scare, is ideologically closer to the spirit of Engels's *The Origin of the Family, Private Property, and the State*. Which is to say that it entertains, even if it finally does not endorse, the view that modern marriage is less a covenant between the sexes or a civil union honorably contracted than an economic institution that flatters, when it does not directly minister to, man's proprietary feelings.

This film doesn't so much want to dispute as to reimagine the economic nature of marriage. It would do so by eliminating the confusion, typically American, between business and work. This is where the film works in romance, in insisting on the romance of work. The intimacy that unites Hildy and Walter is not an intimacy available to every professional association but seems to be unique to the nature of their trade as newspapermen. It is also an intimacy based on their shared professional sense of time as something urgently passing. Hildy and Walter, in work and in love, are always trying to meet some deadline. This is especially true for Walter in his new role as suitor to his ex-wife. The success of his amatory campaign depends on his first postponing, then stopping, her intended departure for Albany, where she will begin what she hopes to be a respectable, halfway normal (deadline-free?) life. Many love stories play on the anxiety of trains being missed; here the anxiety is that they will be caught. This film, justly celebrated for the breathtaking pace of its dialogue, is fast, fast, fast, not just because quickness as well as brevity is the soul of wit, but because it is also the truth of romantic, as it is of filmic, time. Let us call it rampant time.

The first intimate exchange in the film is between Hildy and Bruce, and it is about the meaning of time. About to enter the frenzied precincts of the pressroom, Hildy off-handedly reassures Bruce that she won't be long, a matter of ten minutes. "Even ten minutes is a long time to be away from you," is his doting rejoinder. Hildy pauses, returns to him, and asks him to repeat what he just said. The viewer accustomed to a "normal" life may find the line corny, but to Hildy, for whom even a halfway normal life has so far proved elusive, this way of marking time holds great emotional appeal. She admits to a need to be doted on in this way. Here again we see how work can influence one's sense of time, hence one's relation to romance. Bruce, who sells insurance, is a reassuring but unadventurous suitor because he regards time as something to be insured against, not enlivened or transformed. When Walter, Hildy, and Bruce share a meal in ostensible celebration of the impending marriage, Bruce earnestly remarks the prudence of insuring one's life, then doubtfully adds, "Of course, we don't help you much while you're alive, but afterwards, that's what counts." "Sure," Walter agrees, then fakes a laugh before conceding, in mock ignorance, "I don't get it."

We miss Walter's irony—and his charm—if we miss the downright literalism of that "it"—it being as much the time he will fail to get if he's too busy insuring it, as well as the concept that Bruce is awkwardly expounding. Walter, and in this Hildy is his spiritual mate, brings to the film the dispensation of a future or fantasized time (Walter's seductive fantasy of Hildy's future as a social crusader) or past time (Walter's early, ineffectual appeals to Hildy to remember the times of their shared life or his reminder of the light still burning in his window). I can't agree with Cavell that Walter doesn't get what Bruce is talking about because he is too much of this world to believe or care about an afterlife. Walter doesn't get it because he can make no provision for a time that he is not actively creating or reinventing, a time, indeed, when Walter Burns will no longer be, either on or behind the scene, the male rampant working his mischief. Walter lacks the comic feeling for a social future in which he can play no living part.

In this sense the social time of this film belongs to Walter. It is the fleeting time frantically pursued by the daily newspaper, which traffics in events as if they were transient and which treats history as disposable, instantly revisable, or easily edited. Hence the sly disclaimer with which the film opens, advising us that the story we are about to see "all happened in the 'dark ages' of the newspaper game—when a reporter 'getting that story' justified anything short of murder." Here is that word "get" again, only now it suggests that stories are not so much reported as procured. What it means to get something—a story, a joke, or a girl—is what this comedy means us to "get," and all without ever fooling ourselves that we ever possess the real story, know all the references in the joke, or can ever be sure, as Hildy and Walter head off to Albany, that Walter has finally "got" her. To get a story is a task that justifies doing anything, any time, anywhere. That the film moves from the newspaper office to the Criminal Courts Building begins to seem, in light of the film's opening disclaimer, a morally significant fact. Getting a story verges on outright criminality. Indeed, the comic complications of the film will climax in the handcuffing of Hildy and Walter as alleged criminals (for obstructing justice and harboring a fugitive) and reunited couple.

Hildy is torn between Walter and Bruce because she can entertain two different kinds of time and responds deeply to their separate attractions. Bruce's need for Hildy's affecting presence, which makes even ten minutes seem like a long time, evokes the child's endearing but unavailing protest at separation from the mother, no matter for how brief a time. Hawks emphasizes, though hardly credits, Bruce's appeal to Hildy's dormant maternal feelings. But Bruce's "feminine" side, however attractive, seems attached, at the hip as it were, to his own mother. Hawks retains the mother-in-law of the original play, if for no other reason than to give Walter the satisfaction of insulting her and of showing up the kind of man—Bruce Baldwin, for example—who believes that a boy's best friend is his mother. Bruce does believe it, of course, and has even arranged for his mother to accompany Hildy and himself to Albany, where their marriage will not so much institute a new family as extend an old one.

The film has great fun with what it means to be a mama's boy in the sublime comic mischief when Walter, seeking to meet the "paragon" (a woman's man as opposed to a man's man) Hildy has discovered, heartily shakes the hand of a befuddled elderly gentleman while Bruce vainly tries to introduce himself as the actual suitor. Walter quickly reverses the gag, quick to notice that Bruce has been properly attired in rain gear and rubbers. Bruce is at once too old and too young for Hildy. Our last vision of him is as the child-man reunited with his mother as the door of the pressroom, the domain reserved for grown-up antics, closes on their hapless embrace.

The wisdom of this film, then, does not come to us in the form of moral knowledge but in the realization that the choice of a mate or the filing of a story is implicated in one's attitude toward time and how it is to be filled. The Hecht-MacArthur play accelerated time to dramatize the clamor of the newsroom, where events break quickly: the first act is set at 8:30, the second thirty minutes afterward, the third an astounding "few minutes later." The effect is to create a sense of onrushing time, of events veering recklessly toward a comic catastrophe. This catastrophe is one that threatens not only the action of the comedy but its generic spirit. In this catastrophe, state murder threatens to overshadow the conventional triumph of social time in marriage.

But within the play, the passage of time, while breathtaking, never seems to be anything but a local matter, confined to the newsroom. This is not merely because the play is restricted to the stage, for the film, with its few changes of scene, manages to appear at times even more claustrophobic than the stage. Many of Hawks's medium shots have the effect of intensifying rather than neutralizing the intimacy of close-ups or the impersonality and distance of long shots. The frame seems crowded as the camera focuses on the desk that conceals Earl Williams or the table where Hildy and Walter frantically manage the phones.

Where the play gives us, as it were, local time, the film gives us a *rampant* time, swiftly moving toward a deadline for which there will be no reprieve, no second edition. This is visually as well as emotionally impressed upon us by the first self-conscious cut in the film, a high-angle shot from the pressroom of the Criminal Courts Building onto the prison courtyard below. We do not actually see the gallows going up, only the menacing shadow it casts. This dark image is amplified by the sounds of construction hammering out the last hours of Earl Williams's life. The sights and sounds of death taking on concrete form viscerally remind us that these vintage comedies often locate themselves uncomfortably but honestly in the vicinity of crime melodramas, where the moral licenses of comedy are reinterpreted as socially aberrant behaviors.

Most of the high-angle shots of the film emphasize this potential for sociopathy: the searchlights that scan the prison after Earl Williams's jailbreak seems almost stock footage from one of the crime melodramas of which Hawks was a master; and the interview scene belongs, too, to those quiet, soul-searching interludes of the gangster film when the doomed hooligan (Cagney, most memorably) confesses a stoic and uncharacteristically muted understanding of his "true" nature.

The film itself insists on this by visually linking its hysterical rhythms to the impending execution. The action is dramatically paced by the insertion of two high-angle shots of the gallows under construction that establish, by means of a gruesome visual pun, that the world of *His Girl Friday* is a world of deadlines. We recall here that Hawks took a degree as an engineer; there is a kind of grim professional interest in the gallows as a contraption. A startling shot of the finished gallows completing its test run with a definitive thud punctuates the film with a distinctly professional and moral finality. Those gallows are going up faster than we can catch up with the motive for murder, outpacing even Walter's contagious mania for breaking news.

The shadows cast by the gallows extend the moral reach of Hawks's comedy beyond their immediate use in signaling the imminence of the execution. They seem to be pointing, as they elongate over the course of the film, to a darker relation between the frantic pace of the film and the desperate efforts to secure a reprieve. As they lengthen we seem to be taking the measure of time apportioned by judicial decree. Only two powers can keep time from taking its appointed course: the power of the governor and the power of the press.

In both cases this power is delegated to the two experts in human behavior who can get the real story on Earl Williams and thus decide whether he is sane enough to be executed for murder. One is the court-appointed psychiatrist, and the other is Hildy. Hildy understands something beyond Walter's moral capacity to know—that the truth of a story has consequences not only for one's life, but for one's death. Hildy's greatness as a reporter emerges in comparison to the other press hounds for whom someone's death, perhaps even their own, is a news story, touching on no deeper feeling or reality. Their moral deafness is preserved and counterbalanced by their sensitivity to noise: they yell at the gallows builders to keep the racket down. They can't work when the machinery of death intrudes on their consciousness.

What Hildy understands is time as a dramatic medium. So does Hawks, the storyteller-director in sympathy with Hildy, who finally is, if anyone in the film is, his surrogate. To her he assigns the film's "exclusive," sign of his regard for her professionalism and for her superb instincts for story: its excitements, lulls, surprises, and astonishing culminations. She contributes to the comedy what may be simply called its human interest—an interest not confined to the pursuit of a halfway normal life but somehow and seriously related to it. Human interest visually, as well as ethically, emanates from Hildy in the act of "getting" and writing a story. Walter doesn't know what human interest is; he shows us as much when, in barking frantic directions to Duffy (Frank Orth), his city editor, about the next day's layout, he junks a story on a Chinese earthquake in which a million perished but insist on keeping a story about a rooster: "No, that's human interest!"

Human interest finds its most expressive form in the interview. The interview scene is a kind of interlude that in another comedy would take place in some Arcadian glade. In an uncanny inversion, Hawks makes the prisoner's cell a recess where the truth might be quietly and more honestly told. This scene is the film's only uncynical attempt to "get" at something resembling the truth, the human truth, of what makes us do the things we do so unthinkingly, yet irresistibly. And this attempt belongs to a woman. Many critics have noted the odd and uncharacteristically self-conscious high-angle shot that opens the scene, Hawks's homage to German expressionism and its haunting evocation of the lights and shadows cast by human consciousness. I don't believe it is Hildy's consciousness that is encompassed by the shot, although she possesses the keen-yet-sympathetic intelligence that makes subconsciousness possible. The high-angle shot recalls in the first instance the views down into the courtyard where the gallows were being built and where, minutes later, searchlights scan the walls. Such a shot symbolizes a morally elevated view of dispassion and presumed immunity but does not absolve us of complicity.

This is emphasized by the way the scene is introduced, juxtaposing two short tracking shots, the first of Bruce leaving the newsroom with Diamond Louie, Walter's seedy factotum, tailing him; the second, continuous with the first, of Hildy, who continues Bruce and Louie's trajectory across the screen from right to left. She, like Louie, is on an assignment for Walter, one that involves pursuit and vaguely illegal machinations. This juxtaposition also tells us that there is more than a slight comic resemblance between Earl Williams and Bruce Baldwin, both sexual innocents who can be set up, Williams by the political machinery, Baldwin by Walter's underworld boy Friday, Louie. Hildy finds her "prey," the jail warden Cooley (Pat West), whom she will later tackle when he tries to flee after the jailbreak, and drops a bribe to get her in to see Williams. The succeeding high-angle shot thus breaks the line of that movement toward corruption and entanglement, and in doing so stills the action, interrupts it for a moment, giving us time to separate from the world of bribes and frame-ups and so mentally prepare for the scene to follow.

A tense quiet prevails, one protracted in the one dissolve of the film, in which Hildy moves her chair closer to Earl's cell. This dissolve has the effect of slowing down as well as isolating the action, creating a transition into another order of time, a more *meditative,* certainly less clamorous time than the rest of the film. The mood is one of stillness, and the principal players seem, for once, unrushed. It thus comes as something of a surprise when the guard suddenly announces that Hildy's time is up. We had perhaps forgotten that Hildy's interview, like all her other assignments, was conducted with a heightened awareness of time elapsing, and elapsing perhaps too quickly for any human intentions to be realized, whether those be Walter's desire to stay the execution *and* permanently detain Hildy, or Hildy's intention to get the story that might save Williams and still catch the night train to Albany.

The scene is shot with Hildy dominating the frame, separated from Earl by the grid of cell bars. The basic form of human interchange doesn't change in this scene. There is the same overlap and interruption of lines, but the dramatic and emotional effect achieved here is solemn rather than frenetic. Urgency is now given a human meaning in the quiet insistence with which Hildy coaxes Earl to tell his story before it is too late: What did he do? What did he hear? What was he thinking? She barely permits him to complete a sentence, yet she never seems to rush him or hurriedly extort a confession. And she still has time—and the heart—to notice, before she takes leave of him, the flowers sent by Mollie to cheer him and her picture tacked on the cell bars.

Hildy proves herself to be the film's true, if unaccredited, psychiatrist, out to find an angle, not to work one (like the sheriff and his cohorts, who believe an execution will win them precious votes in the upcoming election). She finds her angle in a phrase picked up and lingering in an aggrieved and distracted mind: production for use. Earl had heard this phrase at a political rally and, Hildy suggests, finding a gun in his hand, put the phrase itself to use.

> Hildy: Now look, Earl, when you found yourself with that gun in your hand, and that policeman coming at you, what did you think about? . . . You must have thought of something. . . . Could it have been, uh, "production for use"? . . . What's a gun for Earl?
>
> Williams: A gun? . . . Why, to shoot, of course.
>
> Hildy: Oh. Maybe that's why you used it.
>
> Williams: Maybe.
>
> Hildy: Seems reasonable?
>
> Williams: Yes, yes it is. You see, I've never had a gun in my hand before. That's what a gun's for, isn't it? Maybe that's why.
>
> Hildy: Sure it is.
>
> Williams: Yes, that's what I thought of. Production for use. Why, it's simple isn't it?
>
> Hildy: Very simple. *[Hildy sighs rather than assert her agreement in a way that suggests at once sympathy and world-weariness.]*

Production for use, as Marilyn Campbell notes, was the memorable slogan of Upton Sinclair's run for governor, a campaign satirized in Budd Schulberg's *What Makes Sammy Run*. Campbell rightly stresses the importance of this phrase to the film's cinematic as well as ideological effects. She got the important structure produced for use, as Hildy's story dramatically concludes, is the gallows. Unlike other commodities and objects that circulate in the film, causing mischief and making visible hidden relationships—stories, money, cigarettes, even desks (they can be used, as Earl discovers, as a hideout)—the gallows have only one use. Production for use reminds us not only that things are produced, but how they are used, to what ends.

Hildy builds a story around this perception, linking Earl's misguided application of this principle. But then she tears up the story in a fit of rage. She is angry at Walter for reneging on his bargain and for having made use of her. Is this what leads her to disassociate herself from a utilitarian economy in which things are put to what seems inhuman use? It is Hildy's anger that blinds her to the higher human interest that her story might serve—saving William's life. We come face-to-face in this moment with a fury not just beyond words, but at their expense—at the expense, that is, of our power to redeem as well as falsify reality.

In the depressed moral economy of this comedy, where language circulates unattached to any standard of truth or even plausibility, Hawks can only revert to the intrinsic authority of cliché and silence as monitors of human value. To this ingenuity we might ascribe the force of Hildy's parting shot, "Good-bye, Earl, and good luck." We had heard something like this line before, when Hildy, after announcing her engagement, had consoled the stunned Walter: "Better luck to you next time." We will hear this formula once again, spoken not by Hildy but by Walter, as he seems, at last, willing to give her up to Bruce: "Good-bye, dear, and good luck." Neither good-bye is final, of course. Earl will escape and entrust his fate to Hildy. Hildy will discover to her relief that Walter's good-bye to her, unlike hers to Williams, is not an act of heartfelt leave-taking but another play to impress on her what it *really* means to leave him. Yet each is rhetorically effective in provoking a necessary breakdown in the frantic clamor of a film that seems demonically intent on banishing the language of real feeling from its precincts.

That even commonplace terms can be produced for moral use is shown when Hildy, by virtue of a single phrase, makes the rabid throng of newspapermen pause for thought, a pause in which something like self-reproach manages to make a brief appearance. It occurs midway in the film after Hildy, in the only moment of female solidarity she displays (in contrast to her superficial deference to her mother-in-law) escorts Mollie out of the pressroom. When Hildy and Mollie exit, they take any vestige of humanity with them, leaving the newspapermen oddly and uncharacteristically disconcerted—and silent. They shuffle around the room, uneasily trying to resume their old rhythms of work, rhythms by which they hope to regain their composure as nonfunctional human beings. Hildy reenters and delivers her inimitable line: "Gentlemen of the press." It's a stock phrase, like "good-bye and good luck," but there is nothing formulaic about the moral impact of that line in the pressroom, filled, for once, with the eerie sound of silence. Those four words reverberate with the unexpressed outrage at the demeaning work of the newspaperman, from peeping through keyholes to harassing kindhearted tarts. Hildy pronounces the word "gentlemen" in a particularly low, grave voice, as if delivering a eulogy for human decency.

All of these silences are full of meanings. Through them we can begin to hear those voices of conscience, remorse, or remonstrance routinely muffled by the sheer din of activity. It is curious how long these moments of morally articulate silence are prolonged in a film justly celebrated for its pace. The truth struggles to be heard in these intervals of quiet but is quickly drowned out by the next onrush of speech, a new burst of sirens.

The self-conscious lighting of the film participates in this moral dramaturgy of the unspoken. As the plot complications intensify, Walter becomes quite busy not only as actor but as stage manager, shutting out lights, pulling down shades. In the determined urbanity of this film, nature is always elsewhere and unreachable—it's where the governor is fishing, it's Niagara Falls, which Hildy, we suspect, will never reach. This is the only comedy I know in which it seems, ironically, entirely *natural* that the romantic lead complains, "Ah, now the moon's out!" Moonlight, of course, signifies the lustrous light of romance, even, as in *Bringing Up Baby,* of the magical mating of species, the leopard and the dog. The filmic apotheosis of moonlight occurs in *It Happened One Night* when Peter Warne (Clark Gable) provokes Ellie Andrews's (Claudette Colbert) declaration of love by describing an island paradise where "you and the moon and the water all become one." In this film, the moon is an obstacle to concealment, and so its glow must be occluded, its light banished.

But if there is no poetic vision of reality, there is the luster of a poetic idea in what Walter offers Hildy: a career as a noble crusader like those honored by statues in the park. There is a grim symmetry in Walter's tempting Hildy with the chance to rise into a completely different class. We recall that when Hildy escorted Mollie Malloy out of reach of the cynical reporters, Mollie cried out, as if in disbelief, "Aren't they inhuman." "I know," Hildy confirms. "They're newspapermen." But Hildy also knows that she is in danger of reverting to something at once more than and yet less than human herself. She finds herself listening, perhaps against her better judgment, to Walter's urging to pursue the "greatest yarn in journalism since Livingstone discovered Stanley." "It's the other way around," Hildy corrects him, but she soon succumbs to his vision of her as a social reformer: "Do you realize what you've done, honey? You've taken a city that's been graft-ridden for forty years under the same old gang. With this yarn, you're kicking 'em out." Walter has turned that doll-faced hick into a first-class newspaperman, and however much we might disapprove of his tutelage, it is clear that Hildy, in accepting the life he offers her, chooses to make a complete break from her past and to renounce any future she might have entertained as a woman leading a halfway normal life.

This break comes in the form of a declaration in the midst of the comic oratorio that gives the film its great concluding set-piece: Walter screaming instructions to Duffy, Hildy trying to rewrite the story of Earl's jailbreak, and Bruce urging Hildy to pay attention and catch that by now emotionally uncatchable nine o'clock train. In the volley of Walter's shouted orders, Hildy's manic rewrites, and Bruce's importuning, she manages to blurt: "I'm no suburban bridge player. I'm a newspaperman." This line, all things considered, is the most amazing kiss-off in movie comedy. It is, first of all, astoundingly casual. Only later will Hildy even remember what she said, just as it will take some time for her to realize that Bruce has indeed left the room, taking with him her chance "to live decent and live like a human being." Though she will complain that Walter has ruined her life, there is little regret and no obvious anguish in the way she bids Bruce good-bye. Yet unlike Tracy Lord's dismissal of her ambitious fiancé, George Kittridge (Katharine Hepburn and John Howard), in *The Philadelphia Story*, Hildy's kiss-off isn't tinged with a "classy" tone of sarcastic triumph. Nor does her brusque, distracted gesture waving Bruce from her side compare to the high romantic kitsch of Ellie Andrews's flight from the high-class altar of emotional immolation to the humble auto cabin where the walls of Jericho come tumbling down. Tracy and Ellie, of course, are heiresses who may choose either to marry within their class or outside or below it. Hildy is a working girl, and her dismissal of her bourgeois suitor is determined less by her class feeling than by the feeling of belonging to a tribe.

In this case it is the tribe of newspapermen, among whom Hildy decides to make her home. She announces this decision to remain a newspaperman rather than become a suburban bridge player in the midst of composing the greatest story of her life, one that Walter assured her would be the making of her career. But more than raw ambition is blurted here, just as more than a callous repudiation of her patient and by this time much-abused suitor is intended. Hildy is not so much rejecting Bruce as choosing between one way of spending her time and another, between the bridge game of the suburbs and the ritual poker game of the pressroom that, as Hecht and MacArthur describe it, "has been going on now for a generation, presumably with the same deck of cards."

The comedy is decided from that point. What remains is the zany poetry of Walter and Hildy's collaboration and the definitive break with Bruce—a break with all the hopes (or perhaps they were pretenses) that Hildy had for becoming a halfway normal woman. She prefers to work, which means she prefers to spend her time with Walter. Walter's suggestion, made supposedly on noble grounds, that she make herself a life without him desolates her, because for her no such life can really exist.

It is at this crisis point that Hildy shows herself to be all too recognizably a more than halfway normal woman who, when all else fails, cries. Cries to get Walter back, cries to forestall the comic catastrophe of Walter's sudden ennoblement. The comic nerve of this film is in insisting that Walter's reformation would be both a human and romantic calamity. Without his diabolic cunning, death might get his due—on schedule. Walter, deaf to human interest, is the demon who understands nature's dark genius for natural selection. The social time of the film is marked by social and natural catastrophes—rigged elections, mine cave-ins, a strike, a world at war with itself. The film will end with the fast-breaking story of a strike in Albany, ironically fulfilling Walter's smug prediction that Hildy, in marrying Bruce, could look forward to a "life of adventure," and in Albany, too!

Comedy instructs us what is gained in pursuing a life of adventure, and what is lost. What is lost is easier to describe: the sense of being settled. We are impressed by the magnitude of this loss not so much by Hildy's yearning to have a home as by Earl Williams's inability to find a refuge. Earl, who at one point finds temporary shelter in a desk, is a figure of anticomedy, a kind of social and emotional black hole that threatens to implode. He's unemployed in a film where everyone is deliriously busy at their job. He complains of being tired, weary of the world, at the point where the comedy is just picking up speed. He's too dimwitted to grasp the comic as well as economic rule of production for use: he meets a tart and talks to her. If the plot didn't give him a reason to stow Williams away in the rolltop desk, Hawks would have had to invent one. Williams is slow, and we never get to see the only quick, smart, and funny thing he does: walking off with the sheriff's gun and shooting the court-appointed psychiatrist in the "classified ads, no ad."

When Hildy heads down the stairs, following Walter and carrying her typewriter, we understand that the female rampant is back in business, clothed in pinstriped suits rather than designer gowns. She has given up the hope of home in her search for a life of adventure, a life whose excitement we might glean from the most piquant memory that Hildy and Walter share in the film, the time they sneaked into the coroner's office and hid out for a week: "We could have gone to jail for that too, you know that," Walter reminds her. Illicit love *would* appeal to Walter, the dapper Mephistopheles, but the film seems more interested not in the legality but in the psychology of their amorous escapades. Love shadowed by death is a keen incitement to action, the more desperate or frenzied the better.

This may be the deeper meaning of the astonishing cut that links Mollie's jump, a futile attempt to rescue Earl from capture, to Walter's entry. I don't mean to imply that Walter is a figure of death. He represents a more fantastical possibility—the evasion of death. An imperturbable belief in his own immunity to mortal accidents may explain why he doesn't "get" life insurance. Or it may be that he simply refuses to bargain with or about death. He stands for life, a life of adventure, not in Albany, but any time, any place, anywhere life presents itself. To accept him is to accept that life and to refuse the notion of a home.

There is, then, something profoundly atavistic as well as exuberantly futuristic in Hawks's new men and women. Hildy Johnson is arguably the most daring of them, going wherever

Walter might send her: into caves that might collapse at any moment, into the depths of the Criminal Courts Building, into the bowels of that moral wilderness, the modern pressroom. What Hildy seeks and finds is not a home but a habitat, often gloomy and subterraneous, where she and Walter might reenact their illicit rites of love. The female rampant, uncontrolled in everything but speech, is a natural denizen of that world. The burst of music, conspicuously absent throughout the rest of the film, seems to act as fanfare to her reentry into that strangely erotic underworld, which is wherever Walter happens to be. Musical time, with its formal promise of harmonic resolution, accompanies this dark duo making their way into that night in which the only measure of time is the deadline.

Yet who is to say that this comic ending is not of the most conventional even as it is of the most aberrant kind? Hildy finally gets to go on her honeymoon, to spend her time in the only way that really matters to her—with Walter, who treats her not as a woman but as a newspaperman.

Disneyland would be a world of Americans, past and present, seen through the eyes of my imagination—a place of warmth and nostalgia, of illusion and color and delight"

—Walt Disney

SHANGRI-LA

I WAS TAUGHT IN grade school about Henry Ford and his assembly lines. They left out the fact that Ford was a hateful pig spewing lies and leaving a trail of slime wherever he walked.

The movie company Dreamworks paid a large amount of money to Jeff Berg for his excellent recent biography of Charles Lindbergh to make into a film by Steven Spielberg. Obviously wanting to do a film about the American hero who first flew the Atlantic, they clearly remembered Billy Wilder's *Spirit of St. Louis* with its stirring score by Franz Waxman. If anyone there reads the book (written with the cooperation of Lindbergh's widow) they'll learn about Lindbergh's suspect political views, including his strong pro-Nazi feelings.

Much of the world's population is searching for enlightenment. A place to go in mind if not in body to experience peace and tranquility and get away from the harshness of their lives. Sometimes a work of art can help you transcend reality.

Ian Burma's review of the book *Virtual Tibet: Searching For Shangri-La from the Himalayas to Hollywood* by Orville Schelle is an entertaining and informative look at the meeting of the Dalai Lama and the laborers of the Dream Factory. Did the producers of *Seven Years In Tibet* know that the character played by Brad Pitt was a Nazi? Did they care?

John Landis

FOUND HORIZON

by Ian Buruma

Traveling recently by bus from Shigatse to Lhasa, squeezed in between a heavily made-up bar hostess from Sichuan who was vomiting her breakfast out the window and a minor Tibetan official in a shiny brown suit who asked me about Manchester United football club before noisily clearing his throat to deposit a green gob of spit beside my left shoe, I wondered what it was about Tibet that has made so many intelligent people go wobbly. The landscape, with its jagged chocolate-colored mountain peaks, its glassy lakes and emerald rivers, is spectacular, to be sure. And some of the other passengers on my bus—a herdsman with finely worked silver daggers, a monk in burgundy robes and Nike shoes, countrywomen with turquoise jewelry threaded through their hair—looked exotic enough. But there was nothing really to suggest that we were in a particularly spiritual place, where wise men knew the meaning of life, and incarnations of great lamas could fly.

But then, of course, it never was the actual place that fired the imagination of romantic seekers; it was the idea of Tibet, far away, impenetrable, isolated in the higher spheres of the earth. To see the real thing was to destroy the illusion. For the enchantment of Tibet lay in its remoteness. Indians and, later, Europeans, and even some Chinese, could project their spiritual fantasies onto a land they had never seen, and probably never would see. Those who felt discontented with their own complicated lives were consoled by the idea that in one isolated spot lived a people who still held the key to happiness, peace, and spiritual salvation, who had, as it were, by some miracle of nature, been spared the expulsion from the Garden of Eden.

It was often the nature of nature itself that caught the fancy of "civilized" men and women. Orville Schell, in his book *Virtual Tibet*, mentions a genteel English lady in 1869 who fell in love with the majestic Himalayan mountains because "no solemn garden parties or funereal dinners, no weary conventionalities of society, follow us here." Another British traveler, in 1903, compared one of the mountains to "a vast cathedral," and when a French Orientalist, around that same time, emerged onto the Tibetan highlands, he felt as though he had risen "through layers of cloud, from hell to heaven, leaving behind and below me this scientifically technical world which has done so much to increase man's misery." Blake would have understood: here, in the thin mountain air, amid those icy peaks, was sweet Jerusalem at last.

But then, these early seekers never sat in a rickety bus, with vomiting Chinese hookers for company. Orville Schell, a seasoned traveler in China, probably has, and his book has the bracing air about it of disenchantment. The fact that he was a bit of a seeker once himself, mesmerized by the idea of Tibet, and of Communist China, makes him the perfect chronicler of such afflictions in others. In an earlier book of his, about the advent of Chinese-style casino capitalism, he expressed a fleeting sense of nostalgia for an earlier China, austere, remote, high-minded, inaccessible, xenophobic, poor. Mao's China, after all, was a kind of Tibet for would-be refugees from Western civilization too.

Having read his book on Tibet, I understand Schell's romantic longings a bit better. Here he is, on the set of the movie *Seven Years in Tibet*, high up in the Andes mountains, gazing in wonder at a replica of Lhasa. He feels "overwhelmed by a yearning for a place like the one I see being set in motion before me—a fantastic island of escape from the prosaic, the rapacious, the speed and falseness of modern life." The fact that he is looking at a movie set adds a nicely poignant touch: this is the genuine stuff of fantasy.

Schell's descriptions of earlier Tibetophiles, trying to make a getaway from the solemn garden parties of life, are lively and interesting enough, but some of them have been told quite a few times before. To me the more arresting parts of his book are about the peculiar symbiosis between Hollywood and Tibet. The number of men and women who go wobbly at the thought of Tibet and its highest representative on earth, His Holiness the Dalai Lama, seems to be remarkably high in the main factory town of American fantasies. Why?

Why would Martin Scorsese, for example, a director of hard-nosed American movies, react like a gushing schoolgirl to the Dalai Lama, about whose life he was inspired to make the film *Kundun*? "Something happened," he is quoted as saying. "I became totally aware of existing in the moment. It was like you could feel your heart beat; and as I left, he looked at me. I don't know, but there was something about the look, something sweet. . . . I just knew I had to make the movie." Scorsese was raised as a Catholic, and Catholics have their own rich tradition of religious ecstasies. Nevertheless, I find it hard to imagine him reacting quite in this way to an audience with the Pope.

Scorsese, in any case, has only a mild case of Tibetitis compared to other Hollywood celebrities. Schell meets most of them. His interviewing technique is feline rather than confrontational; he lets the words of his interlocutors speak for themselves, and sometimes, in my view, leaves the tape recorder running for too long. They certainly sound pretty silly: Richard Gere, for instance, expects to "get 'zapped' every time he is around His Holiness, and believes that Tibet has remained "the last real, living 'wisdom' civilization." But by far the most egregious exponent of this type of thing is the director and star of violent action pictures Steven Seagal. Seagal, as described by Schell, is clearly a *fantaisiste*. An oddball in traditional Chinese clothes, cowboy boots, and a pigtail, he likes to present himself as a pistol-packing tough guy, boasting of affiliations ranging from Japanese gangsters to the CIA, and as an Oriental holy man. Not only does Seagal go wobbly at the sight of His Holiness, but he claims that His Holiness also goes wobbly at the sight of him. The Dalai Lama, in Seagal's account, kissed the action-man's feet as a tribute to a fellow deity. He told Schell:

> I've kept my spiritualism secret because people don't understand it. Friends have never gotten this part of my life, but there are many great lamas who recognize me as something strange and from another time, who refer to me as one of them. I feel a kinship beyond words with them, something really deep. People all over the world come up to me and recognize me as a great spiritual leader.

The problem for the Dalai Lama and his canny government in exile is that he needs the support of such Hollywood Buddhists, but cannot risk having his sacred aura contaminated by too much contact with them. Tibetan worshippers find it unseemly. Somehow, the sight of His Holiness standing on stage at the Beverly-Wilshire Hotel or the Pasadena Civic Auditorium, with Steven Seagal, Richard Gere, and Sharon Stone in a silk pantsuit, renders somewhat implausible his status as the latest incarnation of the ancient God of Compassion. It brings to the proceedings an air of fraudulence. This is not the Dalai Lama's fault. But magic relies on obscurity. The nature of Hollywood magic is different from the religious kind. Or is it?

Schell makes a case that the Hollywood star system is in some ways similar to the order of Tibetan monks and holy men. It is a provocative idea: Grauman's Chinese Theater as the Potala of Tinseltown; Gere, Stone, and Harrison Ford as cinematic lamas; the fans in Bermuda shorts and reversed baseball caps as pilgrims at the sacred shrines of Hollywood Boulevard. As Schell says,

> . . . with its own nobility of stars and celebrities, distinctive rites, costumes, festival-like awards ceremonies, celebrated monuments, potent mythologies, studio complexes as vast as monasteries, and a reigning pantheon of semidivine deities worshiped around the world, Hollywood might well appear as alien and mysterious to outsiders as the forbidden city of Lhasa once did to those Westerners who first breached its carefully guarded perimeters.

The comparison would seem strained if one believed that traditional religious practices were more genuine, or authentic, than the new forms of worship that have taken their place in Hollywood or on television gospel hours. To be sure, tradition creates its own kind of authenticity. Time has a way of legitimizing all manner of human practices, which if they were newly invented would cause outrage: bullfighting, for example. But is it really so implausible to think of Hollywood Buddhism as the result of a natural affinity between a new quasi religious order and a traditional one?

Schell has a few other explanations for Hollywood Buddhism, too, however, some of which are a little too generous for my taste. He believes that the likes of Steven Seagal, having triumphed over "adversity" themselves, "identify with the Dalai Lama and Tibetans as underdogs—the little guy against the big bully." Maybe, but in that case I would like to know a bit more the exact nature of Seagal's or Gere's adversities before I am convinced. I'm sure Gere's ascent to stardom has not been easy, and Seagal has to work hard to administer to his spiritual needs while making his action pictures, but it is rather a long way from these hardships to identification with persecuted Tibetans.

There is another possibility. It is implied in Schell's text without being developed as a theme: the ambivalence of imperialism. British colonialism in Asia, like most forms of colonialism, was a combination of commerce and manifest destiny. The main idea was to make as much money as possible. This meant that markets and sources of production had to be conquered. To justify this enterprise, a mission was concocted to bring civilization to the natives. Meanwhile, however, many an ardent imperialist fell in love with the conquered lands, and developed romantic notions of the cultures his own *mission civilisatrice* was busy converting to modern, Western ways. Schell mentions Lord Curzon and Major Francis Younghusband, who blasted his way to Lhasa in 1904 with Indian troops and Maxim guns. Younghusband certainly believed in the British Empire, but he also went wobbly in Lhasa, being "insensibly suffused with an almost intoxicating sense of elation and good will." Never again could the major "think of evil" or "be at enmity with any man. All nature and all humanity were bathed in a rosy glowing radiancy; and life for the future seemed nought but buoyancy and light." The effusions of Gere or Seagal are hardly more extravagant than this. The point, I think, is that some of the more sensitive imperialists realized what they were destroying, or at least changing forever by their presence, and ended up idealizing it.

I have sometimes wondered what it must be like to be, say, Mick Jagger, and pay a great deal of money for a trip to some outpost of native "authenticity," remote from the vulgar noise of Western civilization—Borneo, say, or, indeed, Tibet—only to find his own voice blaring from a village jukebox. I suppose he might feel flattered, but perhaps—I don't know—also a tiny bit ambivalent, perhaps even a touch disappointed, or even—and I know this is a long shot—guilty. Surely there must be Major Younghusbands among the movie stars and rock idols of the West. Richard Gere, say, or Sting? For their enterprise, as much as that of the Curzons of yesteryear, is touched with the same combination of commerce and claims to a universal civilization. And what better way to resolve any ambivalence about such claims than to make a commercial movie about a lost arcadia?

Hollywood's imperialism is not real, of course, in the sense of territorial conquest. American pop culture only colonizes our imaginations. It is a virtual empire. And Schell traveled all the way to the Andes to see the soldiers and administrators of this great empire in the process of building a virtual Tibet, with a truncated Potala of chicken wire and plywood, and heaps of yak dung made of pottery, and monks recruited from the native Indian population, and Tibetan extras flown in from India and California, and Chinese soldiers played by Japanese Argentines. This movie set arcadia was built for Jean-Jacques Arnaud's *Seven Years in Tibet*, starring Brad Pitt as Heinrich Harrer, the Austrian mountaineer who made it to Tibet in 1943.

The actual story of Harrer's infatuation with Tibet, as Schell recounts, was more sinister than the moviemakers realized when they started their project. Not only was Harrer a successful mountain climber, decorated by Hitler for planting the swastika on top of the Eiger in 1938, but he was a keen member of the Nazi Party, who joined the SA in 1933, when it was illegal for Austrians to do so, and the SS in 1938. The Nazis, especially Heinrich Himmler, had their own Tibetan romance. Central Asia, and Tibet in particular, was believed to be the ancient homeland of the Aryans. To penetrate Tibet and its secrets was, to Himmler and his fellow enthusiasts of mystical racism, part of their effort to trace the bloodlines of the German *Volk*.

News of these facts came rather late in the planning of Arnaud's movie. The idea of Brad Pitt as a Nazi mystic was of course impossible. Harrer's shady past was made a part of his story of redemption: a flawed European, consumed by selfishness and ambition, would be saved by the innocence and ancient wisdom of Tibet—rather like what Younghusband thought he had been. When the real Harrer met the current Dalai Lama in Lhasa, the holy man was already a teenager. In the movie, His Holiness is more childlike, perhaps to emphasize the purity of his extraordinary wisdom. Even Harrer, who idealized Tibet in his book, did not pass over less innocent episodes during his stay, such as armed rebellions in the monasteries. The movie Tibet, however, really is like Richard Gere's "last real 'wisdom' civilization," which lasted until the Chinese arrived in 1950, with their own civilizing mission.

Grafted onto the Nazi myth, then, which is spun out of sight, is another, no less potent myth, that of a land of spiritual purity despoiled by evil foreign forces. This myth, too, fits in well with Hollywood's old obsession with the corruption of innocence—the theme of so many movies about America, from the early westerns to *Apocalypse Now.*

In fact, when the Chinese Communists claimed Tibet as part of China—just as the Nationalists had done, and the Qing government before them—they were careful not to antagonize the Tibetans needlessly. They did not immediately set about insulting the clergy, as shown in the film. Instead they organized lavish banquets for the Lhasa aristocracy, many of whom believed that communism might be the best way to modernize their country, which had gotten stuck in a state of poverty and corruption—not least in the monastic orders.

Most of these early Tibetan Communists were later murdered in Maoist purges. But their intention to find some political solution for Tibet which would be neither theocratic nor entirely dependent on the Chinese was not ignoble. The movie, in which every Chinese is an evil monster, trampling on Tibetan Buddhist images or killing innocent monks, and every Tibetan who tries to negotiate with the Chinese a wicked traitor, suggests that it was. Just as Richard Attenborough's movie *Gandhi* took Indian nationalist myths at face value, so Arnaud's *Seven Years in Tibet* subscribes without a hint of skepticism to the nationalist myths of the Tibetan diaspora. That a half-century of Chinese communism has done a great deal of harm to Tibet is beyond doubt. But sentimental myths of childlike innocence despoiled by absolute evil will not help us see how some of that harm might be undone.

AFTERWORD

The selections you have read in this book are a tiny fraction of the vast amount of words about films and filmmakers written in the past few years. Books and magazines, newspaper articles and Web Sites are multiplying (like film festivals), even as the number of theatrical motion pictures produced each year declines.

It is much easier, and considerably less expensive, to write about a movie than to make one. But movies remain so powerful an emotional and cultural force it seems impossible not to desire to write on the subject.

Agents, producers, managers, publicists, actors, writers, costume designers, stunt men, photographers, hairdressers, critics, scholars, and directors have all written books about their lives and careers. Self-serving autobiographies abound. Hack "revisionist" biographies proliferate like hypocritical politicians.

Statements surrounded by quotation marks magically make true that an individual made the statement—even if the individual never said the words. Journalists and academics reprint the "quotes" and history is made. Since history is based on contemporary accounts and all contemporary accounts are suspect, much of what is written about anything is mythmaking.

Myself a victim of many a printed word, I've learned to approach all "factual" books cautiously.

There are a number of people who have written extensively

about film related subjects with reliably interesting and accurate results. Opinions are just opinions, I'm referring to their facts and writing skills when I say interesting and accurate. In no particular order, I can recommend the works of Thomas Schatz, Bob Thomas, Peter Bogdanovich, Richard Schickel, Peter Biskind, Bill Warren, Kevin Brownlow, Alexander Walker, David J. Skall, John McCabe, William K. Everson, Lotte Eisner, Samuel Marx, Leonard Maltin, Rudy Behlmer, Gavin Lambert, and Aljean Harmetz. I know I've left out many other authors worth reading, but this is a pretty good start if you're interested in reading about the movies.

Working in film and television has given me many gifts. I've met remarkable people, traveled the world and, for the most part, have had a very good time. I intend to make films for as long as I can, and feel privileged and lucky to earn my livelihood doing something I so enjoy.

Using the written word to describe and discuss film is rather like using words to explain the experience of sex. An endlessly fascinating and ongoing discussion.

John Landis

CONTRIBUTORS' NOTES

DOUG ATCHISON has produced, written, and directed over fifteen short films, including the award-winning *Ellen's Father.* He received the 2000 Nicholl Fellowship in Screenwriting for his feature screenplay *Akeelah and the Bee.* He is a contributing writer at *Movie Maker.*

MICHAEL ATKINSON is the author of *Ghosts in the Machine: Speculating on the Dark Heart of Pop Cinema* and *Blue Velvet* for the British Film Institute *Modern Film Classics* series. His film criticism has appeared in the *Village Voice, SPIN, Film Comment, The Guardian, Movieline, Sight & Sound, The Progressive, Maxim,* and elsewhere.

JOHN BAILEY is a cinematographer and director who has photographed many noted films such as *Ordinary People, The Big Chill, The Accidental Tourist, In The Line of Fire, Nobody's Fool,* and *As Good As It Gets,* among the more than 45 theatrical films to his credit. He has contributed to many film magazines, among them: *American Cinematographer; International Camera Guild; The Directors' Guild;* and was anthologized in *Screening Violence.* His most recent release is *The Anniversary Party;* he has just completed production on *Divine Secrets of the Ya Ya Sisterhood.* Bailey is married to acclaimed film editor Carol Littleton.

RUSSEL BANKS is the author of thirteen works of fiction, including *The Angel on the Roof: Stories, CloudSplitter, Rule of the Bone, The Sweet Hereafter, Affliction,* and *Continental Drift. The Sweet Hereafter* and *Affliction* were made into movies. His nonfiction has appeared in *Tin House, Esquire, Harper's,* and *The New York Times,* among others.

WALTER BERNSTEIN started screenwriting in Hollywood with director Robert Rossen. He had collaborated on only one screenplay before he was blacklisted in 1950. He wrote extensively for television over the next decade, then returned to film writing in 1959. His scripts include *The Magnificent Seven, The Money Trap, The Molly Maguires, The Front* and *Semi-Tough.* He is the author of *Inside Out: A Memoir of the Blacklist.*

IAN BURUMA is the author of *God's Dust: A Modern Asian Journey* (1989), *Behind the Mask: On Sexual Demons, Sacred Mothers, Transvestites, Gangsters, Drifters, and Other Japanese Cultural Heroes* (1984), and *The Wages of Guilt: Memories of War in Germany and Japan* (1994). He has also written a novel, *Playing the Game* (1991).

NATHALIE ZEMA DAVIS is Henry Charles Lea Professor of History, Emeritus, Princeton University, and the author of *The Return of Martin Guerre* and *Women on the Margins.*

MARIA DIBATTISTA, author of *Fast-Talking Dames*, is professor of English and Comparative Literature at Princeton University, where she is also the chair of the film studies committee. She has written numerous books and articles on modernist literature and film, including *First Love: The Affections of Modern Fiction* and a coedited volume, *High and Low Moderns: British Literature and Culture 1889-1939.*

DAVID GEFFNER directed two short films, *Wild Blade* and *Easy Money,* both of which went on to successful festival and home video runs. He's a freelance journalist for *RES Magazine, ICG Magazine, Filmmaker, MovieMaker, Variety, L.A. Times Sunday Magazine, DGA Magazine, America West Magazine,* and *Upside* among others. He is the screenwriter of two upcoming indie features, *The Feast,* and *The Sweetest Thing.*

MARY HARRON directed *I Shot Andy Warhol* and *American Psycho.* She writes about film frequently and contributes to such periodicals as *The New York Times.*

MOLLY HASKELL is a film critic and the author of *Holding My Own in No Man's Land,* and *From Reverence to Rape: The Treatment of Women in the Movies.*

MICHAEL HERR is the author of the books *Dispatches, The Big Room* and *Walter Winchell.* He cowrote Francis Ford Coppola's *Apocalypse Now.*

LAWRENCE KASDAN has directed several films including *Body Heat, The Big Chill, Silverado, The Accidental Tourist, I Love You to Death, Grand Canyon, Wyatt Earp, French Kiss,* and *Mumford.* He wrote or cowrote all of these with the exception of *I Love You to Death* and *French Kiss.* Kasdan also wrote or cowrote *Raiders of the Lost Ark, The Empire Strikes Back, Return of the Jedi,* and *The Bodyguard.*

JOHN IRVING is the author of several novels, including *A Widow for One Year, The Cider House Rules, The 158-Pound Marriage, The Hotel New Hampshire, A Son of the Circus, Trying to Save Piggy Sneed,* and *The World According to Garp.* He received an Academy Award for his screenplay for *The Cider House Rules.* His book *My Movie Business* recounts his thirteen-year journey in transforming *The Cider House Rules* into a film.

JACK KEROUAC was a leading chronicler of the beat generation. After studying briefly at Columbia University, he published a series of novels, including *On the Road, The Dharma Bums, The Subterraneans, Doctor Sax, Lonesome Traveler,* and *Big Sur,* among others.

STUART KLAWANS has contributed to *The Nation, New York Daily News, Times Literary Supplement,* NPR, *The Village Voice, Grand Street, Threepenny Review, Entertainment Weekly, Chicago Tribune,* and *The New York Times.* He is included in several anthologies, including *The Best American Essays 1990, Seeing Through Movies,* and *Foreign Affairs.* His book *Film Follies* was nominated for a 1999 National Book Critics Circle Award for Criticism. *Left in the Dark: Film Reviews and Essays, 1988-2001* is forthcoming from Thunder's Mouth Press.

STANLEY KUBRICK directed several award-winning movies, including *Clockwork Orange, Dr. Strangelove, 2001: A Space Odyssey, The Shining, Full Metal Jacket, and Eyes Wide Shut,* among others.

DAVID LEAVITT is the author of several novels and collections of short stories, including *In Maremma: Life and a House in Southern Tuscany, The Page Turner, Martin Bauman; Or, a Sure Thing, Family Dancing,* and *The Lost Language of Cranes.*

LEONARD J. LEFF is a film critic and the author of *Hitchcock and Selznick, Hemingway and His Conspirators, The Dame in the Kimono.* He has written for *Opera News, Film Comment,* and *The Atlantic Monthly.*

RICK LYMAN is bureau chief of *The New York Times* in Houston. He's written and edited for the *Philadelphia Enquirer, Kansas City Star, United Press, The Hammond Indiana Times.* He won the 1993 Overseas Press Club of American Award and shared a Pulitzer Prize in 1983 with a team of reporters at the *Kansas City Star.*

REBECCA MEAD is a staff writer at the *New Yorker.* She has been a contributing editor at *New York* magazine, and a writer for the *Sunday Times* of London.

DARYL G. NICKENS chairs the graduate screenwriting program at the American Film Institute. He is a WGA, Emmy, and Humanitas Award nominee.

ROBERT POLITO is the author of *Savage Art: A Biography of Jim Thompson,* which received the National Book Critics Award in biography, *A Reader's Guide to James Merrill's The Changing Light at Sandover,* and *Doubles* (poems). He edited the Library of American volumes *Crime Novels: American Noir of the 1930's and 1940's, Crime Novels: American Noir of the 1950's.* He is currently finishing a multiperson biography *Detours: Seven Noir Lives.* A contributing editor at *BOMB, The Boston Review,* and *Fence,* he directs the Graduate Writing Program at the New School in New York City.

SAM STAGGS is the author of *All About All About Eve,* and *The Return of Marilyn Monroe.*

TOM WEAVER is the author of *Poverty Row Horrors!, Universal Horrors: The Studio's Classic Films, 1931-1946, Return of the B Science Fiction and Horror Movie Makers, It Came From Weaver 5, Attack of the Monster Movie Makers, Invasion of the Monster Movie Makers,* and more.

ABOUT THE SERIES EDITOR

Jason Shinder's books include the award-winning poetry collections *Every Room We Ever Slept In,* (a New York Public Library noted book) the recently published *Among Women,* and the forthcoming *Lives of the Romantics.* He is the editor of several anthologies including, most recently, *Tales From the Couch: Writers on Therapy, Best American Movie Writing,* of which he is the series editor, and the forthcoming *First Death: Writers on Immortality* and *What Lovest Well Remains: Conversations with Poets on Poets of the Past.* His honors include fellowships from the National Endowment for the Arts, the Yaddo corporation, the Fine Arts Work Center in Provincetown, among others. A teacher in the graduate writing programs at Bennington College, and the New School University, he is the Founder and Director of the YMCA National Writer's Voice, YMCA of the USA Arts & Humanities and the Director of The Writing Program at Sundance Institute.

ABOUT THE GUEST EDITOR

John Landis is the award-winning director (and often writer or cowriter) of many acclaimed movies including: *Animal House, The Blues Brothers, An American Werewolf In London, Trading Places, Three Amigos, Into the Night, Spies Like Us, Coming to America* and *Innocent Blood* among others.

He wrote and directed the groundbreaking music videos *Michael Jackson's Thriller* and *Michael Jackson's Black or White.* Landis has also been active in television as the Executive Producer (and often director) of the Emmy winning HBO series *Dream On.* He has acted in movies as diverse as *Death Race 2000* and *Muppets Take Manhattan.* His many honors include People's Choice Awards, the W.C. Handy Award, the Cable Ace Award, NAACP Image Awards and various international film and television festival awards. He was made a Chevalier dans l'Ordre des Arts et des Lettres by the French Government in 1985 and was recently given the Federico Fellini Prize by Riminicinema, Italy.

PERMISSIONS

Doug Atchison, "How the MPAA Rates Independent Films." Copyright © 2000 Doug Atchison as first appeared in *Movie-Maker.*

Michael Atkinson, "Stop-Motion JimJams: Ray Harryhausen." From *Ghosts in the Machine: The Dark Heart of Pop Cinema* by Michael Atkinson. Copyright © 2000 by Michael Atkinson. Reprinted with permission from Proscenium Publishers.

John Bailey, "Film or Digital: Don't Fight, Coexist." Copyright © 2000 by John Bailey as first published in *The New York Times.*

Russell Banks, "No, But I Saw the Movie." Copyright © 2000 by Russell Banks as first published in *Tin House.* Reprinted by permission of Ellen Levine Literary Agency, Inc.

Walter Bernstein, from *Inside Out: A Memoir of the Blacklist* by Walter Bernstein. Copyright © 2000 Walter Bernstein.

Ian Buruma, "Found Horizon." Reprinted with permission from *The New York Review of Books.* Copyright © 2000 NYREV, Inc.

Natalie Zemon Davis, "Ceremony and Revolt: Burn!" Reprinted by permission of the publisher from *Slaves on Screen* by Natalie Zemon Davis, 43-55, Cambridge, MA: Harvard University Press. Copyright © 2000 by Natalie Zemon Davis.

Maria DiBattista, "Female Rampant." Excerpted from *Fast-Talking Dames* by Maria DiBattista. Copyright © 2001 by Maria DiBattista. Reprinted by permission of Yale University Press.

David Geffner, "People Who Need People." Reprinted from *Filmmaker: The Magazine of Independent Film (Vol 8, #1, Fall 1999)*, with permission of the publisher.

Mary Harron, "The Risky Territory of *American Psycho*. Copyright © 2000 by Mary Harron as first published in *The New York Times*.

Molly Haskell, "High Wire Artist." Copyright © 2000 by Molly Haskell as first published in *The New York Times*.

Michael Herr, *Kubrick*. Copyright © 2000 by Michael Herr. Used by permission of Grove/Atlantic, Inc.

J. Hoberman, "When the Nazis Became Nudniks." Copyright © 2001 by J. Hoberman as published in the *New York Times*.

John Irving, "The Twelve-Year-Old Girl." From *My Movie Business* by John Irving. Copyright © 1999 by Garp Enterprises, Inc. Used by permission of Random House, Inc.

Lawrence Kasdan, "POV." Copyright TK. Reprinted by permission of the author.

Jack Kerouac, "Cody and the Three Stooges." Copyright TK. Reprinted by permission of Sterling Lord Literistic, Inc.

Stuart Klawans, *An Interlude*. From *Film Follies: The Cinema Out of Order* by Stuart Klawans. Copyright © 1999 Stuart Klawans. Reprinted by permission of The Continuum International Publishing Company, Inc.

Stanley Kubrick, "2001: A Film." Copyright 2001. Permission granted by *Action*, the Magazine of the Director's Guild of America, Vol. 4, Number 1, Jan.-Feb. 1969.

David Leavitt, "Lost Among the Pinafores." Copyright © 2000 David Leavitt as first published in *Tin House*.

Leonard J. Leff, "*Gone With the Wind* and Hollywood Racial Politics." Copyright © 2000 Leonard J. Leff, as first published in *The Atlantic Monthly*.

Rick Lyman, "Whoa, Trigger! Auteur Alert!" Copyright © 2000 by Rick Lyman as first published in *The New York Times*.

Rebecca Mead, "Cheese Whiz Sam Raimi, the Auteur of *The Evil Dead*." Copyright ©2000 by Rebecca Mead as first published in *The New Yorker*.

Daryl G. Nickens, "The Great Escape—Or the First Time I Didn't Pay for It." Copyright © 2000 Writers Guild Foundation. Reprinted with permission of International Creative Management.

David Remnick, "Is This the End of Rico?" Copyright © 2001 by David Remnick as first published in *The New Yorker*.

Robert Polito, "Barbara Payton: A Memoir." Copyright © 2000 Robert Polito. Piece originally appeared in the *San Diego Reader*. Printed by permission of the author.

Sam Staggs, *All About All About Eve*. Copyright © 2000 Sam Staggs from *All About All About Eve* by Sam Staggs. Reprinted by permission of St. Martin's Press, LLC.

Tom Weaver, "Hats off to Charles Gemora, Hollywood's Greatest Ape." Copyright © 2000 Tom Weaver as first published in *MonsterKid Magazine*.

INDEX

Symbols

1900, 5
2001: A Space Odyssey, 179–184
The 7th Voyage of Sinbad, 257
8mm, 60

A

Absalom, Absalom!, 178
Ackerman, Forrest J., 2
Adams, Jane, 250
Adams, Marjorie, 180
Adler, Renata, 239
Affliction, 89, 91, 94–96, 98–101, 103
Africa Screams, 26
Agin, Joerg, 252
Aldrich, Robert, 7
Alexander, Jane, 109
Alexander Nevsky, 183
Algren, Nelson, 92–93
All About "All About Eve", 37–53
Allen, Woody, 123, 147–148
Allyson, June, 129
Almendros, Néstor, 248
The Amazing Dr. Clitterhouse, 273
American Gigolo, 248
American Movie, 213, 222–224
American Pie, 67
American Psycho, 53–58, 67
Angels With Dirty Faces, 273
The Anniversary Party, 247–249, 251, 253
Anywhere but Here, 93
The Ape Man, 20
Apocalypse Now, 173, 317
Arloria, Franco Giorgio, 205
Army of Darkness, 194
Arnaud, Jean-Jacques, 316–317
Aronofsky, Darren, 59
The Art of War, 178
As Good as It Gets, 248
Atchison, Doug, Separate And Unequal?, 59–69
Atkinson, Michael, Stop-Motion Jimjams, 254–259
Atlantic City, 7
Attenborough, Richard, 318
Aurthur, Bob, 142–143
Aurthur, Robert Alan, 130
Auster, Paul, 93, 103
Austin Powers, 193

B

Badie, Mina, 250
Bailey, John, Film or Digital?, 246–254
Baker, Rick, 3
Ball of Fire, 273
Banks, Russell, No, But I Saw The Movie, 88–105
Barbara Payton: A Memoir, 1, 8–15
Barcroft, Roy, 20
Baretzki, Stefan, 230
Barrows, George, 3, 23–24
Basketball Diaries, 54
Battle of Algiers, 150, 203–204
Battlefield Earth, 179
Beals, Jennifer, 250
The Beast from 20,000 Fathoms, 256
Beatty, Warren, 147
Beckhard, Arthur, 240
Being John Malkovitch, 98

Bel Geddes, Norman, 229
Bellamy, Ralph, 279, 283–284
Beloved, 93
Berkeley, Busby, 241, 277
Berman, Shelly, 241
Bernardi, Herschel, 148
Bernardo, Paul, 55–57
Bernstein, Walter, 88
  Inside Out: A Memoir of the Blacklist, 123–148
Berra, Yogi, 149
Bertolucci, Bernardo, 5
The Big Chill, 251
The Big Sleep, 273
Birdman of Alcatraz, 6
Birdwell, Russell, 78
The Birth of a Nation, 73, 77, 79
Black and White, 65
Black Caesar, 277
Black Zoo, 23
Blair Witch Project, 98
Blazing Saddles, 271
Blobel, Paul, 232
Body and Soul, 164
Boetticher, Budd, 186
Bogdanovich, Peter, 190
Bolt, Robert, 158
The Bonnie Parker Story, 189–190
Bonnie and Clyde, 241
Bonomo, Joe, 27
Boogie Nights, 61–62, 68
Borchardt, Mark, 222–224
Borsos, Phillip, 111
Boudin, Leonard, 138, 141
Bourne, Saint Clair, 216
Bracco, Lorraine, 266–267
Brackett, Charles, 45
Brando, Marlon, 150, 207, 209, 211, 273
The Brandon Teena Story, 216
Braun, Alfred, 232
Breen, Joseph Ignatius, 46–47, 49–53, 77, 80
Bride of the Gorilla, 14
Bridges of Madison County, 64
Bringing Up Baby, 281, 304
Broderick, Matthew, 274
Brooks, Mel, 238–243
Brown, Kay, 72, 76–77
Bruce, Lenny, 242
Brynner, Yul, 142–143
Buford, Kate, 1, 3–5
Burn!, 203–204, 207–212
Burns, Bob, 2–3
  Hats Off To Charles Gemora, Hollywood's Greatest Ape, 20–33
Burroughs, William, 178
Burson, Colette, 67
Burt Lancaster, An American Life, 1, 3
Burton, Tim, 197
Buruma, Ian, Found Horizon, 310–318

C

Cabaret, 243
The Cabinet of Dr. Caligari, 139
Caesar, Sid, 239
Cagney, James, 5, 271, 297
Calciano, Sal, 263
Calley, John, 175
Cameron, John, 200
Campbell, Bruce, 194, 198–200, 202
Campbell, Joseph, 256
Campbell, Marilyn, 301
Capone, Al, 271–272
Carey, Macdonald, 190
Carey, Peter, 93, 103
Carroll, Nancy, 133
Casablanca, 85
Caspar, Horst, 235
Cates, Phoebe, 250
Cavell, Stanley, 292, 294
The Celebration, 98
The Cell, 67
censorship, 35–37
  and *Gone With the Wind*, 70–85
  and MPAA rating of independent films, 59–69, 59
  and Production Code, 46–49
Ceremony and Revolt, 203–212
Chandler, Raymond, 87
Chaney, Lon, 26
Chang, Wah, 27
Chaplin, Charlie, 183, 194
Chase, David, 264–266, 268–271, 274–275
Cheese Whiz, 193–203
Cheever, John, 93

The Chimp, 26
Chong, Annabel, 218–219
Chressanthis, James, 253
The Cider House Rules, 106–107, 109, 111–112
The Civil War, 200
Clark, Fred, 45
Clarke, Arthur C., 183
Clash of the Titans, 255
Cleopatra, 39
Clinton, Bill, 36
Cobb, Lee J., 273
Coburn, James, 91, 96
Cody & The Three Stooges, 2, 16–20
Coen, Joel and Ethan, 195–196, 198, 201
Cohn, Harry, 142
Cohn, Sidney, 132
Cokor, George, 75
Colbert, Claudette, 287, 304
The Colossus of New York, 30
Come Back Little Sheba, 6
Coming Soon, 67
Conrad, Joseph, 204
Continental Drift, 103
Conversation Piece, 5
Cooper, Gary, 7, 133
Coppola, Francis Ford, 103, 250, 273
Corman, Roger, 261
Cornwell, David, 172, 174
Corrigan, Crash, 3, 20, 23, 32
Costner, Kevin, 196
Courshon, Jerome, 65–66
Coven, 224
Cravat, Nick, 27–28
Craven, Wes, 193
Crime and Punishment, 57
The Crimson Pirate, 4, 7, 28
Cripps, Thomas, 71
Criss Cross, 6
Crouching Tiger, Hidden Dragon, 253
The Cruise, 213, 215, 217–218, 221–222, 225
Crumb, 213, 219, 224
Crumb, Robert, 219
Cumming, Alan, 247, 249, 251
Curse of the Faceless Man, 30
Curtis, Tony, 7
Curts, Jamie Lee, 194

D

Dafoe, Willem, 96, 101, 103
Darkman, 194
Darktown Strutters, 188
Darnell, Linda, 38
David Copperfield, 108
Davis, Bette, 45
Davis, Natalie Zemon, 150
 Ceremony and Revolt, 203–212
Days of Heaven, 248
de Havilland, Olivia, 71, 83
De Palma, Brian, 250
De Toth, Andre, 186
Dead End, 273
DeCavalcante, Simone Rizzo, 262–264
Dee, Sandra, 140
Delbanco, Nicholas, 151–152, 168–169
The Destruction of the European Jews, 174, 176
Detour, 15
DeVries, Peter, 104
Di Battista, Maria, Fast-Talking Dames, 278–308
Diamonds, 64
DiCaprio, Leonardo, 194
Dick, Kirby, 213, 218–225
Dickens, Charles, 108
Diessl, Gustav, 235
Digital Filmmaking, 246–254
Disney, Walt, 309
Divine Secrets of the Ya-Ya Sisterhood, 253
Dmytryk, Edward, 273
Donnie Brasco, 274
Douglas, Kirk, 64, 133
Dream Novel, 173
Dunne, John Gregory, 160

E

Earth vs. the Flying Saucers, 257
Ebert, Roger, 238
The Eddy Duchin Story, 129
Edge of the City, 130–131
Egoyan, Atom, 95, 100–102
Eisenstein, Sergei, 183
The Eleanor Roosevelt Story, 242
Elliott, Denholm, 172

Ellis, Bret Easton, 53
Elmer Gantry, 4, 6
The English Patient, 93
The Eternal Jew, 230
Evans, Dale, 185, 190
Evil Dead, 193–195, 201–202
Evil Dead II-Dead by Dawn, 193–194, 202
Exodus, 133
Eyes Wide Shut, 63, 174

F

Fairbanks, Douglas, 6
Falco, Edie, 270
Fantasia, 156
Farber, Manny, 281
Fargo, 198
Farrow, Mia, 52
Fast-Talking Dames, 278–308
Fiddler on the Roof, 241
Film or Digital?, 246–254
The Flame and the Arrow, 28
Flanagan, Bob, 213, 217, 221
Flight of the Lost Balloon, 30–31
For Love of the Game, 196, 202
Force of Evil, 164
Ford, Harrison, 314
Ford, John, 131, 186
Foreman, Carl, 132
Forster, E. M., 112–119
Found Horizon, 310–318
Franciosa, Anthony, 131
Freeman, Y. Frank, 144–146
The Freshman, 274
Friedkin, William, 250
From Here to Eternity, 8
From Kubrick, 171–178
The Front, 123, 147
The Front Page, 279, 283
Frost, Robert, 270
The Full Monty, 119

G

Gable, Clark, 84, 304
Gallo, Joe, 262
Gandhi, 318
Gandolfini, James, 264, 266–268
Geffner, David, 150
  People Who Need People, 213–225
Gemora, Charlie, 3
George, Heinrich, 235
Gere, Richard, 313–317
Gibson, Buzz, 31
Gillette, Paul J., 10
Girosi, Marcello, 135–136
Glazier, Sidney, 242
The Glenn Miller Story, 129
God, Sex & Apple Pie, 65
The Godfather, 57, 264, 273–275
The Godfather III, 274
Godfellas, 264, 274
Goebbels, Joseph, 229–231, 233–236
The Golden Bough, 175, 178
The Golden Stallion, 185, 187, 189, 192
Gone With the Wind, 37, 70–85, 236
Gordon Parks, 216
Gorilla at Large, 23
Gotti, John, 276
Gough, Lloyd, 148
The Graduate, 241
Grant, Cary, 19, 133, 279, 281, 284
Graubard, Wally, 133–134
The Great Escape, 120–123
The Great Sacrifice, 232
Green, 68
Green Pastures, 75
Greene, Lorne, 197
Greene, Ray, 62–64
Griffith, D. W., 79, 271
Gussow, Mel, 39
Guterson, David, 93

H

Halloween: H20, 194
The Happy Valley Kid, 200
Hardy, Oliver, 240
Harlan, Veit, 230–236
Harris, Richard, 10
Harrison, Jim, 93
Harron, Mary, 37
  The Risky Territory of *American Psycho*, 53–58
Harryhausen, Ray, 3, 254–259
Hasford, Gustav, 171, 178
Haskell, Molly, 1
  High-Wire Artist, 3–8

Hathaway, Henry, 273
Hats Off To Charles Gemora, Hollywood's Greatest Ape, 20–33
Hawks, Howard, 186, 271–273, 280, 280–283, 286, 289, 298–299, 302
Hays, David, 251
Hays, Will, 46, 272
Hayward, Susan, 38
Hecht, Ben, 93, 99, 272, 279, 280, 282–283, 286, 305
Hecht, Harold, 6
Hellman, Monte, 248
Hemingway, Ernest, 92, 155, 177
Hepburn, Katherine, 287, 305
Herr, Michael, 150
    From Kubrick, 171–178
Hewitt, Christopher, 239
Hickey, John, 250
High-Wire Artist, 3–8
Hilberg, Raul, 174
Hill, James, 7
Hill, Napoleon, 155
Hippler, Fritz, 230
Hirsch, Karl T., 68
His Girl Friday, 278–308
Hitchcock, Alfred, 10, 88, 149–150, 286
Hitler, a Film From Germany, 243
Hoberman, J., When The Nazis Became Nudniks, 238–243
Hodson, Joel, 158
Hoffman, Dustin, 241
Holden, William, 10, 45
Hollywood Goes Ape, 32
Hollywood Screwballs, 10
Holm, Ian, 91, 96
Homolka, Karla, 57
Hoodlum, 277
Hoop Dreams, 221, 223
Hoskins, Bob, 275
House of Strangers, 38
Howard, John, 305
Howard, Sidney, 71–73, 78, 80
Howards End, 112–114, 118–119
The Hudsucker Proxy, 195
Hughes, Howard, 47, 49
Hunter, Tab, 139
Hurt, William, 161
Huston, John, 119, 273

I

I Am Not Ashamed, 10, 12, 15
I, Claudius, 268
I Married a Monster From Outer Space, 30
The Ice Storm, 95
Imperioli, Michael, 274, 277
In a Door, Into a Fight, Out a Door, Into a Chase, 188
Inside Out: A Memoir of the Blacklist, 88, 123–148
An Interlude, 228–238
Invasion of the Body Snatchers, 128
Invisible Darkness, 57
Ironweed, 95
Irving, John, 88, 93, 103
    The Twelve-Year-Old Girl, 105–112
Is This The End Of Rico?, 262–277
It Came From Beneath the Sea, 257–258
It Came From Bob's Basement, 2
It Happened One Night, 287, 304

J

Jack Frost, 197
Jack the Giant Killer, 30
Jackie Brown, 188
Jackson, Carton, 77
Jacobins, 208
Jagger, Mick, 315
James Bombed, 200
James, C. L. R., 208
Jason and the Argonauts, 256, 258
Jayne Mansfield's Wild, Wild World, 9
The Jerk, 174–175
The Jimmy Hoffa Story, 200
Johnson, Diane, 174
Johnson, Hall, 74
Johnson, Lillian, 84
Johnston, Eric, 46
Jolson, Al, 72
Joy, Jason, 48–51, 272
Jud Süss, 230–231
Julia, 163
Jurassic Park, 255

K

Kael, Pauline, 153, 179, 239
Kafka, Franz, 177–178
Kapo, 203

Kasdan, Jon, 166, 169
Kasdan, Lawrence, 251
    POV, 151–170
Kasdan, Meg, 166, 169
Kauffman, George, 240
Kauffmann, Stanley, 239
Kazan, Elia, 123
Kazin, Alfred, 151
Keeping Up Appearances, 119
Kelley, David, 275
Kennedy, William, 95
Kerouac, Jack, 2, 103
    Cody & The Three Stooges, 16–20
Kerr, Deborah, 8
Khouri, Callie, 253
The Killers, 6–7
King Kong, 31
King of New York, 275
Kiss of Death, 273
Kiss Tomorrow Goodbye, 10, 14
Klawans, Stuart, An Interlude, 228–238
Kline, Kevin, 250
Knight, Wilder, 216
Kolberg, 231–238
Kreimeier, Klaus, 232
Krim, Arthur, 143
Kubrick, Stanley, 63, 149, 171–184, 209
    2001: A Film, 179–184

L

Lady and the Tramp, 193
Lancaster, Burt, 1–8, 27–28, 143–144
Lang, Fritz, 227
Langlois, Henri, 2
Last Night, 98
Laurel and Hardy, 2, 26
Laurel, Stan, 30, 240
LaVigne, Emile, 21
Lawrence of Arabia, 156, 158
Lawrence, T. E., 158–160
Lazar, Irving, 133, 136–137, 140–141, 144, 146
Lean, David, 156
Leavitt, David, 88
    Lost Among The Pinafores, 112–119
Leff, Leonard J., 37
    Gone With the Wind and Hollywood's Racial Politics, 70–85
Lehrer, Tom, 242
Leigh, Jennifer Jason, 247, 249, 251
Leigh, Vivien, 84
Leiser, Erwin, 230
Leno, Jay, 2
Leone, Sergio, 277
The Leopard, 5
LeRoy, Mervyn, 271
A Letter to Three Wives, 37
Levine, Joseph H., 239
Levitch, Timothy, 215, 217, 221
Levy, Al, 134
Lewis, Gough, 218–220
Lewis, Sinclair, 153–154
Lewton, Val, 79
Life Is Beautiful, 243
Little Caesar, 271–272
Little Odessa, 277
Lloyd, Harold, 194
The Long Good Friday, 275
Lopez, Jennifer, 67
Loren, Sophia, 133, 135–136, 139–140
Lost Among The Pinafores, 112–119
Lucas, George, 248
Luciano, Lucky, 262
Lumet, Sidney, 133
Lyman, Rick, 150
    Whoa, Trigger! Auteur Alert!, 184–193

M

MacArthur, Charles, 279, 280, 282–283, 286, 305
Macgowan, Kenneth, 48
Mack, Helen, 285
MacLeish, Archibald, 151
Macy, William H., 62
Maddin, Guy, 257
Maddow, Ben, 131
Magenty, Adrian Ross, 118
Magic Island, 27
The Magnificent Seven, 142–143
Mailer, Norman, 151
Majd, Hooman, 65
Malden, Karl, 24
Malick, Terrence, 248
The Maltese Falcon, 273

A Man Is Ten Feet Tall, 130
The Man with the Golden Arm, 92
Mankiewicz, Joe, 37–46, 49–52
Mann, Anthony, 186
Mann, Michael, 266
The Many Loves of Casanova, 10
Marchand, Nancy, 268
Marcovicci, Andrea, 148
The Mark of Zorro, 6
Mars, Kenneth, 239
Marshman, Jr., D. M., 45
Martin, Steve, 174–175
Marty, 1, 6
Marx Brothers, 2, 27
Masella, Joseph, 263
May, Elaine, 242
McCarthy, Joseph, 123, 128, 132
McCarthy, Todd, 272
McDaniel, Hattie, 70–71, 75, 77–79, 81–84
McLaglen, Victor, 131
McQueen, Butterfly, 75, 77–78
Mead, Rebecca, 150
    Cheese Whiz, 193–203
Mean Streets, 274
Medina, Patricia, 24, 28
Meisel, Kurt, 235
Mendel, Barry, 103
Menjou, Adolphe, 131
Merrick, David, 240
Merrill, Gary, 45
Michlig, John, 2
Midnight Cowboy, 36
A Midsummer Night's Dream, 151
Mighty Joe Young, 255
Miller, Bennett, 215, 217, 222, 224
Miller's Crossing, 195
Milliken, Mike, 251
Minot, Susan, 93
Mitchell, Margaret, 70–71, 78, 80
Monkey Business, 281
The Monster and the Girl, 3, 20, 26
The Monte Stratton Story, 129
Moody, Rick, 95
The Moon Is Blue, 47
Morricone, Ennio, 209, 212
Morrison, Toni, 93
Moss, Carlton, 83
Mostel, Zero, 123, 148, 239–241
Motion Picture Producers and Distributors of America (MPPDA), 46
    rating of independent films, 59–69
Mumford, 152
Murder Is My Beat, 14–15
Murder My Sweet, 273
Murders in the Rue Morgue, 20, 27
The Musketeers of Pig Alley, 271
Myrick, Susan, 76
Mysterious Island, 256, 258

N

Natural Born Killers, 54
Neal, Tom, 10, 13, 15
Neeson, Liam, 194
New Jack City, 277
Nichols, MIke, 197, 241
Nickens, Daryl G., 88
    The Great Escape, 120–123
No, But I Saw The Movie, 89–105
No Down Payment, 131
No Way Out, 38–39
Nolte, Nick, 91, 96
Noonan, Chris, 103
Northwestern, 224
Nostromo, 204
Notorious, 286
Nozaki, Al, 28

O

Oberon, Merle, 280
O'Brien, Pat, 280
O'Brien, Willis, 255
O'Connor, Flannery, 119
O'Connor, Harvey, 138
O'Connor, Jesse, 138
On the Road, 103
On the Ropes, 213
On the Waterfront, 273
Once Upon a Time in America, 277
Ondaatje, Michael, 93
One-Eyed Jacks, 31
Only the Valiant, 12, 14
Ordinary People, 248
Orgazmo, 60–62, 68
The Origin of the Family, Private Property, and the State, 292
Orr, Mary, 37–38, 45–46
Orth, Frank, 298

Oscar and Lucinda, 93
The Outlaw, 47, 49
Ovitz, Michael, 178
The Ox-Bow Incident, 85

P

Paisan, 203
Pal, George, 28
Palermo, Vincent, 263
Paltrow, Gwyneth, 250
Paratroop Command, 190
Parker, Trey, 60
Parrish, Bob, 136
Parsons, Wilfrid, 48
Patterson, John, 266–267
Paul, Edna, 201
Paxton, Bill, 198
Payne, John, 181
Peck, Gregory, 12
People Who Need People, 213–225
People Will Talk, 39
Perelman, S. J., 93
Perils of Nyoka, 20
Phantom of the Rue Morgue, 20, 24–28, 30–31
The Philadelphia Story, 287, 305
Pitt, Brad, 310, 317
Playboy's Freshman Class, 193
Poitier, Sidney, 38
Polito, Robert, 1
    Barbara Payton: A Memoir, 8–15
Polk, Oscar, 75, 79, 81
Polley, Sarah, 91
Polonsky, Abraham, 164
Pontecorvo, Gillo, 150, 203–212
Ponti, Carlo, 133, 135–136, 141–142, 146
The Pornographer, 59, 61–62, 68
Portnoy's Complaint, 241, 264
Posey, Parker, 250
Post, Don, 33
The Postman Always Rings Twice, 11
POV, 151–170
Powers, Mala, 30
Preminger, Otto, 47, 92, 130, 133
Price, Richard, 93
Price, Sarah, 223
Pride and Prejudice, 116
Prinz, LeRoy, 27
The Producers, 238–243
Production Code, 46–49, 52
Prohaska, Janos, 3
Provine, Dorothy, 189
Psychodynamics of Unconventional Sex Behavior, 10
The Public Enemy, 268, 271
Pulp Fiction, 99, 185

Q

Qualen, John, 285
Quek, Grace, 220–221
The Quick and the Dead, 194

R

Raimi, Sam, 150, 194–203
Randall, Tony, 131
Rapf, Michael, 179
Rashomon, 99
Ratoff, Gregory, 52
Rawshanks, Joan, 18
Redford, Robert, 147
The Regeneration, 271
Reilly, John C., 250
The Remains of the Day, 119, 270
Remnick, David, Is This The End Of Rico?, 262–277
Rentschler, Eric, 230
Requiem for a Dream, 59–60, 65–66, 69
Reservoir Dogs, 184
Reynolds, Burt, 62
Rhapsody, 173
Riefenstahl, Leni, 228
Rimawi, David, 61
The Rise and Fall of Bug Manousous, 265
The Risky Territory of *American Psycho*, 53–58
Ritt, Martin, 130, 140, 147–148
Ritter, Thelma, 51
The Roaring Twenties, 273
Robards, Jason, 10
Robbins, Harold, 155
Robinson, Edward G., 38, 272
Roger and Me, 221
Rogers, Roy, 185–186, 189–190
A Room With a View, 119
Roosevelt, Eleanor, 75
Rosamond, Clinton, 75

The Rose Tattoo, 6
Rose, Sheree, 221
Rossellini, Roberto, 203
Roth, Philip, 241
Rotondo, Anthony, 264–265
Rowe, Kenneth, 157–158
Rudin, Scott, 197
Rule of the Bone, 103
Russell, Charley, 136
Russell, Jane, 49, 51
Russell, Rosiland, 279, 287, 289

S

Sahl, Mort, 241
Samuels, Lesser, 38
Sarandon, Susan, 7
Sargent, Alvin, 163
Sarris, Andrew, 239
Satyricon: Memoirs of a Lusty Roman, 10
Saving Private Ryan, 57, 64
Scarface, 271–273
Scary Movie, 60
Schell, Orville, 311–316
Schneider, Aaron, 253
Schnitzler, Arthur, 173–174
Schrader, Paul, 88, 95–96, 100–101, 250
Schulberg, Budd, 301
Sclafani, Joseph, 264–265
Scorsese, Martin, 250, 274, 312
Scott, Randolph, 181
Scott, Ridley, 266
Scream, 193
Scream 2, 2, 57, 193
Seagal, Steven, 313–315
Secret Ceremony, 52
Seldes, Gilbert, 287
Sellers, Peter, 242
Selznick, David O., 37, 70–82, 84–85
Separate And Unequal?, 59–69
Seven Days in May, 7
Seven Samurai, 142, 144
Seven Years In Tibet, 310, 312, 316, 318
Sex: The Annabel Chong Story, 213, 218–221
Shapiro, Victor, 77–78
Shaw, Irwin, 133, 140–141
Shawn, Dick, 239
Shelley, Joshua, 148
The Shining, 172, 175
Shopworn Angel, 133
The Short-Timers, 178
Sick: The Life and Death of Bob Flanagan, Supermasochist, 213, 217–218, 221
A Simple Plan, 196–198, 202
Simpson, Mona, 93
Sinatra, Frank, 143
Sinclair, Upton, 301
Siodmak, Robert, 6–7
Six Months to Live, 200
Skouras, Spyros, 131–132
Skratz, G. P., 2
Slave Ship, 75
Sliver, 66
Smith, Bessie, 122
Smith, Chris, 223
Smith, Scott, 196
Snodgrass, W. D., 151
Snow Falling on Cedars, 93
Solinas, Franco, 204–205, 208
The Sopranos, 264–266, 268–270, 274, 277
South Park, 60–61, 68, 194
Southern, Terry, 171
Sowa, Mike, 251
Spacek, Sissy, 96
Spartacus, 133, 207–210, 212
Speaking of Writing, 152
Speer, Albert, 228–229
Spiegel, Scott, 200
Spielberg, Steven, 64, 249, 309
Spirit of St. Louis, 309
Springtime for Hitler, 239–240
Staggs, Sam, All About "All About Eve", 37–53
Stanwyck, Barbara, 15
Stapleton, Oliver, 106
Star Wars, 255
Star Wars, Episode II, 248
Starr, Ken, 36
Stewart, James, 133
Stiller, Ben, 197
Sting, 316
Stone, Matt, 60, 68–69
Stone, Sharon, 66, 195, 267, 313–314
Stop-Motion Jimjams, 254–259
Strange, Glenn, 20

Stranger at My Door, 189
Sturridge, Charles, 119
Sullavan, Margaret, 133
Sunset Boulevard, 45
Suspicion, 286
Susskind, David, 130
The Sweet Hereafter, 89, 91, 94–103
Sweet Smell of Success, 1, 6
Swiss Miss, 26, 28
Syberberg, Hans-Jürgen, 242–243

T
Tan, Amy, 93
Tapert, Robert, 195, 197, 200
Tarantino, Quentin, 99, 150, 184–193
Taxi Driver, 58
Taylor, Elizabeth, 52
Taylor, Robert, 131
That Kind of Woman, 135, 139, 141
That Uncertain Feeling, 280
The Theory of the Leisure Class, 178
There's Something About Mary, 238
Think and Grow Rich, 155
Thompson, Emma, 118
Thompson, Marshall, 30
Thornton, Billy Bob, 198
Three Stooges, 2, 199
Thurman, Uma, 184, 188
Time for Drunken Horses, 253
Titanic, 193
To the Manor Born, 119
Toback, James, 65
Too Late, 253
Tracy, Spencer, 1
Trainspotting, 119
Trapeze, 4
Trapped, 14
Traumnovelle, 173–175
The Treasure of the Sierra Madre, 198
Triumph of the Will, 228
Trumbo, Dalton, 130, 133
Twain, Mark, 36
The Twelve-Year-Old Girl, 105–112
Two-Lane Blacktop, 248

U
Ulmer, Edgar, 1, 14–15
Ulzanas Raid, 7
Underworld, 271
Unforgiven, 271
The Unholy Three, 26

V
Valenti, Jack, 64, 68–69
The Valley of Gwangi, 256
Van Horn, Emil, 3, 20, 23–24, 32
Velasquez, Chico, 18
Vera Cruz, 7
Vinterberg, Thomas, 250
Virtual Tibet, 311
Visconti, Luchino, 5
von Harbou, Thea, 232
von Sternberg, Josef, 271
Von Trier, Lars, 250

W
Wagner, Richard, 237
Waiting for God, 119
Walken, Christopher, 275
Walker, William, 204–212
Wallace, Adelaide, 38
Walsh, Raoul, 271
War of the Worlds, 21–22, 28
Warren, Earl, 129
Warshow, Robert, 271
Watson, Eric, 59–60, 65–66, 69
Waxman, Franz, 309
Wayne, John, 131
Weaver, Tom, Hats Off To Charles Gemora, Hollywood's Greatest Ape, 20–33
Wegener, Paul, 235
Welch, Raquel, 257
Welles, Orson, 183, 245
Wellman, William, 271
Welty, Eudora, 103, 105
West, Mae, 27, 35, 47
West, Pat, 299
Wharton, John, 84
What Makes Sammy Run, 301
When The Nazis Became Nudniks, 238–243
Where Angels Fear to Tread, 119
Whipper, Leigh, 85
White Heat, 273
White, Walter, 74, 76–78
Whitten, David, 218–220
Whoa, Trigger! Auteur Alert!, 184–193

Widmark, Richard, 38
The Wild Bunch, 57, 271
Wilder, Billy, 45, 309
Wilder, Gene, 239–241
Wilkes, Ashley, 85
Williams, Robin, 58
Williams, Stephen, 57
Wilson, Dooley, 85
Wilson, Michael, 158
Winwood, Estelle, 241
Wise Blood, 119
Wiseman, Frederick, 214, 221
Witney, William, 185–192
The Wizard of Oz, 84
Wonder Bar, 72
World Without End, 21
Wray, Fay, 3

X

Xena: Warrior Princess, 195

Y

Yordan, Philip, 131
You Are Not the Target, 155
Younghusband, Francis, 315
Youngman, Henny, 36

Z

Zanuck, Daryl F., 38–46, 49–50, 52
Zwigoff, Terry, 219, 22